First World, Emerging Markets and Globalization: The Development of the World's Nations

Beatriz Scaglia

The role of the book within our culture is changing. The change is brought on by new ways to acquire & use content, the rapid dissemination of information and real-time peer collaboration on a global scale. Despite these changes one thing is clear--"the book" in it's traditional form continues to play an important role in learning and communication. The book you are holding in your hands utilizes the unique characteristics of the Internet -- relying on web infrastructure and collaborative tools to share and use resources in keeping with the characteristics of the medium (user-created, defying control, etc.)--while maintaining all the convenience and utility of a real book.

Contents

Articles

Pre-Emerging Markets

References

Three Worlds Theory

Three Worlds Theory

Part of the Politics series on

Maoism

⚒ **Communism Portal**
Politics portal

The **Three Worlds Theory** (simplified Chinese: 三个世界的理论; traditional Chinese: 三個世界的理論; pinyin: *Sān gè Shìjiè de Lǐlùn*), developed by Chinese Communist leader Mao Zedong (1893–1976), posited that international relations comprise three politico–economic worlds: the First World, the superpowers, the Second World, the superpowers' allies, and the Third World, the nations of the Non-Aligned Movement.

Notably, Chairman Mao included the US and the Soviet Union in the First World group of countries. In 1974, then Chinese Vice-Premier Deng Xiaoping (1904–97), explained the Three Worlds Theory in a speech to the United Nations, explaining the politico-economic alliances of the People's Republic of China with Right-wing, reactionary governments in the late 1970s and the 1980s.

The Three Worlds Theory developed by Mao Zedong was different from the Western theory of the Three Worlds. The Western theory said that the First World was the United States and its allies, the Second World was the Soviet Union and its allies, and the Third World was the neutral and nonaligned countries.

Some anti-revisionist political parties and organizations were disillusioned by the Three Worlds Theory. Subsequently, in Albania, Enver Hoxha (1908–85), leader of the Party of Labour of Albania, presented and practised a critical ideological alternative form of government and basic ideology, distanced from the Three Worlds Theory and the Communist Party of the Soviet Union's revisionism. After debate, many anti-revisionist parties, previously allied with the Communist Party of China, transferred their loyalties to the Party of Labour of Albania.

See also

- First World
- Second World
- Third World
- Fourth World
- Seven Worlds Index
- Anti-revisionism

External links

- http://www.revolutionarydemocracy.org/rdv10n1/mao.htm
- http://maoist.wikia.com/wiki/Three_Worlds_Theory (contains exchange above, also without exact attribution)
- http://www.fmprc.gov.cn/eng/ziliao/3602/3604/t18008.htm
- http://www.marxists.org/reference/archive/deng-xiaoping/1974/04/10.htm
- http://www.marxists.org/reference/archive/hoxha/works/imp_rev/imp_ch4.htm

First World

The concept of the **First World** first originated during the Cold War, where it was used to describe countries that were aligned with the United States. These countries were democratic and capitalistic. After the fall of the Soviet Union and the end of the Cold War, the term "First World" took on a new meaning that was more applicable to the times. Since its original definition, the term First World has come to be largely synonymous with developed and/or highly developed countries (depending on which definition is being used).

The three worlds as they were separated during the Cold War era, each with its respective allies. Colors do not represent current economical development. First World: the United States and its allies. Second World: the Soviet Union and its allies. Third World: Non-aligned and neutral countries.

First World countries in general have very advanced economies and very high Human Development indices. On the other hand, the United Nations defined the First World on the wealth of the nation's Gross National Product (GNP). The definition of the First World is now less concrete than during the Cold War.

Global dynamics between the First World and the other Worlds were essentially split into two. Relationships with the Second World were competitive, ideological and hostile. Relationships with Third World countries were normally positive in theory, while some were quite negative in practice (e.g. wars). Present inter-world relationships are not so rigid, although there is a disparity in terms of the First World having more influence, wealth, information and advancements than the other worlds.

Globalization is an increasingly important phenomenon which has been fueled largely by the First World and its connections with the other worlds. An example of globalization within the First World is the European Union which has brought much cooperation and integration to the region. Multinational corporations also provide examples of the First World's impact on globalization, as they have brought economic, political and social integration in many countries. With the rise of the multinational corporation, the problem of outsourcing has risen in many First World countries.

Definition

After World War II the world split into two large geopolitical blocs, separating into spheres of communism and capitalism. This led to the Cold War, during which the term First World was highly used because of its political, social, and economic relevance. The term itself was first introduced in in the late 1940s by the United Nations. Today, the First World is slightly outdated and has no official definition, however it is generally thought of as the capitalist, industrial, developed countries who aligned with the United States after World War II. This definition included most of the countries of North America, Western Europe, Australia and Japan. In today's society the First World is viewed as countries who have the most advanced economies, the greatest influence, the highest standards of living, and the greatest technology. After the Cold War these countries of the First World included member states of NATO, US aligned states, neutral countries who were developed and industrialized, and former British Colonies. Countries were also placed into the First World based on how civilized the country was. According to Nations Online the member countries of NATO after the Cold War included:

- Belgium, Canada, Denmark, France, West Germany, Greece, Iceland, Italy, Luxembourg, Netherlands, Norway, Portugal, Spain, Turkey, United Kingdom and the United States

The US aligned countries included:

- Israel, Japan, and South Korea

The neutral countries included:

- Austria, Finland, Ireland, Sweden, Switzerland and Yugoslavia

The former British colonies also included in the First World were:

- Australia and New Zealand

Human Development Index

Main article: Human Development Index

The Human Development Index is a worldwide organization where different indicators are used to classify countries based on their developmental status. Statistics like GDP, GNP, literacy, and education are combined to form a list of countries ranging from very high human development to low human development. The

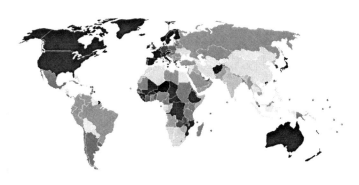

Global Human Development Indices

countries with very high human development ratings are said to be the most developed and industrialized countries in the world. If the classification of the First World is based on the definition above, the Human Development Index is a good indicator in identifying First World countries. Hence, according to the Human Development Index, thirty eight countries are ranked as having very high human development. Most of the countries on this list coincide with the data on countries listed in Nations Online. The countries that are on the Human Development Index but not on the NATO list above include

- Finland, Liechtenstien, Singapore, Hong Kong, Andorra, Slovenia, Kuwait, Cyprus, Qatar, Czech Republic, Barbados, Malta, United Arab Emirates, and Brunei Darussalam.

Variations in definitions

Since the end of the Cold War, the original definition of First World is no longer necessarily applicable. There are varying definitions of the First World, however they follow the same idea. John D. Daniels, past president of the Academy of International Business, defines the First World to be consisting of "high-income industrial countries." Scholar and Professor George J. Bryjak defines the First World to be the "modern, industrial, capitalist countries of North America and Europe." L. Robert Kohls, former director of training for the U.S. Information Agency and the Meridian International Center in Washington, uses First World and "fully developed" as synonyms.

Other indicators

Varying definitions of the term First World and the uncertainty of the term in today's world leads to different indicators of First World status. In 1945, the United Nations (UN) used the terms first, second, third, and fourth worlds to define the relative wealth of nations (although popular use of the term fourth world did not come about until later). They were defined in terms of Gross National Product (GNP), measured in U.S. dollars, along with other socio-political factors. The first world included the large industrialized, democratic (free elections, etc.) nations. The second world included modern, wealthy, industrialized nations, but they were all under communist control. Most of the rest of the world was deemed part of the third world, while the fourth world was considered to be those nations whose people were living on less than US$100 annually. If we use the term to mean high income industrialized economies, then the World Bank classifies countries according to their GNI or gross national income per capita. The World Bank separates countries into four categories: high-income, upper-middle-income, lower-middle-income, and low-income economies. The First World is considered to be countries with high-income economies. The high-income economies are equated to mean developed and industrialized countries. According to the World Bank the countries with the top GNP include:

- Bermuda, Luxembourg, Norway, Kuwait, Brunei, Singapore, United States, Hong Kong, Switzerland and the Netherlands.

Three World Model

The terms First World, Second World, and Third World were used originally to divide the world's nations into three categories. The model did not emerge to its end state all at once. The complete overthrow of the status quo post-World War II, known as the Cold War, left two superpowers (the United States and the Soviet Union) vying for ultimate global

NATO Countries

supremacy. They created two camps, known as blocs. These blocs formed the basis of the concepts of the First and Second Worlds.

Early in the Cold War era, NATO and the Warsaw Pact were created by the United States and The Soviet Union, respectively. They were also referred to as the Western Bloc and the Eastern Bloc. The circumstances of these two blocks were so different that they were essentially two worlds, however they were not numbered first and second. The onset of the Cold War is marked by Winston Churchill's famous "Iron Curtain" speech. In this speech, Churchill describes the division of the West and East to be so solid that it could be called an iron curtain.

In 1952, the French demographer Alfred Sauvy coined the term Third World in reference to the three estates in pre-revolutionary France. The first two estates being the nobility and clergy and everybody else comprising the third estate. He compared the capitalist world (i.e. First World) to the nobility and the communist world (i.e. Second World) to the clergy. Just as the third estate comprised everybody else, Sauvy called the Third World all the countries that were not in this Cold War division, i.e. the unaligned and uninvolved states in the "East-West Conflict." With the coining of the term Third World directly, the first two groups came to be known as the "First World" and "Second World," respectively. Here the three world system emerged.

However, Shuswap Chief George Manuel believes the **Three World Model** to be outdated. In his 1974 book *The Fourth World: An Indian Reality*, he describes the emergence of the Fourth World while coining the term. The fourth world refers to "nations," e.g. cultural entities and ethnic groups, of indigenous people who do not compose states in the traditional sense. Rather, they live within or across state boundaries (see First Nations). One example is the American Indians of North America, Central America, and the Caribbean.

Post Cold War

With the fall of the Soviet Union in 1991, the Eastern Bloc ceased to exist; with it, so did all applicability of the term Second World. The definitions of the First World and Third World changed slightly, yet generally described the same concepts.

Relationships with the other worlds

Historic

During the Cold War Era, the relationships between the First World and the Second World and the First World and the Third World were very rigid. The First World and Second World were at constant odds with one another via the tensions between their two cores, the United States and the Soviet Union, respectively. The Cold War, by virtue of its name, was a primarily ideological struggle between the First and Second Worlds, or more specifically the U.S. and the Soviet Union. Multiple doctrines and plans dominated Cold War dynamics including the Truman Doctrine, Marshall Plan (from the U.S) and the Molotov Plan (from the Soviet Union). The extent of the odds between the two worlds is evident in Berlin - which was then split into East and West. In order to stop their citizens in East Berlin from having too much exposure to Western and Capitalistic wealth and happiness, the Soviet Union put up the Berlin Wall within the actual city.

The relationship between the First World and the Third World is characterized by the very definition of the Third World. Because countries of the Third World were noncommittal and non-aligned with both the First World and the Second World, they were targets for recruitment. In the quest for expanding their sphere of influence, the United States (core of the First World) tried to establish democracy and capitalism in the Third World. In addition, because the Soviet Union (core of the Second World) also wanted to expand, the Third World often became a site for proxy wars.

Some examples include Vietnam and Korea. Success lay with the First World if at the end of the War the country became capitalistic and democratic, and with the Second World if the country became communist. While Vietnam as a whole was eventually communized, only the northern

The Domino Theory

half of Korea remained to be communist. The Domino Theory largely governed United States policy regarding the Third World and their rivalry with the Second World. In light of the Domino Theory, the U.S. saw winning the proxy wars in the Third World as a measure of the "credibility of US commitments all over the world."

Present

The movement of people and information largely characterizes the inter-world relationships in the present day. A majority of breakthroughs and innovation originate in Western Europe and the U.S. and later their effects permeate globally. As judged by the Wharton School of Business at the University of Pennsylvania, most of the Top 30 Innovations of the Last 30 Years were from former First World countries (e.g. the U.S. and countries in Western Europe).

The disparity between knowledge in the First World as compared to the Third World is evident in healthcare and medical advancements. Deaths from water-related illnesses have largely been eliminated in "wealthier nations," while they are still a "major concern in the developing world." Widely treatable diseases in the developed countries of the First World, malaria and tuberculosis

Global distribution of Malaria risk.

needlessly claim many lives in the developing countries of the Third World. 900,000 people die from malaria each year and combating malaria accounts for 40% of health spending in many African countries. Malaria as well as other diseases already conquered in the First World, wreak havoc in the Third World, trapping "communities in a downward spiral of poverty." However, many First World countries are making plans to help Third World countries gain access to information and advancements. U.S. President Barack Obama has pledged to "end deaths by malaria by 2015" by achieving "universal access to proven, low-cost malaria treatment and prevention efforts."

The International Corporation for Assigned Names and Numbers (ICANN) recently announced that the first Internationalized Domain Names (IDNs) will be available as soon as the summer of 2010. These include non-Latin domains such as Chinese, Arabic, and Russian. This is one way that the flow of information between the First and Third Worlds may become more even.

The movement of information and technology from the First World to various Third World countries has created a general "aspir(ation) to First World living standards." The Third World has lower living standards as compared to the First World. Information about the comparatively higher living standards of the First World come through television, commercial advertisements and foreign visitors to their countries. This exposure causes two changes: a) living standards in some Third World countries rises and b) this exposure creates hopes and many from Third World countries immigrate - both legally and illegally - to these First World countries in hopes to attain that living standard and prosperity. In fact, this immigration is the "main contributor to the increasing populations of U.S. and Europe." While these immigrations have greatly contributed to globalization, they have also precipitated trends like brain drain and problems with repatriation. They have also created immigration and governmental burden problems for the countries (i.e. First World) to which people are immigrating to.

Environmental impact

It has been argued that the most important human population problem for the world is not the high rate of population increase in certain Third World countries, but rather the "increase in total human impact." The per-capita impact - the resources consumed and the wastes created by each person - is varied globally; the highest being in the First World and the lowest in the Third World: inhabitants of the U.S., Western

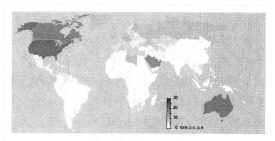

CO_2 emissions per capita

Europe and Japan consume 32 times as much resources and put out 32 times as much waste than those in the Third World. Also, for example, first world countries, such as America, Australia, Japan, Canada are producing the most CO_2 in the world, contributing to the greenhouse gas emissions in a massive way. These first world countries use natural resources until near depletion occurs; this happens because the country has the wealth to buy these products. There are the exceptions, first world countries like Norway, Sweden, and Germany have worked with the environment and benefited economically from being environmentally sustainable.

However, China leads the world in total emissions, but its large population skews its per-capita statistic lower than those of more developed nations.

As large consumers of fossil fuels, First World countries drew attention to environmental pollution. The Kyoto Protocol is a treaty that is based on the United Nations Framework Convention on Climate

Change, which was finalized in 1992 at the Earth Summit in Rio. It proposed to place the burden of protecting the climate on the United States and other First World countries. Countries that were considered to be developing, such as China and India, were not required to approve the treaty because they were more concerned that restricting emissions would further restrain their development.

International relations

Until the recent past, little attention was paid to the interests of Third World countries. This is because most international relations scholars have come from the industrialized, First World nations. As more countries have continued to become more developed, the interests of the world have slowly started to shift. However, First World nations still have many more universities, professors, journals, and conferences, which has made it very difficult for Third World countries to gain legitimacy and respect with their new ideas and methods of looking at the world.

Development theory

During the Cold War, the modernization theory and development theory developed in the West as a result of their economic, political, social, and cultural response to the management of former colonial territories. Western scholars and practitioners of international politics hoped to theorize ideas and then create policies based on those ideas that would cause newly independent colonies to change into politically developed sovereign nation-states. However, most of the theorists were from the United States, and they were not interested in Third World countries achieving development by any model. They wanted those countries to develop through liberal processes of politics, economics, and socialization; that is to say, they wanted them to follow the Western liberal capitalist example of a so-called "First World state." Therefore, the modernization and development tradition consciously originated as a Western (mostly U.S.) alternative to the Marxist and neo-Marxist strategies promoted by the "Second World states" like the Soviet Union. It was used to explain how developing Third World states would naturally *evolve* into developed First World States, and it was partially grounded in liberal economic theory and a form of Talcott Parsons' sociological theory.

Globalization

The United Nations's ESCWA has written that globalization "is a widely-used term that can be defined in a number of different ways." Joyce Osland from San Jose State University wrote, "Globalization has become an increasingly controversial topic, and the growing number of protests around the world has focused more attention on the basic assumptions of globalization and its effects." "Globalization is not new, though. For thousands of years, people—and, later, corporations—have been buying from and selling to each other in lands at great distances, such as through the famed Silk Road across Central Asia that connected China and Europe during the Middle Ages. Likewise, for centuries, people and corporations have invested in enterprises in other countries. In fact, many of the features of the current wave of globalization are similar to those prevailing before the outbreak of the First World War in 1914."

World Trade Organization

As defined by its website, the World Trade Organization (WTO) is "is the only global international organization dealing with the rules of trade between nations." Established not long ago in 1995, its predecessor was the General Agreement on Tariffs and Trade (GATT). This organization focuses on economic growth and development in regards to negotiations amongst international trading.

Some of the 153 countries belonging to the WTO are considered developed countries like the United States, and the European Union. Countries like China, Brazil, India and South Africa are considered some of the most influential members within the WTO. Developing countries are said to receive special treatment and provisions according to certain agreements held by the WTO. This special treatment could be defined as: "including longer time periods to implement agreements and commitments, measures to increase their trading opportunities and support to help them build the infrastructure for WTO work, handle disputes, and implement technical standards." The use (or misuse) of these privileges can be, and ofen are, questioned and challenged by other members. Amongst these developing countries are smaller, more intricate groups a.k.a. alliances. The Cairns group of seventeen is composed of developed and developing nations, and has existed since the mid-1980s. While this alliance has seemed to disappear over the years, another group of twenty or "G-20" has risen; made up of countries like India, China Egypt, Argentina and South Africa. Various groups continues to develop to handle such issues as development, membership, and regional trade.

European Union

The most prominent example of globalization in the first world is the European Union (EU). The European Union is an agreement in which countries voluntarily decide to build common governmental institutions to which they delegate some individual national sovereignty so that decisions can be made democratically on a higher level of common interest for Europe as a whole. The result is a union of 27 Member States covering 4324782 square kilometres (1669808 sq mi) with roughly half a billion people. In total, the European Union produces almost a third of the world's gross national product and the member states speak more than 23 languages. All of the European Union countries are joined together by a hope to promote and extend peace, democracy, cooperativeness, stability, prosperity, and the rule of law. In a 2007 speech, Benita Ferrero-Waldner, the European Commissioner for External Relations, said herself, "The future of the EU is linked to globalization...the EU has a crucial role to play in making globalization work properly...".

Just as the concept of the First World came about as a result of World War II, so did the European Union. In 1951 the beginnings of the EU were founded with the creation of European Coal and Steel Community (ECSC). From the beginning of its inception, countries in the EU were judged by many standards, including economic ones. This is where the relation between globalization, the EU, and First World Countries arises. Especially during the 1990s when the EU focused on economic policies such as the creation and circulation of the Euro, the creation of the European Monetary Institute, and the opening of the European Central Bank.

In 1993, at the Copenhagen European Council, the European Union took a decisive step towards expanding the EU, what they called the Fifth Enlargement, agreeing that "the associated countries in Central and Eastern Europe that so desire shall become members of the European Union." Thus, enlargement was no longer a question of if, but when and how. The European Council stated that accession could occur when the prospective country is able to assume the obligations of membership, that is that all the economic and political conditions required are attained. Furthermore, it defined the membership criteria, which are regarded as the Copenhagen criteria, as follows:

- stability of institutions guaranteeing democracy, the rule of law, human rights and respect for and protection of minorities
- the existence of a functioning market economy as well as the capacity to cope with competitive pressure and market forces within the Union
- the ability to take on the obligations of membership including adherence to the aims of political, economic & monetary union

It is clear that all these criteria are characteristics of developed countries. Therefore, there is a direct link between globalization, developed nations, and the European Union.

Multinational corporations

A majority of multinational corporations find their origins in First World countries. After the fall of communism, multinational corporations proliferated as more countries focused on global trade. The series of General Agreement on Tariffs and Trade (GATT) and later the World Trade Organization (WTO) essentially ended the protectionist measures that were dissuading global trade. The eradication of these protectionist measures, while creating avenues for economic interconnection, mostly benefited developed countries, who by using their power at GATT summits, forced developing and underdeveloped countries to open their economies to Western goods.

As the world starts to globalize, it is accompanied by criticism of the current forms of globalization, which are feared to be overly corporate-led. As corporations become larger and multinational, their influence and interests go further accordingly. Being able to influence and own most media companies, it is hard to be able to publicly debate the notions and ideals that corporations pursue. Some choices that corporations take to make profits can affect people all over the world. Sometimes fatally.

The third industrial revolution is spreading from the developed world to some, but not all, parts of the developing world. To participate in this new global economy, developing countries must be seen as attractive offshore production bases for multinational corporations. To be such bases, developing countries must provide relatively well-educated workforces, good infrastructure (electricity, telecommunications, transportation), political stability, and a willingness to play by market rules.

If these conditions are in place, multinational corporations will transfer via their offshore subsidiaries or to their offshore suppliers the specific production technologies and market linkages necessary to participate in the global economy. By themselves, developing countries, even if well educated, cannot produce at the quality levels demanded in high-value-added industries and cannot market what they produce even in low-value-added industries such as textiles or shoes. Put bluntly, multinational companies possess a variety of factors that developing countries must have if they are to participate in the global economy.

Outsourcing

Outsourcing according to Grossman and Helpman refers to the process of "subcontracting an ever expanding set of activities, ranging from product design to assembly, from research and development to marketing, distribution and after-sales service." Many companies have moved to outsourcing services in which they no longer specifically need or have the capability of handling themselves. Why? What it all comes down to is what the companies can have more control over. Whatever companies tend to not have much control, or need to have control, will outsource activities to firms that they consider "less competing." According to SourcingMag.com, the process of outsourcing can take four phases: 1) Strategic Thinking, 2) Evaluation and Selection, 3) Contract Development and 4) Outsourcing Management.

Outsourcing is among some of the many reasons for increased competition within developing countries. Aside from being a reason for competition, many First World countries see outsourcing, in particular Offshore outsourcing, as an opportunity for increased income. As a consequence, the skill level of production in foreign countries handling the outsourced services increases within the economy; and the skill level within the domestic developing countries can decrease. It is because of competition (including outsourcing) that Robert Feenstra and Gordon Hanson predict that there will be a rise of 15-33 percent in inequality amongst these countries.

See also

- Three Worlds Theory
- Second World
- Third World
- Fourth World
- Seven Worlds Index
- Globalization
- Multinational Corporation
- North-South divide
- Digital divide

Second World

See also: Three Worlds Theory

The term "**Second World**" is a phrase that was used to describe the Communist states within the Soviet Union's sphere of influence or those countries that had centrally-planned economies. Along with "First World" and "Third World", the term was used to divide the nations of Earth into three broad categories. In other words, the concept of "Second World" was a construct of the Cold War and the term has largely fallen out of use since the "Autumn of Nations" in 1989. Subsequently, the actual meaning of the terms "First World" and "Third World" changed from being based on political ideology to an economic definition (see the terms *developed country* and *developing country*).

The three worlds as they were separated during the Cold War era, each with its respective allies. Colors do not represent current economical development.   First World: the United States and its allies.   Second World: the Soviet Union and its allies.   Third World: Non-aligned and neutral countries.

See also

- Three Worlds Theory
- First World
- Third World
- Fourth World
- Eastern Europe
- Eastern Bloc
- Cold War
- Communism
- Soviet Union

Third World

See also: Three Worlds Theory

The term **'Third World'** arose during the Cold War to define countries that remained non-aligned or not moving at all with either capitalism and NATO (which along with its allies represented the First World) or communism and the Soviet Union (which along with its allies represented the Second World). This definition provided a way of broadly categorizing the nations of the Earth into three groups based on social, political, and economic divisions.

The term continues to be used colloquially to describe the poorest countries in the world.

The three worlds as they were separated during the Cold War era, each with its respective allies. Colors do not represent current economical development.   First World: the United States and its allies.   Second World: the Soviet Union and its allies.   Third World: Non-aligned and neutral countries.

Etymology

French demographer, anthropologist and historian Alfred Sauvy, in an article published in the French magazine *L'Observateur*, August 14, 1952, coined the term *Third World*, referring to countries particularly in the Middle East, South Asia, Latin America, Africa, and Oceania, that were unaligned with either the Communist Soviet bloc or the Capitalist NATO bloc during the Cold War. His usage was a reference to the Third Estate, the commoners of France who, before and during the French Revolution, opposed priests and nobles, who composed the First Estate and Second Estate, respectively. Sauvy wrote, *"Like the third estate, the Third World is nothing, and wants to be something,"* He conveyed the concept of political non-alignment with either the capitalist or communist bloc.

The growing use of the term Developing World led to a growing sense of solidarity among the nations of the so-called Third World to unite against interference from either major bloc. In 1955, leaders of 29 countries from Asia and Africa met at the Bandung Conference to discuss cooperation. The First Prime Minister of India, Jawaharlal Nehru, notably said:

> I have no doubt that an equally able disposition could be made on the part of the other bloc. I belong to neither [the First or Second World] and I propose to belong to neither whatever happens in the world. If we have to stand alone, we will stand by ourselves, whatever happens...

We do not agree with the communist teachings, we do not agree with the anti-communist teachings, because they are both based on wrong principles."

Nehru's speech led several delegates to call for India to lead a "third bloc" composed of the nations of Africa and Asia, however he declined and no other state chose to fill the proposed role.

In addition, Mao Zedong, the Chairman of China Communist Party, in February 22, 1974 with the President of the Republic of Zambia Kenneth Kaunda had said: "I think the United States and the Soviet Union was the first world. Centrist, Japan, Europe, Australia, Canada, is the Second World. We are the Third World." This definition, basically according to human development index, with the first popular—Cold War framework focusing on the difference between patterns that subconsciously—take a completely different point of view.

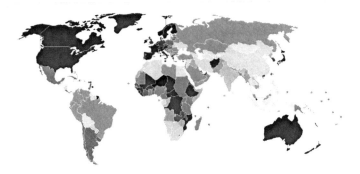

World map indicating a Human Development Index (2009 Update)

History

A number of *Third World* countries were former colonies and with the end of imperialism many of these countries, especially the smaller ones, were faced with the challenges of nation and institution-building on their own for the first time. Due to this common background many of these nations were for most of the 20th century, and are still today, "developing" in economic terms. This term when used today generally denotes countries that have not "developed" to the same levels

An abandoned Mogadishu street in 1993

as OECD countries, and which are thus in the process of "developing". In the 1980s, economist Peter Bauer offered a competing definition for the term *Third World*. He claimed that the attachment of Third World status to a particular country was not based on any stable economic or political criteria, and was a mostly arbitrary process. The large diversity of countries that were considered to be part of the Third

World, from Indonesia to Afghanistan, ranged widely from economically primitive to economically advanced and from politically non-aligned to Soviet- or Western-leaning. An argument could also be made for how parts of the U.S. are more like the Third World. The only characteristic that Bauer found common in all *Third World* countries was that their governments "demand and receive Western aid" (the giving of which he strongly opposed). Thus, the aggregate term "Third World" was challenged as misleading even during the Cold War period.

See also

- Three Worlds Theory
- First World
- Second World
- Fourth World
- Seven Worlds Index
- Non-Aligned Movement

Further reading

- Aijaz Ahmad, In Theory: Classes, Nations, Literatures. (1992)
- P. T. Bauer, Equality, the Third World, and Economic Delusion. (1981) ISBN 0-674-25986-6.
- J. Cole, Development and Underdevelopment. (1987)
- A. Escobar, Encountering Development. The Making and Unmaking of the Third World. (1995)
- E. Hermassi, The Third World Reassessed. (1980)
- A. R. Kasdan, The Third World: A New Focus for Development. (1973)
- P. W. Porter and E. S. Sheppard, A World of Difference: Society, Nature, and Development. (1998)
- H. A. Reitsma and J. M. Kleinpenning, The Third World in Perspective. (1985)
- Alan Whaites, States in Development, UK Department for International Development, London 2007, * [1]

External links

- Hans Rosling at TED 2006 [2]

Fourth World

See also: Three Worlds Theory

The **Fourth World** is either (i) sub-populations socially excluded from global society, or (ii) nomadic, pastoral, and hunter-gatherer peoples living beyond the modern industrial norm. Since publication of *The Fourth World: An Indian Reality* (1974), by George Manuel, Chief of the National Indian Brotherhood and Assembly of First Nations, the term *Fourth World* is synonymous with stateless, poor, and marginal nations. The term originated with a remark by Mbuto Milando, first secretary of the Tanzanian High Commission, that "When Native peoples come into their own, on the basis of their own cultures and traditions, that will be the Fourth World," in conversation with Manuel. Since 1979, think tanks such as the Center for World Indigenous Studies have used the term in defining the relationships between ancient, tribal, and non-industrial nations and modern industrialised nation-states. With the 2007 UN Declaration on the Rights of Indigenous Peoples, communications and organizing amongst Fourth World peoples have accelerated in the form of international treaties between aboriginal nations for the purposes of trade, travel, and security.

Etymologically, *Fourth World* follows the First World, Second World, and Third World hierarchy of nation-state status; however, unlike the former categories, *Fourth World* denotes nations without a sovereign state, emphasising the non-recognition and exclusion of ethnically- and religiously-defined peoples from the politico-economic world system, e.g. the Romani people worldwide, the Basque, Sami, pre-First World War Ashkenazi Jews in the Pale of Settlement, the Assyrians, and the Kurds in the Middle East, the indigenous peoples of the Americas and First Nations groups throughout North, Central and South America, and indigenous Africans and Asians. Spanish sociologist Manuel Castells of the University of Southern California Annenberg School for Communication has made extensive use of the term *fourth world* in the *International Journal of Communication*.

Generosity being the essential attitude that generates Fourth World cultural ambience, the abiding principles of Fourth World societies are conservation, cooperation and reciprocity.

See also

- Three Worlds Theory
- Seven Worlds Index

Further reading

- Castells, Manuel (1998, second edition, 2000). *End of Millenium, The Information Age: Economy, Society and Culture Vol. III*. Oxford, UK: Blackwell. ISBN 978-0631221395.

External links

- Fourth World Journal [1]
- Fourth World Center for the Study of Indigenous Law and Politics [2] at University of Colorado at Denver
- Fourth World: Nations without a State - Nadesan Satyendra [3]
- Fourth World Eye [4]
- Fourth World Documentation Program [5]

Seven Worlds Index

Seven Worlds Index

The **Seven Worlds Index** classifies the countries of the world according to their political systems, societies, and economies, as (I) Liberal Democracy, (II) Communist and Post-Communist, (III) Newly Industrializing Countries (NICs), (IV) Less Developed Countries (LDCs), (V) the Islamic Worlds, (VI) Marginal States, and (VII) Microstates. The British political scientist John McCormick developed this classification system in an attempt to analyze, explain, and understand the world's international relations after the conclusion of the Russo–American Cold War (1945–91).

Liberal Democracy

Liberal democracies possess legitimate, defined, and predictable political processes and institutions. Usually, these nations are wealthier than other types of nation states, and have a relatively-high respect for the civil rights and civil liberties of their citizens; most liberal democracies were comprehended in the First World. Examples: Australia, Canada, France, New Zealand, Sweden, Germany, Israel, Japan, United Kingdom, and United States.

Communist and Post Communist

This category could now also be described as "states in transition," but they are all linked by the common experience of Marxist-Leninist government and economy. Most of these states turned their backs on communism at the end of the Cold War. Eventually many of these nation-states will probably disperse into other categories like the liberal democracies, newly industrializing countries, or even regress and fall into the less developed countries or marginal states categories. All are former Second World countries. Examples: China, Cuba, North Korea, Poland, Russia, and Vietnam.

Newly Industrializing Countries

Most of these states are undergoing economic, political, and social transformation as a result of industrialization like the kind that Europe experienced in the 18th and 19th century. Their political systems are stabilizing, and the economy of these states is industrializing rapidly. Examples: Brazil, India, Malaysia, Mexico, Thailand, Egypt, the Philippines, South Africa, and Turkey.

Less Developed Countries

Largely located in Latin America as well as sub-Saharan Africa, these nation states have some potential to build political, economic, or social stability, but face many long-term obstacles. Some have stable political systems, but poor economies. Some have growing economies but unstable governments due to corruption and or questionable human rights records. Examples: Bangladesh, Nigeria, and Tanzania.

Islamic World

A group characterized by the dominance of the religion of Islam in the societies. This is distinct because Islamic faith informs all other aspects of a nation-state's character including the ideological foundation for their political institution , economics, social values, and often the legal system in the form of Sharia law. Examples: Brunei, Iran, Oman, Pakistan, Saudi Arabia, Yemen.

Marginal States

This group is the most transitional of all nation-states. This transitional period is due to the fact they are actually failed states. To enter into the status of a failed state is because of political, social, or economic upheaval due to extended warfare, environmental disaster, or political and economic islolation. Examples: Afghanistan, Burma, Haiti, Iraq, Somalia, Sudan, and Zimbabwe.

Microstates

These nations are put into a single category because of their size seems to be the most important factor that distinguishes them from the rest of the world. They have populations ranging from 800 to 5,000,000. They are usually highly dependent on larger neighboring countries for trade, protection, and other natural resources. Examples: Barbados, The Bahamas, Luxembourg, Malta, Monaco, Nauru, Singapore, and Vatican City.

See also

• Three Worlds Theory

References

• Le Roy, Michael K.. *Comparative Politics Using MicroCase ExplorIt*.

Globalization

Globalization

Globalization (or **globalisation**) describes the process by which regional economies, societies, and cultures have become integrated through a global network of communication, transportation, and trade. The term is sometimes used to refer specifically to economic globalization: the integration of national economies into the international economy through trade, foreign direct investment, capital flows, migration, and the spread of technology. However, globalization is usually recognized as being driven by a combination of economic, technological, sociocultural, political, and biological factors. The term can also refer to the transnational circulation of ideas, languages, or popular culture through acculturation.

Definitions

According to the Oxford English Dictionary, the word 'globalization' was first employed in 1930, to denote a holistic view of human experience in education. An early description of globalization was penned by the American entrepreneur-turned-minister Charles Taze Russell who coined the term 'corporate giants' in 1897, although it was not until the 1960s that the term began to be widely used by economists and other social scientists. The term has since then achieved widespread use in the mainstream press by the later half of the 1980s. Since its inception, the concept of globalization has inspired numerous competing definitions and interpretations, with antecedents dating back to the great movements of trade and empire across Asia and the Indian Ocean from the 15th century onwards.

The United Nations ESCWA has globalization "is a widely-used term that can be defined in a number of different ways. When used in an economic context, it refers to the reduction and removal of barriers between national borders in order to facilitate the flow of goods, capital, services and labor... although considerable barriers remain to the flow of labor... Globalization is not a new phenomenon. It began in the late nineteenth century, but it slowed down during the period from the start of the First World War until the third quarter of the twentieth century. This slowdown can be attributed to the inward-looking policies pursued by a number of countries in order to protect their respective industries... however, the pace of globalization picked up rapidly during the fourth quarter of the twentieth century..."

Saskia Sassen writes that "a good part of globalization consists of an enormous variety of micro-processes that begin to denationalize what had been constructed as national — whether policies, capital, political subjectivity, urban spaces, temporal frames, or any other of a variety of dynamics and domains."

Tom J. Palmer of the Cato Institute defines globalization as "the diminution or elimination of state-enforced restrictions on exchanges across borders and the increasingly integrated and complex global system of production and exchange that has emerged as a result."

Thomas L. Friedman has examined the impact of the "flattening" of the world, and argues that globalized trade, outsourcing, supply-chaining, and political forces have changed the world permanently, for both better and worse. He also argues that the pace of globalization is quickening and will continue to have a growing impact on business organization and practice.

Noam Chomsky argues that the word globalization is also used, in a doctrinal sense, to describe the neoliberal form of economic globalization.

Herman E. Daly argues that sometimes the terms internationalization and globalization are used interchangeably but there is a significant formal difference. The term "internationalization" (or internationalisation) refers to the importance of international trade, relations, treaties etc. owing to the (hypothetical) immobility of labor and capital between or among nations.[citation needed]

Finally, Takis Fotopoulos argues that globalization is the result of systemic trends manifesting the market economy's grow-or-die dynamic, following the rapid expansion of transnational corporations. Because these trends have not been offset effectively by counter-tendencies that could have emanated from trade-union action and other forms of political activity, the outcome has been globalization. This is a multi-faceted and irreversible phenomenon within the system of the market economy and it is expressed as: economic globalization, namely, the opening and deregulation of commodity, capital and labour markets which led to the present form of neoliberal globalization; political globalization, i.e., the emergence of a transnational elite and the phasing out of the all powerful-nation state of the statist period; cultural globalization, i.e., the worldwide homogenisation of culture; ideological globalization; technological globalization; social globalization.

Effects

Globalization has various aspects which affect the world in several different ways

- *Industrial* - emergence of worldwide production markets and broader access to a range of foreign products for consumers and companies. Particularly movement of material and goods between and within national boundaries. International trade in manufactured goods increased more than 100 times (from $95 billion to $12 trillion) in the 50 years since 1955. China's trade with Africa rose sevenfold during 2000-07 alone.
- *Financial* - emergence of worldwide financial markets and better access to external financing for borrowers. By the early part of the 21st century more than $1.5 trillion in national currencies were traded daily to support the expanded levels of trade and investment. As these worldwide structures grew more quickly than any transnational regulatory regime, the instability of the global financial infrastructure dramatically increased, as evidenced by the Financial crisis of 2007–2010.

- *Economic* - realization of a global common market, based on the freedom of exchange of goods and capital. The interconnectedness of these markets, however, meant that an economic collapse in one area could impact other areas.[citation needed] With globalization, companies can produce goods and services in the lowest cost location. This may cause jobs to be moved to locations that have the lowest wages, least worker protection and lowest health benefits. For Industrial activities this may cause production to move to areas with the least pollution regulations or worker safety regulations.

As of 2005–2007, the Port of Shanghai holds the title as the World's busiest port.

- *Health Policy* - On the global scale, health becomes a commodity. In developing nations under the demands of Structural Adjustment Programs, health systems are fragmented and privatized. Global health policy makers have shifted during the 1990s from United Nations players to financial institutions. The result of this power transition is an increase in privatization in the health sector. This privatization fragments health policy by crowding it with many players with many private interests. These fragmented policy players emphasize partnerships and specific interventions to combat specific problems (as opposed to comprehensive health strategies). Influenced by global trade and global economy, health policy is directed by technological advances and innovative medical trade. Global priorities, in this situation, are sometimes at odds with national priorities where increased health infrastructure and basic primary care are of more value to the public than privatized care for the wealthy.

- *Political* - some use "globalization" to mean the creation of a world government which regulates the relationships among governments and guarantees the rights arising from social and economic globalization. Politically, the United States has enjoyed a position of power among the world powers, in part because of its strong and wealthy economy. With the influence of globalization and with the help of The United States' own economy, the People's Republic of China has experienced some tremendous growth within the past decade. If China continues to grow at the rate projected by the trends, then it is very likely that in the next twenty years, there will be a major reallocation of power among the world leaders. China will have enough wealth, industry, and technology to rival the United States for the position of leading world power.

- *Informational* - increase in information flows between geographically remote locations. Arguably this is a technological change with the advent of fibre optic communications, satellites, and increased availability of telephone and Internet.

- *Language* - the most popular first language is Mandarin (845 million speakers) followed by Spanish (329 million speakers) and English (328 million speakers). However the most popular second language is undoubtedly English, the "lingua franca" of globalization:

- About 35% of the world's mail, telexes, and cables are in English.
- Approximately 40% of the world's radio programs are in English.
- About 50% of all Internet traffic uses English.

- *Competition* - Survival in the new global business market calls for improved productivity and increased competition. Due to the market becoming worldwide, companies in various industries have to upgrade their products and use technology skillfully in order to face increased competition.

- *Ecological* - the advent of global environmental challenges that might be solved with international cooperation, such as climate change, cross-boundary water and air pollution, over-fishing of the ocean, and the spread of invasive species. Since many factories are built in developing countries with less environmental regulation, globalism and free trade may increase pollution and impact on precious fresh water resources (Hoekstra and Chapagain 2008). On the other hand, economic development historically required a "dirty" industrial stage, and it is argued that developing countries should not, via regulation, be prohibited from increasing their standard of living.

- *Cultural* - growth of cross-cultural contacts; advent of new categories of consciousness and identities which embodies cultural diffusion, the desire to increase one's standard of living and enjoy foreign products and ideas, adopt new technology and practices, and participate in a "world culture". Some bemoan the resulting consumerism and loss of languages. Also see Transformation of culture.

  London is a city of considerable diversity. As of 2008, estimates were published that stated that approximately 30% of London's total population was from an ethnic minority group. The latest official figures show that in 2008, 590,000 people arrived to live in the UK whilst 427,000 left, meaning that net inward migration was 163,000.

  - Spreading of multiculturalism, and better individual access to cultural diversity (e.g. through the export of Hollywood). Some consider such "imported" culture a danger, since it may supplant the local culture, causing reduction in diversity or even assimilation. Others consider multiculturalism to promote peace and understanding between people. A third position that gained popularity is the notion that multiculturalism to a new form of monoculture in which no distinctions exist and everyone just shift between various lifestyles in terms of music, cloth and other aspects once more firmly attached to a single culture. Thus not mere cultural assimilation as mentioned above but the obliteration of culture as we know it today. In reality, as it happens in countries like the United Kingdom, Canada, Australia or New Zealand, people who always lived in their native countries maintain their cultures without feeling forced by any reason to accept another and are

    proud of it even when they're acceptive of immigrants, while people who are newly arrived simply keep their own culture or part of it despite some minimum amount of assimilation, although aspects of their culture often become a curiosity and a daily aspect of the lives of the people of the welcoming countries.

- Greater international travel and tourism. WHO estimates that up to 500,000 people are on planes at any one time.[citation needed] In 2008, there were over 922 million international tourist arrivals, with a growth of 1.9% as compared to 2007.
- Greater immigration, including illegal immigration. The IOM estimates there are more than 200 million migrants around the world today. Newly available data show that remittance flows to developing countries reached $328 billion in 2008.
- Spread of local consumer products (e.g., food) to other countries (often adapted to their culture).
- Worldwide fads and pop culture such as Pokémon, Sudoku, Numa Numa, Origami, Idol series, YouTube, Orkut, Facebook, and MySpace. Accessible to those who have Internet or Television, leaving out a substantial segment of the Earth's population.

- Worldwide sporting events such as FIFA World Cup and the Olympic Games.
- Incorporation of multinational corporations into new media. As the sponsors of the All-Blacks rugby team, Adidas had created a parallel website with a downloadable interactive rugby game for its fans to play and compete.

The construction of continental hotels is a major consequence of globalization process in affiliation with tourism and travel industry, Dariush Grand Hotel, Kish, Iran

- *Social* - development of the system of non-governmental organisations as main agents of global public policy, including humanitarian aid and developmental efforts.
- *Technical*
  - Development of a Global Information System, global telecommunications infrastructure and greater transborder data flow, using such technologies as the Internet, communication satellites, submarine fiber optic cable, and wireless telephones
  - Increase in the number of standards applied globally; e.g., copyright laws, patents and world trade agreements.
- *Legal/Ethical*
  - The creation of the international criminal court and international justice movements.
  - Crime importation and raising awareness of global crime-fighting efforts and cooperation.
  - The emergence of Global administrative law.
- *Religious*
  - The spread and increased interrelations of various religious groups, ideas, and practices and their ideas of the meanings and values of particular spaces.

Cultural effects

"Culture" is defined as patterns of human activity and the symbols that give these activities significance. Culture is what people eat, how they dress, the beliefs they hold, and the activities they practice. Globalization has joined different cultures and made it into something different.

One classic culture aspect is food. Someone in America can be eating Japanese noodles for lunch while someone in Sydney, Australia is eating classic Italian meatballs. India is known for its curry and exotic spices. France is known for its cheeses. North America is known for its burgers and fries. McDonald's is a North American company which is now a global enterprise with 31,000 locations worldwide. This company is just one example of food causing cultural influence on the global scale.

Globalization has influenced the use of language across the world. This street in Hong Kong, a former British colony, shows various signs, a few of which incorporate both Chinese and British English.

Another common practice brought about by globalization is the usage of Chinese characters in tattoos. These tattoos are popular with today's youth despite the lack of social acceptance of tattoos in China. Also, there is a lack of comprehension in the meaning of Chinese characters that people get, making this an example of cultural appropriation.

The internet breaks down cultural boundaries across the world by enabling easy, near-instantaneous communication between people anywhere in a variety of digital forms and media. The Internet is associated with the process of cultural globalization

Japanese McDonald's fast food as evidence of corporate globalization and the integration of the same into different cultures.

because it allows interaction and communication between people with very different lifestyles and from very different cultures. Photo sharing websites allow interaction even where language would otherwise be a barrier.

Negative effects

See also: Alter-globalization, Participatory economics, and Global Justice Movement

Globalization has generated significant international opposition over concerns that it has increased inequality and environmental degradation. In the Midwestern United States, globalization has eaten away at its competitive edge in industry and agriculture, lowering the quality of life.

Some also view the effect of globalization on culture as a rising concern. Along with globalization of economies and trade, culture is being imported and exported as well. The concern is that the stronger, bigger countries such as the United States, may overrun the other, smaller countries' cultures, leading to those customs and values being faded away. This process is also sometimes referred to as Americanization or McDonaldization.

Sweatshops

In many poorer nations globalization is the result of foreign businesses utilizing workers in a country to take advantage of the lower wage rates.

A maquila in Mexico

One example used by anti-globalization protestors is the use of sweatshops by manufacturers. According to Global Exchange these "Sweat Shops" are widely used by sports shoe manufacturers and mentions one company in particular – Nike. There are factories set up in the poor countries where employees agree to work for low wages. Then if labour laws alter in those countries and stricter rules govern the manufacturing process the factories are closed down and relocated to other nations with more business favorable policies.[citation needed]

There are several agencies that have been set up worldwide specifically designed to focus on anti-sweatshop campaigns and education of such. In the USA, the National Labor Committee has proposed a number of bills as part of The Decent Working Conditions and Fair Competition Act, which have thus far failed in Congress. The legislation would legally require companies to respect human and worker rights by prohibiting the import, sale, or export of sweatshop goods.

Specifically, these core standards include no child labor, no forced labor, freedom of association, right to organize and bargain collectively, as well as the right to decent working conditions.

There are also concerns about the emergence of "electronic sweatshops." Shehzad Nadeem writes that the outsourcing of service work, such as customer service and Information Technology work, to India has resulted in "longer work hours, an intense work pace, and temporal displacement manifested in health problems and alienation from family and friends."

Negative effects of economic liberalization

Further information: Neoliberalism

The world today is so interconnected that the collapse of the subprime mortgage market in the U.S. has led to a global financial crisis and recession on a scale not seen since the Great Depression. Government deregulation and failed regulation of Wall Street's investment banks were important contributors to the subprime mortgage crisis.

A flood of consumer goods such as televisions, radios, bicycles, and textiles into the United States, Europe, and Japan has helped fuel the economic expansion of Asian tiger economies in recent decades. However, Chinese textile and clothing exports have recently encountered criticism from Europe, the United States and some African countries. In South Africa, some 300,000 textile workers have lost their jobs due to the influx of Chinese goods. The increasing U.S. trade deficit with China has cost 2.4 million American jobs between 2001 and 2008, according to a study by the Economic Policy Institute (EPI). A total of 3.2 million – one in six U.S. factory jobs – have disappeared between 2000 and 2007.

Brain drain

Opportunities in richer countries drives talent away from poorer countries, leading to brain drains. Brain drain has cost the African continent over $4.1 billion in the employment of 150,000 expatriate professionals annually. Indian students going abroad for their higher studies costs India a foreign exchange outflow of $10 billion annually.

Environmental degradation

The Worldwatch Institute said the booming economies of China and India are planetary powers that are shaping the global biosphere. In 2007, China overtook the United States as the world's biggest producer of CO_2. Only 1 percent of the country's 560 million city inhabitants (2007) breathe air deemed safe by the European Union. At present rates, tropical rainforests in Indonesia would be logged out in 10 years, Papua New Guinea in 13 to 16 years. A major source of deforestation is the logging industry, driven spectacularly by China and Japan. China and India are quickly becoming large oil consumers. China has seen oil consumption grow by 8% yearly since 2002, doubling from 1996–2006. *State of the World 2006* report said the two countries' high economic growth hid a reality of severe pollution. The report states:

> *The world's ecological capacity is simply insufficient to satisfy the ambitions of China, India, Japan, Europe and the United States as well as the aspirations of the rest of the world in a sustainable way*

Without more recycling, zinc could be used up by 2037, both indium and hafnium could run out by 2017, and terbium could be gone before 2012. It is said that if China and India were to consume as much resources per capita as United States or Japan in 2030 together they would require a full planet Earth to meet their needs. In the longterm these effects can lead to increased conflict over dwindling resources and in the worst case a Malthusian catastrophe.

Food security

The head of the International Food Policy Research Institute, stated in 2008 that the gradual change in diet among newly prosperous populations is the most important factor underpinning the rise in global food prices. From 1950 to 1984, as the Green Revolution transformed agriculture around the world, grain production increased by over 250%. The world population has grown by about 4 billion since the beginning of the Green Revolution and most believe that, without the Revolution, there would be greater famine and malnutrition than the UN presently documents (approximately 850 million people suffering from chronic malnutrition in 2005).

It is becoming increasingly difficult to maintain food security in a world beset by a confluence of "peak" phenomena, namely peak oil, peak water, peak phosphorus, peak grain and peak fish. Growing populations, falling energy sources and food shortages will create the "perfect storm" by 2030, according to the UK government chief scientist. He said food reserves are at a 50-year low but the world requires 50% more energy, food and water by 2030. The world will have to produce 70% more food by 2050 to feed a projected extra 2.3 billion people and as incomes rise, the United Nations' Food and Agriculture Organisation (FAO) warned. Social scientists have warned of the possibility that global civilization is due for a period of contraction and economic re-localization, due to the decline in fossil fuels and resulting crisis in transportation and food production. One paper even suggested that the future might even bring about a restoration of sustainable local economic activities based on hunting and gathering, shifting horticulture, and pastoralism.

The journal *Science* published a four-year study in November 2006, which predicted that, at prevailing trends, the world would run out of wild-caught seafood in 2048.

Disease

Further information: Globalization and disease

Globalization has also helped to spread some of the deadliest infectious diseases known to humans. Starting in Asia, the Black Death killed at least one-third of Europe's population in the 14th century. Even worse devastation was inflicted on the American supercontinent by European arrivals. 90% of the populations of the civilizations of the "New World" such as the Aztec, Maya, and Inca were killed by small pox brought by European colonization. Modern modes of transportation allow more people and products to travel around the world at a faster pace, but they also open the airways to the transcontinental movement of infectious disease vectors. One example of this occurring is AIDS/HIV. Due to immigration, approximately 500,000 people in the United States are believed to be infected with Chagas disease. In 2006, the tuberculosis (TB) rate among foreign-born persons in the United States was 9.5 times that of U.S.-born persons.

Drug and illicit goods trade

The United Nations Office on Drugs and Crime (UNODC) issued a report that the global drug trade generates more than $320 billion a year in revenues. Worldwide, the UN estimates there are more than 50 million regular users of heroin, cocaine and synthetic drugs. The international trade of endangered species is second only to drug trafficking. Traditional Chinese medicine often incorporates ingredients from all parts of plants, the leaf, stem, flower, root, and also ingredients from animals and minerals. The use of parts of endangered species (such as seahorses, rhinoceros horns, saiga antelope horns, and tiger bones and claws) has created controversy and resulted in a black market of poachers who hunt restricted animals. In 2003, 29% of open sea fisheries were in a state of collapse.

Advocates

Supporters of free trade claim that it increases economic prosperity as well as opportunity, especially among developing nations, enhances civil liberties and leads to a more efficient allocation of resources. Economic theories of comparative advantage suggest that free trade leads to a more efficient allocation of resources, with all countries involved in the trade benefiting. In general, this leads to lower prices, more employment, higher output and a higher standard of living for those in developing countries.

Dr. Francesco Stipo, Director of the USA Club of Rome suggests that "the world government should reflect the political and economic balances of world nations. A world confederation would not supersede the authority of the State governments but rather complement it, as both the States and the world authority would have power within their sphere of competence".

Proponents of laissez-faire capitalism, and some libertarians, say that higher degrees of political and economic freedom in the form of democracy and capitalism in the developed world are ends in themselves and also produce higher levels of material wealth. They see globalization as the beneficial spread of liberty and capitalism.

Supporters of democratic globalization are sometimes called pro-globalists. They believe that the first phase of globalization, which was market-oriented, should be followed by a phase of building global political institutions representing the will of world citizens. The difference from other globalists is that they do not define in advance any ideology to orient this will, but would leave it to the free choice of those citizens via a democratic process.[citation needed]

Some, such as former Canadian Senator Douglas Roche, O.C., simply view globalization as inevitable and advocate creating institutions such as a directly elected United Nations Parliamentary Assembly to exercise oversight over unelected international bodies.

Critics

Main article: Anti-globalization movement

See also: Alter-globalization, Participatory economics, and Global Justice Movement

"Anti-globalization" can involve the process or actions taken by a state or its people in order to demonstrate its sovereignty and practice democratic decision-making. Anti-globalization may occur in order to maintain barriers to the international transfer of people, goods and beliefs, particularly free market deregulation, encouraged by business organizations and organizations such as the International Monetary Fund or the World Trade Organization. Moreover, as Naomi Klein argues in her book No Logo, anti-globalism can denote either a single social movement or an umbrella term that encompasses a number of separate social movements such as nationalists and socialists. In either case, participants stand in opposition to the unregulated political power of large, multi-national corporations, as the corporations exercise power through leveraging trade agreements which in some instances create unemployment, and damage the democratic rights of citizens[citation needed], the environment particularly air quality index and rain forests[citation needed], as well as national government's sovereignty to determine labor rights,[citation needed] including the right to form a union, and health and safety legislation, or laws as they may otherwise infringe on cultural practices and traditions of developing countries.[citation needed]

Some people who are labeled "anti-globalist" or "sceptics" (Hirst and Thompson) consider the term to be too vague and inaccurate. Podobnik states that "the vast majority of groups that participate in these protests draw on international networks of support, and they generally call for forms of globalization that enhance democratic representation, human rights, and egalitarianism."

Joseph Stiglitz and Andrew Charlton write:

> The anti-globalization movement developed in opposition to the perceived negative aspects of globalization. The term 'anti-globalization' is in many ways a misnomer, since the group represents a wide range of interests and issues and many of the people involved in the anti-globalization movement do support closer ties between the various peoples and cultures of the world through, for example, aid, assistance for refugees, and global environmental issues.

Some members aligned with this viewpoint prefer instead to describe themselves as the "Global Justice Movement", the "Anti-Corporate-Globalization Movement", the "Movement of Movements" (a popular term in Italy), the "Alter-globalization" movement (popular in France), the "Counter-Globalization" movement, and a number of other terms.

Critiques of the current wave of economic globalization typically look at both the damage to the planet, in terms of the perceived unsustainable harm done to the biosphere, as well as the perceived human costs, such as poverty, inequality, miscegenation, injustice and the erosion of traditional culture which, the critics contend, all occur as a result of the economic transformations related to globalization. They challenge directly the metrics, such as GDP, used to measure progress promulgated by institutions such as the World Bank, and look to other measures, such as the Happy Planet Index, created by the New

Economics Foundation. They point to a "multitude of interconnected fatal consequences–social disintegration, a breakdown of democracy, more rapid and extensive deterioration of the environment, the spread of new diseases, increasing poverty and alienation" which they claim are the unintended but very real consequences of globalization.

The terms globalization and anti-globalization are used in various ways. Noam Chomsky believes that

> The term "globalization" has been appropriated by the powerful to refer to a specific form of international economic integration, one based on investor rights, with the interests of people incidental. That is why the business press, in its more honest moments, refers to the "free trade agreements" as "free investment agreements" (Wall St. Journal). Accordingly, advocates of other forms of globalization are described as "anti-globalization"; and some, unfortunately, even accept this term, though it is a term of propaganda that should be dismissed with ridicule. No sane person is opposed to globalization, that is, international integration. Surely not the left and the workers movements, which were founded on the principle of international solidarity — that is, globalization in a form that attends to the rights of people, not private power systems.

> The dominant propaganda systems have appropriated the term "globalization" to refer to the specific version of international economic integration that they favor, which privileges the rights of investors and lenders, those of people being incidental. In accord with this usage, those who favor a different form of international integration, which privileges the rights of human beings, become "anti-globalist." This is simply vulgar propaganda, like the term "anti-Soviet" used by the most disgusting commissars to refer to dissidents. It is not only vulgar, but idiotic. Take the World Social Forum, called "anti-globalization" in the propaganda system – which happens to include the media, the educated classes, etc., with rare exceptions. The WSF is a paradigm example of globalization. It is a gathering of huge numbers of people from all over the world, from just about every corner of life one can think of, apart from the extremely narrow highly privileged elites who meet at the competing World Economic Forum, and are called "pro-globalization" by the propaganda system. An observer watching this farce from Mars would collapse in hysterical laughter at the antics of the educated classes.

Critics argue that globalization results in:

- **Poorer countries suffering disadvantages**: While it is true that globalization encourages free trade among countries, there are also negative consequences because some countries try to save their national markets. The main export of poorer countries is usually agricultural goods. Larger countries often subsidise their farmers (like the EU Common Agricultural Policy), which lowers the market price for the poor farmer's crops compared to what it would be under free trade.

- **The exploitation of foreign impoverished workers**: The deterioration of protections for weaker nations by stronger industrialized powers has resulted in the exploitation of the people in those nations to become cheap labor. Due to the lack of protections, companies from powerful industrialized nations are able to offer workers enough salary to entice them to endure extremely long hours and unsafe working conditions, though economists question if consenting workers in a competitive employers' market can be decried as "exploited". It is true that the workers are free to leave their jobs, but in many poorer countries, this would mean starvation for the worker, and possible even his/her family if their previous jobs were unavailable.

- **The shift to outsourcing**: Globalization has allowed corporations to move manufacturing and service jobs from high cost locations to locations with the lowest wages and worker benefits. This results in loss of jobs in the high cost locations. [citation needed] This has contributed to the deterioration of the middle class[citation needed] which is a major factor in the increasing economic inequality in the United States .[citation needed] Families that were once part of the middle class are forced into lower positions by massive layoffs and outsourcing to another country. This also means that people in the lower class have a much harder time climbing out of poverty because of the absence of the middle class as a stepping stone.

- **Weak labor unions**: The surplus in cheap labor coupled with an ever growing number of companies in transition has caused a weakening of labor unions in the United States. Unions lose their effectiveness when their membership begins to decline. As a result unions hold less power over corporations that are able to easily replace workers, often for lower wages, and have the option to not offer unionized jobs anymore.

- **An increase in exploitation of child labor**: for example, a country that experiencing increases in labor demand because of globalization and an increase the demand for goods produced by children, will experience greater a demand for child labor. This can be "hazardous" or "exploitive", e.g., quarrying, salvage, cash cropping but also includes the trafficking of children, children in bondage or forced labor, prostitution, pornography and other illicit activities.

In December 2007, World Bank economist Branko Milanovic has called much previous empirical research on global poverty and inequality into question because, according to him, improved estimates of purchasing power parity indicate that developing countries are worse off than previously believed. Milanovic remarks that "literally hundreds of scholarly papers on convergence or divergence of countries' incomes have been published in the last decade based on what we know now were faulty numbers." With the new data, possibly economists will revise calculations, and he also believed that there are considerable implications estimates of global inequality and poverty levels. Global inequality was estimated at around 65 Gini points, whereas the new numbers indicate global inequality to be at 70 on the Gini scale.

The critics of globalization typically emphasize that globalization is a process that is mediated according to corporate interests, and typically raise the possibility of alternative global institutions and policies, which they believe address the moral claims of poor and working classes throughout the globe, as well as environmental concerns in a more equitable way.

The movement is very broad[citation needed], including church groups, national liberation factions, peasant unionists, intellectuals, artists, protectionists, anarchists, those in support of relocalization and others. Some are reformist, (arguing for a more moderate form of capitalism) while others are more revolutionary (arguing for what they believe is a more humane system than capitalism) and others are reactionary, believing globalization destroys national industry and jobs.

One of the key points made by critics of recent economic globalization is that income inequality, both between and within nations, is increasing as a result of these processes. One article from 2001 found that significantly, in 7 out of 8 metrics, income inequality has increased in the twenty years ending

2001. Also, "incomes in the lower deciles of world income distribution have probably fallen absolutely since the 1980s". Furthermore, the World Bank's figures on absolute poverty were challenged. The article was skeptical of the World Bank's claim that the number of people living on less than $1 a day has held steady at 1.2 billion from 1987 to 1998, because of biased methodology.

A chart that gave the inequality a very visible and comprehensible form, the so-called 'champagne glass' effect, was contained in the 1992 United Nations Development Program Report, which showed the distribution of global income to be very uneven, with the richest 20% of the world's population controlling 82.7% of the world's income.

Distribution of world GDP, 1989

Quintile of Population	Income
Richest 20%	82.7%
Second 20%	11.7%
Third 20%	2.3%
Fourth 20%	2.4%
Poorest 20%	0.2%

Source: United Nations Development Program. 1992 Human Development Report

Economic arguments by fair trade theorists claim that unrestricted free trade benefits those with more financial leverage (i.e. the rich) at the expense of the poor.

Americanization related to a period of high political American clout and of significant growth of America's shops, markets and object being brought into other countries. So globalization, a much more diversified phenomenon, relates to a multilateral political world and to the increase of objects, markets and so on into each others countries.

Critics of globalization talk of Westernization. A 2005 UNESCO report showed that cultural exchange is becoming more frequent from Eastern Asia but Western countries are still the main exporters of cultural goods. In 2002, China was the third largest exporter of cultural goods, after the UK and US. Between 1994 and 2002, both North America's and the European Union's shares of cultural exports declined, while Asia's cultural exports grew to surpass North America. Related factors are the fact that Asia's population and area are several times that of North America.

Some opponents of globalization see the phenomenon as the promotion of corporatist interests. They also claim that the increasing autonomy and strength of corporate entities shapes the political policy of countries.

History

The historical origins of globalization are the subject of on-going debate. Though some scholars situate the origins of globalization in the modern era, others regard it as a phenomenon with a long history.

Perhaps the most extreme proponent of a deep historical origin for globalization was Andre Gunder Frank, an economist associated with dependency theory. Frank argued that a form of globalization has been in existence since the rise of trade links between Sumer and the Indus Valley Civilization in the third millennium B.C. Critics of this idea point out that it rests upon an over-broad definition of globalization.

Extent of the Silk Road and Spice trade routes blocked by the Ottoman Empire in 1453 spurring exploration

An early form of globalized economics and culture existed during the Hellenistic Age, when commercialized urban centers were focused around the axis of Greek culture over a wide range that stretched from India to Spain, with such cities as Alexandria, Athens, and Antioch at its center. Trade was widespread during that period, and it is the first time the idea of a cosmopolitan culture (from Greek "Cosmopolis", meaning "world city") emerged. Others have perceived an early form of globalization in the trade links between the Roman Empire, the Parthian Empire, and the Han Dynasty. The increasing articulation of commercial links between these powers inspired the development of the Silk Road, which started in western China, reached the boundaries of the Parthian empire, and continued onwards towards Rome. With 300 Greek ships a year sailing between the Greco-Roman world and India, the annual trade may have reached 300,000 tons.

The Islamic Golden Age was also an important early stage of globalization, when Jewish and Muslim traders and explorers established a sustained economy across the Old World resulting in a globalization of crops, trade, knowledge and technology. Globally significant crops such as sugar and cotton became widely cultivated across the Muslim world in this period, while the necessity of learning Arabic and completing the Hajj created a cosmopolitan culture.

Portuguese carrack in Nagasaki, 17th
century Japanese Nanban art

Native New World crops exchanged
globally: Maize, Tomato, Potato, Vanilla,
Rubber, Cacao, Tobacco

The advent of the Mongol Empire, though destabilizing to the commercial centers of the Middle East and China, greatly facilitated travel along the Silk Road. This permitted travelers and missionaries such as Marco Polo to journey successfully (and profitably) from one end of Eurasia to the other. The so-called Pax Mongolica of the thirteenth century had several other notable globalizing effects. It witnessed the creation of the first international postal service, as well as the rapid transmission of epidemic diseases such as bubonic plague across the newly unified regions of Central Asia. These pre-modern phases of global or hemispheric exchange are sometimes known as archaic globalization. Up to the sixteenth century, however, even the largest systems of international exchange were limited to the Old World.

The Age of Discovery brought a broad change in globalization, being the first period in which Eurasia and Africa engaged in substantial cultural, material and biologic exchange with the New World. It began in the late 15th century, when the two Kingdoms of the Iberian Peninsula - Portugal and Castile - sent the first exploratory voyages around the Horn of Africa and to the Americas, "discovered" in 1492 by Christopher Columbus. Shortly before the turn of the 16th century, Portuguese started establishing trading posts (factories) from Africa to Asia and Brazil, to deal with the trade of local products like gold, spices and timber, introducing an international business center under a royal monopoly, the House of India.

Global integration continued with the European colonization of the Americas initiating the Columbian Exchange, the enormous widespread exchange of plants, animals, foods, human populations (including slaves), communicable diseases, and culture between the Eastern and Western hemispheres. It was one of the most significant global events concerning ecology, agriculture, and culture in history. New crops that had come from the Americas via the European seafarers in the 16th century significantly contributed to the world's population growth.

This phase is sometimes known as proto-globalization. It was characterized by the rise of maritime European empires, in the 16th and 17th centuries, first the Portuguese and Spanish Empires, and later the Dutch and British Empires. In the 17th century, globalization became also a private business phenomenon when chartered companies like British East India Company (founded in 1600), often described as the first multinational corporation, as well as the Dutch East India Company (founded in

1602) were established. Because of the large investment and financing needs and high risks involved in international trade, the British East India Company became the first company in the world to share risk and enable joint ownership of companies through the issuance of shares of stock: an important driver for globalization.[citation needed]

The 19th century witnessed the advent of globalization approaching its modern form. Industrialization allowed cheap production of household items using economies of scale, while rapid population growth created sustained demand for commodities. Globalization in this period was decisively shaped by nineteenth-century imperialism. After the Opium Wars and the completion of British conquest of India, vast populations of these regions became ready consumers of European exports. It was in this period that areas of sub-Saharan Africa and the Pacific islands were incorporated into the world system. Meanwhile, the conquest of new parts of the globe, notably sub-Saharan Africa, by Europeans yielded valuable natural resources such as rubber, diamonds and coal and helped fuel trade and investment between the European imperial powers, their colonies, and the United States.[citation needed] Said John Maynard Keynes,

Animated map showing Colonial empires evolution from 1492 to present

19th century Great Britain become the first global economic superpower, because of superior manufacturing technology and improved global communications such as steamships and railroads.

> The inhabitant of London could order by telephone, sipping his morning tea, the various products of the whole earth, and reasonably expect their early delivery upon his doorstep. Militarism and imperialism of racial and cultural rivalries were little more than the amusements of his daily newspaper. What an extraordinary episode in the economic progress of man was that age which came to an end in August 1914.

The first phase of "modern globalization" began to break down at the beginning of the 20th century, with the first world war. The novelist VM Yeates criticised the financial forces of globalization as a factor in creating World War I. The final death knell for this phase came during the gold standard crisis and Great Depression in the late 1920s and early 1930s.[citation needed]

In the middle decades of the twentieth century globalization was largely driven by the global expansion of multinational corporations based in the United States and Europe, and worldwide exchange of new developments in science, technology and products, with most significant inventions of this time having their origins in the Western world according to Encyclopedia Britannica. Worldwide export of western culture went through the new mass media: film, radio and television and recorded music. Development and growth of international transport and telecommunication played a decisive role in modern globalization.

In late 2000s, much of the industrialized world entered into a deep recession. Some analysts say the world is going through a period of deglobalization after years of increasing economic integration. China has recently become the world's largest exporter surpassing Germany.

Post-World War II

Globalization, since World War II, is largely the result of planning by politicians to break down borders hampering trade. Their work led to the Bretton Woods conference, an agreement by the world's leading politicians to lay down the framework for international commerce and finance, and the founding of several international institutions intended to oversee the processes of globalization.

These institutions include the International Bank for Reconstruction and Development (the World Bank), and the International Monetary Fund. Globalization has been facilitated by advances in technology which have reduced the costs of trade, and trade negotiation rounds, originally under the auspices of the General Agreement on Tariffs and Trade (GATT), which led to a series of agreements to remove restrictions on free trade.

Since World War II, barriers to international trade have been considerably lowered through international agreements — GATT. Particular initiatives carried out as a result of GATT and the World Trade Organization (WTO), for which GATT is the foundation, have included:

- Promotion of free trade:
  - elimination of tariffs; creation of free trade zones with small or no tariffs
  - Reduced transportation costs, especially resulting from development of containerization for ocean shipping.
  - Reduction or elimination of capital controls
  - Reduction, elimination, or harmonization of subsidies for local businesses
  - Creation of subsidies for global corporations
  - Harmonization of intellectual property laws across the majority of states, with more restrictions
  - Supranational recognition of intellectual property restrictions (e.g. patents granted by China would be recognized in the United States)

Cultural globalization, driven by communication technology and the worldwide marketing of Western cultural industries, was understood at first as a process of homogenization, as the global domination of American culture at the expense of traditional diversity. However, a contrasting trend soon became evident in the emergence of movements protesting against globalization and giving new momentum to the defense of local uniqueness, individuality, and identity.

The Uruguay Round (1986 to 1994) led to a treaty to create the WTO to mediate trade disputes and set up a uniform platform of trading. Other bilateral and multilateral trade agreements, including sections of Europe's Maastricht Treaty and the North American Free Trade Agreement (NAFTA) have also been signed in pursuit of the goal of reducing tariffs and barriers to trade.

World exports rose from 8.5% in 1970, to 16.2% of total gross world product in 2001.

In the 1990s, the growth of low cost communication networks allowed work done using a computer to be moved to low wage locations for many job types. This included accounting, software development, and engineering design.

Measurement

Economic globalization can be measured in different ways. These center around the four main economic flows that characterize globalization:

- Goods and services, e.g., exports plus imports as a proportion of national income or per capita of population
- Labor/people, e.g., net migration rates; inward or outward migration flows, weighted by population
- Capital, e.g., inward or outward direct investment as a proportion of national income or per head of population
- Technology, e.g., international research & development flows; proportion of populations (and rates of change thereof) using particular inventions (especially 'factor-neutral' technological advances such as the telephone, motorcar, broadband)

As globalization is not only an economic phenomenon, a multivariate approach to measuring globalization is the recent index calculated by the Swiss think tank KOF. The index measures the three main dimensions of globalization: economic, social, and political. In addition to three indices measuring these dimensions, an overall index of globalization and sub-indices referring to actual economic flows, economic restrictions, data on personal contact, data on information flows, and data on cultural proximity is calculated. Data is available on a yearly basis for 122 countries, as detailed in Dreher, Gaston and Martens (2008). According to the index, the world's most globalized country is Belgium, followed by Austria, Sweden, the United Kingdom and the Netherlands. The least globalized countries according to the KOF-index are Haiti, Myanmar, the Central African Republic and Burundi.

A.T. Kearney and *Foreign Policy Magazine* jointly publish another Globalization Index. According to the 2006 index, Singapore, Ireland, Switzerland, the Netherlands, Canada and Denmark are the most globalized, while Indonesia, India and Iran are the least globalized among countries listed.

International social fora

See also: European Social Forum, Asian Social Forum, and World Social Forum

The first World Social Forum in 2001 was an initiative of the administration of Porto Alegre, Brazil. The slogan of was "Another World Is Possible". It was here that the WSF's Charter of Principles was adopted to provide a framework for the fora.

The WSF became a periodic meeting: in 2002 and 2003 it was held again in Porto Alegre and became a rallying point for worldwide protest against the American invasion of Iraq. In 2004 it was moved to Mumbai, India, to make it more accessible to the populations of Asia and Africa. This last appointment saw the participation of 75,000 delegates.

Regional fora took place following the example of the WSF, adopting its Charter of Principles. The first European Social Forum was held in November 2002 in Florence. The slogan was "Against the war, against racism and against neo-liberalism". It saw the participation of 60,000 delegates and ended with a huge demonstration against the war of 1,000,000 people according to the organizers. The other two ESFs took place in Paris and London, in 2003 and 2004 respectively.

Recently there has been some discussion behind the movement about the role of the social forums. Some see them as a "popular university", an occasion to make many people aware of the problems of globalization. Others would prefer that delegates concentrate their efforts on the coordination and organization of the movement and on the planning of new campaigns. However it has often been argued that in the dominated countries (most of the world) the WSF is little more than an 'NGO fair' driven by Northern NGOs and donors most of which are hostile to popular movements of the poor.

Relation to Americanization

In the past, the argument that globalization could be equated in actuality to the spreading of American culture was made. The thorough spreading of American culture throughout the world was apparent. For example, there were cola products shipped and sold in nearly every country in the world. American fashion also seemed to be trending in most other countries. The United States was known as a hyperpower due to its economic and military dominance at the time; the relative power of the US waned as other developing nations such as the BRIC nations grew in strength, decreasing the forcefulness of the argument that current globalization is simply Americanization.

See also

- Alter-globalization
- American Imperialism
- Archaic globalization
- Civilizing mission
- Columbian Exchange
- Cultural assimilation
- Deglobalization
- Development criticism
- Faith and Globalisation initiative
- Global civics
- Global information system
- Global Trade Watch (Australia)
- Globalism
- Globality
- Great Transition
- Impact of globalization on women in China
- Interdependence
- New world order (politics)
- Postmodernism
- Transnational cinema
- Vermeer's Hat: The Seventeenth Century and the Dawn of the Global World
- World economy

References

Globalization: An Innovation Imperative (Keynote Presentation by Mr. Pari Natarajan, CEO, Zinnov) [1]

Further reading

- Barbara, Christopher (2008). *International legal personality: Panacea or pandemonium? Theorizing about the individual and the state in the era of globalization* [2]. Saarbrücken: Verlag Dr. Müller. ISBN 3639115147.
- Barzilai, Gad (2008). *Beyond Relativism: Where is Political Power in Legal Pluralism* [3]. The Berkeley Electronic Press. pp. 395–416.
- Bastardas-Boada, Albert (2002), "World Language Policy in the Era of Globalization: Diversity and Intercommunication from the Perspective of 'Complexity'", *Noves SL, Revista de Sociolingüística*

(Barcelona), http://www6.gencat.net/llengcat/noves/hm02estiu/metodologia/a_bastardas1_9.
htm.

- von Braun, Joachim; Eugenio Diaz-Bonilla (2007). *Globalization of Food and Agriculture and the Poor* [4]. Oxford: Oxford University Press. ISBN 9780195695281.

- Peter Berger, *Four Faces of Global Culture* [5]*Wikipedia:Link rot* (The National Interest, Fall 1997).

- Friedman, Thomas L. (2005). *The World Is Flat*. New York: Farrar, Straus and Giroux. ISBN 0-374-29288-4.

- Glyn, Andrew (2006). *Capitalism Unleashed: Finance, Globalization, and Welfare* [6]. Oxford: Oxford University Press. ISBN 0199226792.

- Gowan, Peter (1999). *The Global Gamble: Washington's Faustian Bid for World Dominance* [7]. London: Verso. ISBN 1859842712.

- Grinin, Leonid. *Globalization and Sovereignty: Why do States Abandon their Sovereign Prerogatives?* [8].

- Haggblade, Steven; et al. (2007). *Transforming the Rural Nonfarm Economy: Opportunities and Threats in the Developing World* [9]. Johns Hopkins University Press. p. 512. ISBN 978-0-8018-8663-8.

- Kitching, Gavin (2001). *Seeking Social Justice through Globalization. Escaping a Nationalist Perspective* [10]. Penn State Press. ISBN 0271021624.

- Gernot Kohler and Emilio José Chaves (Editors) "Globalization: Critical Perspectives" Hauppauge, New York: Nova Science Publishers <http://www.novapublishers.com/> ISBN 1-59033-346-2. With contributions by Samir Amin, Christopher Chase Dunn, Andre Gunder Frank, Immanuel Wallerstein

- Mander, Jerry; Edward Goldsmith (1996). *The case against the global economy : and for a turn toward the local*. San Francisco: Sierra Club Books. ISBN 0-87156-865-9.

- Moore, Karl; David Lewis (2009). *Origins of Globalization* [11]. New York: Routledge. ISBN 978-0-415-80598-8.

- Murray, Warwick E. (2006). *Geographies of Globalization*. New York: Routledge. ISBN 0415317991.

- Neumann, Iver B.; Ole Jacob Sending (2010). *Governing the Global Polity: Practice, Mentality, Rationality* [12]. Ann Arbor: University of Michigan Press. ISBN 9780472070930.

- Osterhammel, Jurgen; Niels P. Petersson (2005). *Globalization: A Short History* [13]. Princeton, New Jersey: Princeton University Press. ISBN 0-691-12165-6.

- Raffaele Feola, La Globalizzazione dell'Arte. L'UTOPIA DEL GLOBALE, Napoli 2009.

- Reinsdorf, Marshall and Matthew J. Slaughter (2009). *International Trade in Services and Intangibles in the Era of Globalization*. Chicago: The University of Chicago Press. ISBN 9780226709598.

- Sen, Amartya (1999). *Development as Freedom*. Oxford, New York: Oxford University Press. ISBN 019289330.

- Sirkin, Harold L; James W. Hemerling and Arindam K. Bhattacharya (2008). *Globality: Competing with Everyone from Everywhere for Everything* [14]. New York: Business Plus. p. 292. ISBN 0446178292.
- Smith, Charles (2007). *International Trade and Globalisation, 3rd edition*. Stocksfield: Anforme. ISBN 1905504101.
- Steger, Manfred (2002). *Globalism: the new market ideology*. Lanham, Maryland: Rowman & Littlefield Publishers. ISBN 0742500721.
- Steger, Manfred (2003). *Globalization: A Very Short Introduction*. Oxford, New York: Oxford University Press. ISBN 0-19-280359-X.
- Stiglitz, Joseph E. (2002). *Globalization and Its Discontents*. New York: W.W. Norton. ISBN 0-393-32439-7.
- Stiglitz, Joseph E. (2006). *Making Globalization Work*. New York: W.W. Norton. ISBN 0-393-06122-1.
- Tausch, Arno (2008). *Multicultural Europe: Effects of the Global Lisbon Process* [15]. Hauppauge, New York: Nova Science Publishers. ISBN 978-1-60456-806-6.
- Tausch, Arno (2009). *Titanic 2010? The European Union and its failed "Lisbon strategy* [16]. Hauppauge, New York: Nova Science Publishers. ISBN 978-1-60741-826-9.
- Rafael Domingo Osle, *The New Global Law* (Cambridge University Press, 2010)
- Wolf, Martin (2004). *Why Globalization Works*. New Haven: Yale University Press. ISBN 978-0300102529.

External links

- YaleGlobal Online [17] Online Magazine focusing on Globalization
- Latin Business Chronicle, Dec.10, 2008 [18] Latin America More Globalized
- Arno Tausch (2006), 'From the "Washington" towards a "Vienna Consensus"? A quantitative analysis on globalization, development and global governance'. Paper, prepared for the discussion process leading up to the EU-Latin America and Caribbean Summit 2006, May 11, 2006 to May 12, 2006, Vienna, Austria. Centro Argentino de Estudios Internacionales, Buenos Aires [19]
- '"Destructive Creation"? Some long-term Schumpeterian reflections on the Lisbon process' [20] PDF. Arno Tausch (2007), Entelequia e-Books, University of Cadiz/Malaga (Spain), Munich Personal Repec Archive, Global Development Network, University of Sussex and University of Connecticut, Ideas/Repec]
- Embracing the Challenge of Free Trade: Competing and Prospering in a Global Economy [21] a speech by Federal Reserve chairman Ben Bernanke
- BBC News Special Report - Globalisation [22]
- Guardian Special Report - Globalisation [23]
- Inequality Project [24] from University of Texas

- Institute for Research on World-Systems [25] at UC Riverside
- Resilience, Panarchy, and World-Systems Analysis [26] from the Ecology and Society Journal
- OECD Globalization statistics [27]
- Globalization theories [28]
- The Sociology of Globalization [29]
- Mapping Globalization [30] — globalization project with a collection of maps
- Globalization from the Canadian Encyclopedia [31]
- Globalization and Me [32] Blog and Viewpoints on Globalization

Multimedia

- CBC Archives [33] CBC Television reports on the opening of Moscow McDonald's (1990) - sample of Western business expanding into former communist countries.
- Squeezed: The Cost of Free Trade in the Asia-Pacific [34] 2007 film about the impacts of globalisation in Thailand and the Philippines.

krc:Глобализация mwl:Globalizaçon pnb:گلوبلائزیشن ckb:گڵۆ□□□ یاری□ت

Developed Country

Developed country

The term **developed country** is used to describe countries that have a high level of development according to some criteria. Which criteria, and which countries are classified as being developed, is a contentious issue and is surrounded by fierce debate. Economic criteria have tended to dominate discussions. One such criterion is income per capita;

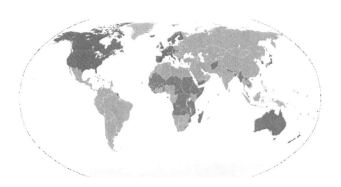

Developed countries are shown in blue (According to the IMF, as of 2008).

countries with high gross domestic product (GDP) per capita would thus be described as developed countries. Another economic criterion is industrialization; countries in which the tertiary and quaternary sectors of industry dominate would thus be described as developed. More recently another measure, the Human Development Index (HDI), which combines an economic measure, national income, with other measures, indices for life expectancy and education has become prominent. This criterion would define developed countries as those with a very high (HDI) rating. However, many anomalies exist when determining "developed" status by whichever measure is used.Wikipedia:Please clarify

Countries not fitting such definitions are classified as developing countries.

Similar terms

Terms similar to **developed country** include **advanced country**, **industrialized country**, **more developed country** (MDC), **more economically developed country** (MEDC), **Global North country**, **first world country**, and **post-industrial country**. The term industrialized country may be somewhat ambiguous, as industrialization is an ongoing process that is hard to define. The term MEDC is one used by modern geographers to specifically describe the status of the countries referred to: more economically developed. The first industrialised country was Britain, followed by Belgium, Germany, United States, France and other Western European countries. According to some economists such as

Jeffrey Sachs, however, the current divide between the developed and developing world is largely a phenomenon of the 20th century.

Definition

Kofi Annan, former Secretary General of the United Nations, defined a developed country as follows: "A developed country is one that allows all its citizens to enjoy a free and healthy life in a safe environment." But according to the United Nations Statistics Division,

> There is no established convention for the designation of "developed" and "developing" countries or areas in the United Nations system.

And it notes that

> The designations "developed" and "developing" are intended for statistical convenience and do not necessarily express a judgement about the stage reached by a particular country or area in the development process.

The UN also notes

> In common practice, Japan in Asia, Canada and the United States in North America, Australia and New Zealand in Oceania, and most European countries are considered "developed" regions or areas. In international trade statistics, the Southern African Customs Union is also treated as a developed region and Israel as a developed country; countries emerging from the former Yugoslavia are treated as developing countries; and countries of eastern Europe and of the Commonwealth of Independent States (code 172) in Europe are not included under either developed or developing regions.

According to the classification from IMF before April 2004, all the countries of Eastern Europe (including Central European countries that still belong to the Eastern Europe Group in the UN institutions) as well as the former Soviet Union (U.S.S.R.) countries in Central Asia (Kazakhstan, Uzbekistan, Kyrgyzstan, Tajikistan and Turkmenistan) and Mongolia, were not included under either developed or developing regions, but rather were referred to as "countries in transition"; however they are now widely regarded (in the international reports) as "developing countries". In the 21st century, the original Four Asian Tigers (which are Hong Kong, Taiwan, Singapore and South Korea) are considered "developed" region or areas, along with Cyprus, Czech republic, Israel, Malta, Slovakia and Slovenia.

Human Development Index

Main articles: Human Development Index and List of countries by Human Development Index

The UN HDI is a statistical measure that gauges a country's level of human development. While there is a strong correlation between having a high HDI score and a prosperous economy, the UN points out that the HDI accounts for more than income or

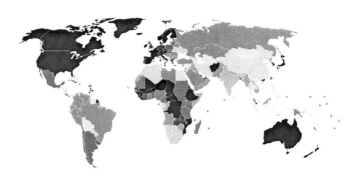

World map indicating the Human Development Index (based on 2007 data, published on October 5, 2009)[Wikipedia:Citation neededcitation needed](Color-blind compliant map) For red-green color vision problems.

productivity. Unlike GDP per capita or per capita income, the HDI takes into account how income is turned "*into education and health opportunities and therefore into higher levels of human development.*" A few examples are Italy and the United States. Despite a relatively large difference in GDP per capita, both countries rank roughly equal in term of overall human development. Since 1980, Norway (2001–2006 and 2009), Japan (1990–91 and 1993), Canada (1992 and 1994–2000) and Iceland (2007–08) have had the highest HDI score. Countries with a score of over 0.800 are considered to have a "high" standard of human development. The top 38 countries have scores ranging from 0.902 in Malta to 0.971 in Norway.

Many countries listed by IMF or CIA as "advanced" (as of 2009), possess an HDI over 0.9 (as of 2007). Many countries possessing an HDI of 0.9 and over (as of 2007), are also listed by IMF or CIA as "advanced" (as of 2009). Thus, many "advanced economies" (as of 2009) are characterized by an HDI score of 0.9 or higher (as of 2007).

The latest index was released on October 5, 2009 and covers the period up to 2007. The following are the 38 countries classified as possessing a "Very high human development" with an HDI at or above 0.900.

- Norway 0.971 (═)
- Australia 0.970 (═)
- Iceland 0.969 (═)
- Canada 0.966 (═)
- Ireland 0.965 (═)
- Netherlands 0.964 (▲ 1)
- Sweden 0.963 (▼ 1)
- France 0.961 (▲ 3)
- Switzerland 0.960 (═)

- Japan 0.960 (═)
- Luxembourg 0.960 (▼ 3)
- Finland 0.959 (▲ 1)
- United States 0.956 (▼ 1)

- Austria 0.955 (▲ 2)
- Spain 0.955 (═)
- Denmark 0.955 (▼ 2)
- Belgium 0.953 (═)
- Italy 0.951 (▲ 1)
- Liechtenstein 0.951 (▼ 1)
- New Zealand 0.950 (═)
- United Kingdom 0.947 (═)
- Germany 0.947 (═)

- Singapore 0.944 (▲ 1)
- Hong Kong 0.944 (▼ 1)
- Greece 0.942 (═)
- South Korea 0.937 (═)

- Israel 0.935 (▲ 1)
- Andorra 0.934 (▼ 1)
- Slovenia 0.929 (═)
- Brunei 0.920 (═)
- Kuwait 0.916 (═)
- Cyprus 0.914 (═)
- Qatar 0.910 (▲ 1)
- Portugal 0.909 (▼ 1)
- United Arab Emirates 0.903 (▲ 2)

- Czech Republic 0.903 (═)
- Barbados 0.903 (▲ 2)
- Malta 0.902 (▼ 3)

Other lists of Developed Countries

Only three institutions have produced lists of "developed countries". The three institutions and their lists are the UN list (shown above), the CIA list and the FTSE Group's list, whose list is not included because its association of developed countries with countries with both high incomes and developed markets is not deemed as directly relevant here. However many institutions have created lists which are sometimes referred to when people are discussing developed countries. The IMF identifies 34 "advanced economies", The OECD, also widely known as the 'developed countries club' has 30 members. The World Bank identifies 66 "high income countries". The EIU's Quality-of-life survey and a list of countries with welfare states are also included here. The criteria for using all these lists and for countries' inclusion on these lists are often not properly spelt out, and several of these lists are based on old data.

IMF advanced economies

According to the International Monetary Fund the following 34 countries are classified as "**advanced economies**":

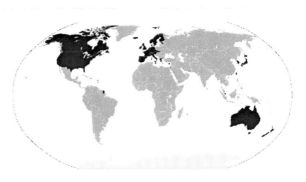

Countries described as Advanced Economies by the IMF.

- 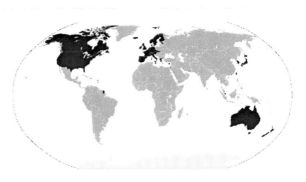 Australia
- Austria
- Belgium
- Canada
- Cyprus
- Czech Republic
- Denmark
- Finland
- France
- Germany
- Greece
- Hong Kong
- Iceland
- Ireland
- Israel
- Italy
- Japan
- Luxembourg
- Malta
- Netherlands
- New Zealand
- Norway
- Portugal
- San Marino
- Singapore
- Slovakia
- Slovenia
- South Korea
- Spain
- Sweden
- Switzerland
- Taiwan

-  United Kingdom
- United States

The CIA has a modified version of an old version of the IMF's list of Advanced Economies. The CIA notes that the IMF's Advanced Economies list "would presumably also cover" some smaller countries. They are:

- Andorra
- Bermuda
- Faroe Islands
- Holy See
- Liechtenstein
- Monaco

Development Assistance Committee members

There are 24 members—select 23 OECD member countries and the European Commission—in the Development Assistance Committee, a group of the world's major donor countries that discuss issues surrounding development aid and poverty reduction in developing countries. As of 2010, the following OECD member countries are DAC members:

Members of the OECD Development Assistance Committee.

- Australia
- Austria
- Belgium
- Canada
- Denmark
- Finland
- France
- Germany
- Greece
- Ireland
- Italy
- Japan
- Luxembourg
- Netherlands
- New Zealand
- Norway

- Portugal
- South Korea
- Spain
- Sweden
- Switzerland
- United Kingdom
- United States

The DAC membership excludes the following OECD members: Chile, Czech Republic, Hungary, Iceland, Israel, Mexico, Poland, Slovakia, Slovenia and Turkey.

High-income OECD members

There are 30 **High-income OECD members**, although there are three other OECD members (Mexico, Turkey, and Chile) that are not high-income members (but rather are upper-middle-income economies), while Estonia (being a high income economy) is expected to join OECD in 2010. As of 2010, the High-income OECD membership is as follows:

23 countries in Europe:

- Austria
- Belgium
- Czech Republic
- Denmark
- Finland
- France
- Germany
- Greece
- Hungary
- Iceland
- Ireland
- Italy
- Luxembourg
- Netherlands
- Norway
- Poland
- Portugal
- Slovakia
- Slovenia
- Spain
- Sweden

- ⊞ Switzerland
- ▓▓ United Kingdom

3 countries in Asia:

- ▬ Israel
- ● Japan
- South Korea

2 countries in North America:

- ▐◆▌ Canada
- ▬ United States

2 countries in Oceania:

- ▓▓ Australia
- ▓▓ New Zealand

Economist's Quality-of-life survey of 2005

Research about standards of living and quality of life by the Economist Intelligence Unit resulted in a quality-of-life index. As of 2005, the highest-ranked economies are

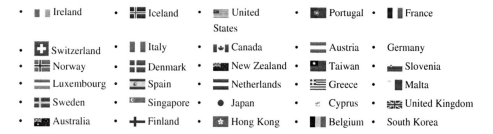

- ▐▐ Ireland
- ▓▓ Iceland
- ▓▓ United States
- ◉ Portugal
- ▐ France
- ⊞ Switzerland
- ▐▐ Italy
- ▐◆▌ Canada
- ▬ Austria
- Germany
- ▓▓ Norway
- ▓▓ Denmark
- ▓▓ New Zealand
- ▐▓ Taiwan
- ▬ Slovenia
- ▬ Luxembourg
- ▬ Spain
- ▬ Netherlands
- ▓▓ Greece
- ▐ Malta
- ▓▓ Sweden
- ▓ Singapore
- ● Japan
- Cyprus
- ▓▓ United Kingdom
- ▓▓ Australia
- ✚ Finland
- ▓ Hong Kong
- ▐▐ Belgium
- South Korea

Newsweek's Quality-of-life survey of 2010

Research about standards of living and quality of life by Newsweek, resulted in the "world's best countries" index, measuring: "health, education, economy, and politics". As of 15/8/2010, the highest-ranked countries are:

- Finland
- Canada
- New Zealand
- Belgium
- Czech Republic
- Switzerland
- Netherlands
- United Kingdom
- Singapore
- Greece
- Sweden
- Japan
- South Korea
- Spain
- Portugal
- Australia
- Denmark
- France
- Israel
- Croatia
- Luxembourg
- United States
- Ireland
- Italy
- Poland
- Norway
- Germany
- Austria
- Slovenia
- Chile

See also

- Developed market
- Emerging markets

External links

- IMF [1] (advanced economies)
- The Economist [2] (quality of life survey)
- The World Factbook [3] (developed countries)
- United Nations Statistics Division [4] (definition)
- United Nations Statistics Division [5] (developed regions)
- World Bank [6] (high-income economies)

Criterion for Judging the Development of Countries

Gross domestic product

The **gross domestic product (GDP)** or **gross domestic income (GDI)** is a measure of a country's overall economic output. It is the market value of all final goods and services made within the borders of a country in a year. It is often positively correlated with the standard of living, though its use as a stand-in for measuring the standard of living has come under increasing criticism and many countries are actively exploring alternative measures to GDP for that purpose.

Gross domestic product comes under the heading of national accounts, which is a subject in macroeconomics.

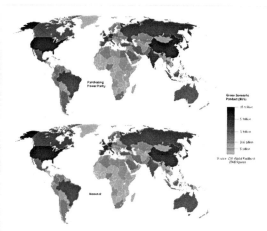

CIA World Factbook 2008 figures of total nominal GDP (bottom) compared to PPP-adjusted GDP (top)

Countries by 2008 GDP (nominal) per capita (IMF, October 2008 estimate)

GDP (PPP) per capita

Determining GDP

Economics

General categories
Microeconomics · Macroeconomics History of economic thought Methodology · Heterodox approaches
Techniques
Mathematical · Econometrics Experimental · National accounting
Fields and subfields
Behavioral · Cultural · Evolutionary Growth · Development · History International · Economic systems Monetary and Financial economics Public and Welfare economics Health · Education · Welfare Population · Labour · Managerial Business · Information · Game theory Industrial organization · Law Agricultural · Natural resource Environmental · Ecological Urban · Rural · Regional · Geography
Lists

Journals · Publications
Categories · Topics · Economists

The economy: concept and history

Business and Economics Portal

GDP can be determined in three ways, all of which should in principle give the same result. They are the product (or output) approach, the income approach, and the expenditure approach.

The most direct of the three is the product approach, which sums the outputs of every class of enterprise to arrive at the total. The expenditure approach works on the principle that all of the product must be bought by somebody, therefore the value of the total product must be equal to people's total expenditures in buying things. The income approach works on the principle that the incomes of the productive factors ("producers," colloquially) must be equal to the value of their product, and determines GDP by finding the sum of all producers' incomes.

Example: the expenditure method:

GDP = private consumption + gross investment + government spending + (exports − imports),

or

$$GDP = C + \text{Inv} + G + (eX - i)$$

Note: "Gross" means that GDP measures production regardless of the various uses to which that production can be put. Production can be used for immediate consumption, for investment in new fixed assets or inventories, or for replacing depreciated fixed assets.

"Domestic" means that GDP measures production that takes place within the country's borders. In the expenditure-method equation given above, the exports-minus-imports term is necessary in order to null out expenditures on things not produced in the country (imports) and add in things produced but not sold in the country (exports).

Economists (since Keynes) have preferred to split the general consumption term into two parts; private consumption, and public sector (or government) spending. Two advantages of dividing total consumption this way in theoretical macroeconomics are:

- **Private consumption** is a central concern of welfare economics. The private investment and trade portions of the economy are ultimately directed (in mainstream economic models) to increases in long-term private consumption.

- If separated from endogenous private consumption, **government consumption** can be treated as exogenous,[citation needed] so that different government spending levels can be considered within a meaningful macroeconomic framework.

Income Approach

This method measures GDP by adding incomes that firms pay households for the factors of production they hire- wages for labor, interest for capital, rent for land and profits for entrepreneurship.

The US "National Income and Expenditure Accounts" divide incomes into five categories:

1. Wages, salaries, and supplementary labour income
2. Corporate profits
3. Interest and miscellaneous investment income
4. Farmers' income
5. Income from non-farm unincorporated businesses

These five income components sum to net domestic income at factor cost.

Two adjustments must be made to get GDP:

1. Indirect taxes minus subsidies are added to get from factor cost to market prices.
2. Depreciation (or capital consumption) is added to get from net domestic product to gross domestic product.

Expenditure approach

In economies, most things produced are produced for sale, and sold. Therefore, measuring the total expenditure of money used to buy things is a way of measuring production. This is known as the expenditure method of calculating GDP. Note that if you knit yourself a sweater, it is production but does not get counted as GDP because it is never sold. Sweater-knitting is a small part of the economy, but if one counts some major activities such as child-rearing (generally unpaid) as production, GDP ceases to be an accurate indicator of production. Similarly, if there is a long term shift from non-market provision of services (for example cooking, cleaning, child rearing, do-it yourself repairs) to market provision of services, then this trend toward increased market provision of services may mask a dramatic decrease in actual domestic production, resulting in overly optimistic and inflated reported GDP. This is particularly a problem for economies which have shifted from production economies to service economies.

Components of GDP by expenditure

GDP (Y) is a sum of **Consumption (C)**, **Investment (I)**, **Government Spending (G)** and **Net Exports (X - M)**.

$$Y = C + I + G + (X - M)$$

Here is a description of each GDP component:

- **C (consumption)** is normally the largest GDP component in the economy, consisting of private (household final consumption expenditure) in the economy. These personal expenditures fall under one of the following categories: durable goods, non-durable goods, and services. Examples include food, rent, jewelry, gasoline, and medical expenses but does not include the purchase of new housing.

- **I (investment)** includes business investment in equipments for example and does not include exchanges of existing assets. Examples include construction of a new mine, purchase of software, or purchase of machinery and equipment for a factory. Spending by households (not government) on new houses is also included in Investment. In contrast to its colloquial meaning, 'Investment' in GDP does not mean purchases of financial products. Buying financial products is classed as 'saving', as opposed to **investment**. This avoids double-counting: if one buys shares in a company, and the company uses the money received to buy plant, equipment, etc., the amount will be counted toward GDP when the company spends the money on those things; to also count it when one gives it to the company would be to count two times an amount that only corresponds to one group of products. Buying bonds or stocks is a swapping of deeds, a transfer of claims on future production, not directly an expenditure on products.
- **G (government spending)** is the sum of government expenditures on final goods and services. It includes salaries of public servants, purchase of weapons for the military, and any investment expenditure by a government. It does not include any transfer payments, such as social security or unemployment benefits.
- **X (exports)** represents gross exports. GDP captures the amount a country produces, including goods and services produced for other nations' consumption, therefore exports are added.
- **M (imports)** represents gross imports. Imports are subtracted since imported goods will be included in the terms **G, I**, or **C**, and must be deducted to avoid counting foreign supply as domestic.

A fully equivalent definition is that **GDP (Y)** is the sum of **final consumption expenditure (FCE)**, **gross capital formation** [1] **(GCF)**, and **net exports (X - M)**.

$$Y = FCE + GCF + (X - M)$$

FCE can then be further broken down by three sectors (households, governments and non-profit institutions serving households) and GCF by five sectors (non-financial corporations, financial corporations, households, governments and non-profit institutions serving households [2]). The advantage of this second definition is that expenditure is systematically broken down, firstly, by type of final use (final consumption or capital formation) and, secondly, by sectors making the expenditure, whereas the first definition partly follows a mixed delimitation concept by type of final use and sector.

Note that **C, G**, and **I** are expenditures on final goods and services; expenditures on intermediate goods and services do not count. (Intermediate goods and services are those used by businesses to produce other goods and services within the accounting year.)

According to the U.S. Bureau of Economic Analysis, which is responsible for calculating the national accounts in the United States, :In general, the source data for the expenditures components are considered more reliable than those for the income components [see income method, below]."

Examples of GDP component variables

C, I, G, and **NX**(net exports): If a person spends money to renovate a hotel to increase occupancy rates, the spending represents private investment, but if he buys shares in a consortium to execute the renovation, it is saving. The former is included when measuring GDP (in **I**), the latter is not. However, when the consortium conducted its own expenditure on renovation, that expenditure would be included in GDP.

If a hotel is a private home, spending for renovation would be measured as consumption, but if a government agency converts the hotel into an office for civil servants, the spending would be included in the public sector spending, or **G**.

If the renovation involves the purchase of a chandelier from abroad, that spending would be counted as **C, G**, or **I** (depending on whether a private individual, the government, or a business is doing the renovation), but then counted again as an import and subtracted from the GDP so that GDP counts only goods produced within the country.

If a domestic producer is paid to make the chandelier for a foreign hotel, the payment would not be counted as **C, G**, or **I**, but would be counted as an export.

Income approach

Another way of measuring GDP is to measure total income. If GDP is calculated this way it is sometimes called Gross Domestic Income (GDI), or GDP(I). GDI should provide the same amount as the expenditure method described above. (By definition, GDI = GDP. In practice, however, measurement errors will make the two figures slightly off when reported by national statistical agencies.)

GDP real growth rates for 2008

Total income can be subdivided according to various schemes, leading to various formulae for GDP measured by the income approach. A common one is:

> *GDP = compensation of employees + gross operating surplus + gross mixed income + taxes less subsidies on production and imports*

$$GDP = COE + GOS + GMI + T_{P\,\&\,M} - S_{P\,\&\,M}$$

- **Compensation of employees** (COE) measures the total remuneration to employees for work done. It includes wages and salaries, as well as employer contributions to social security and other such programs.
- **Gross operating surplus** (GOS) is the surplus due to owners of incorporated businesses. Often called profits, although only a subset of total costs are subtracted from gross output to calculate GOS.

- **Gross mixed income** (GMI) is the same measure as GOS, but for unincorporated businesses. This often includes most small businesses.

The sum of **COE**, **GOS** and **GMI** is called total factor income; it is the income of all of the factors of production in society. It measures the value of GDP at factor (basic) prices. The difference between basic prices and final prices (those used in the expenditure calculation) is the total taxes and subsidies that the government has levied or paid on that production. So adding taxes less subsidies on production and imports converts GDP at factor cost to GDP(I).

Total factor income is also sometimes expressed as:

Total factor income = Employee compensation + Corporate profits + Proprietor's income + Rental income + Net interest

Yet another formula for GDP by the income method is:[citation needed]

$$GDP = R + I + P + SA + W$$

where R : rents

I : interests

P : profits

SA : statistical adjustments (corporate income taxes, dividends, undistributed corporate profits)

W : wages

Note the mnemonic, "ripsaw".

A "production boundary" that delimits what will be counted as GDP.

> "One of the fundamental questions that must be addressed in preparing the national economic accounts is how to define the production boundary—that is, what parts of the myriad human activities are to be included in or excluded from the measure of the economic production."

All output for market is at least in theory included within the boundary. Market output is defined as that which is sold for "economically significant" prices; economically significant prices are "prices which have a significant influence on the amounts producers are willing to supply and purchasers wish to buy." An exception is that illegal goods and services are often excluded even if they are sold at economically significant prices (Australia and the United States exclude them).

This leaves non-market output. It is partly excluded and partly included. First, "natural processes without human involvement or direction" are excluded. Also, there must be a person or institution that owns or is entitled to compensation for the product. An example of what is included and excluded by these criteria is given by the United States' national accounts agency: "the growth of trees in an uncultivated forest is not included in production, but the harvesting of the trees from that forest is included."

Within the limits so far described, the boundary is further constricted by "functional considerations." The Australian Bureau for Statistics explains this: "The national accounts are primarily constructed to assist governments and others to make market-based macroeconomic policy decisions, including analysis of markets and factors affecting market performance, such as inflation and unemployment." Consequently, production that is, according to them, "relatively independent and isolated from markets," or "difficult to value in an economically meaningful way" [i.e., difficult to put a price on] is excluded. Thus excluded are services provided by people to members of their own families free of charge, such as child rearing, meal preparation, cleaning, transportation, entertainment of family members, emotional support, care of the elderly. Most other production for own (or one's family's) use is also excluded, with two notable exceptions which are given in the list later in this section.

Nonmarket outputs that *are* included within the boundary are listed below. Since, by definition, they do not have a market price, the compilers of GDP must *impute* a value to them, usually either the cost of the goods and services used to produce them, or the value of a similar item that is sold on the market.

- Goods and services provided by governments and non-profit organisations free of charge or for economically insignificant prices are included. The value of these goods and services is estimated as equal to their cost of production. This ignores the consumer surplus generated by an efficient and effective government supplied infrastructure. For example, government-provided clean water confers substantial benefits above its cost. Ironically, lack of such infrastructure which would result in higher water prices (and probably higher hospital and medication expenditures) would be reflected as a higher GDP. This may also cause a bias that mistakenly favors inefficient privatizations since some of the consumer surplus from privatized entities' sale of goods and services are indeed reflected in GDP.
- Goods and services produced for own-use by businesses are attempted to be included. An example of this kind of production would be a machine constructed by an engineering firm for use in its own plant.
- Renovations and upkeep by an individual to a home that she owns and occupies are included. The value of the upkeep is estimated as the rent that she could charge for the home if she did not occupy it herself. This is the largest item of production for own use by an individual (as opposed to a business) that the compilers include in GDP. If the measure uses historical or book prices for real estate, this will grossly underestimate the value of the rent in real estate markets which have experienced significant price increases (or economies with general inflation). Furthermore, depreciation schedules for houses often accelerate the accounted depreciation relative to actual depreciation (a well built house can be lived in for several hundred years - a very long time after it has been fully depreciated). In summary, this is likely to grossly underestimate the value of existing housing stock on consumers' actual consumption or income.
- Agricultural production for consumption by oneself or one's household is included.
- Services (such as chequeing-account maintenance and services to borrowers) provided by banks and other financial institutions without charge or for a fee that does not reflect their full value have a value imputed to them by the compilers and are included. The financial institutions provide these services by giving the customer a less advantageous interest rate than they would if the services were absent; the value imputed to these services by the compilers is the difference between the

interest rate of the account with the services and the interest rate of a similar account that does not have the services. According to the United States Bureau for Economic Analysis, this is one of the largest imputed items in the GDP.

GDP vs GNP

GDP can be contrasted with **gross national product (GNP)** or **gross national income (GNI)**. The difference is that GDP defines its scope according to location, while GNP defines its scope according to ownership. In a global context, world GDP and world GNP are therefore equivalent terms.

GDP is product produced within a country's borders; GNP is product produced by enterprises owned by a country's citizens. The two would be the same if all of the productive enterprises in a country were owned by its own citizens, but foreign ownership makes GDP and GNP non-identical. Production within a country's borders, but by an enterprise owned by somebody outside the country, counts as part of its GDP but not its GNP; on the other hand, production by an enterprise located outside the country, but owned by one of its citizens, counts as part of its GNP but not its GDP.

To take the United States as an example, the U.S.'s GNP is the value of output produced by American-owned firms, regardless of where the firms are located. Similarly, if a country becomes increasingly in debt, and spends large amounts of income servicing this debt this will be reflected in a decreased GNI but not a decreased GDP. Similarly, if a country sells off its resources to entities outside their country this will also be reflected over time in decreased GNI, but not decreased GDP. This would make the use of GDP more attractive for politicians in countries with increasing national debt and decreasing assets.

Gross national income (GNI) equals GDI plus income receipts from the rest of the world minus income payments to the rest of the world.

In 1991, the United States switched from using GNP to using GDP as its primary measure of production. The relationship between United States GDP and GNP is shown in table 1.7.5 of the *National Income and Product Accounts* .

International standards

The international standard for measuring GDP is contained in the book *System of National Accounts* (1993), which was prepared by representatives of the International Monetary Fund, European Union, Organization for Economic Co-operation and Development, United Nations and World Bank. The publication is normally referred to as SNA93 to distinguish it from the previous edition published in 1968 (called SNA68) [citation needed] Wikipedia:Avoid weasel words.

SNA93 provides a set of rules and procedures for the measurement of national accounts. The standards are designed to be flexible, to allow for differences in local statistical needs and conditions.

National measurement

Within each country GDP is normally measured by a national government statistical agency, as private sector organizations normally do not have access to the information required (especially information on expenditure and production by governments).

Main article: National agencies responsible for GDP measurement

Interest rates

Net interest expense is a transfer payment in all sectors except the financial sector. Net interest expenses in the financial sector are seen as production and value added and are added to GDP.

Adjustments to GDP

When comparing GDP figures from one year to another, it is desirable to compensate for changes in the value of money—inflation or deflation. The raw GDP figure as given by the equations above is called the nominal, or historical, or current, GDP. To make it more meaningful for year-to-year comparisons, it may be multiplied by the ratio between the value of money in the year the GDP was measured and the value of money in some base year. For example, suppose a country's GDP in 1990 was $100 million and its GDP in 2000 was $300 million; but suppose that inflation had halved the value of its currency over that period. To meaningfully compare its 2000 GDP to its 1990 GDP we could multiply the 2000 GDP by one-half, to make it relative to 1990 as a base year. The result would be that the 2000 GDP equals $300 million x one-half = $150 million, *in 1990 monetary terms.* We would see that the country's GDP had, realistically, increased 1.5 times over that period, not 3 times, as it might appear from the raw GDP data. The GDP adjusted for changes in money-value in this way is called the real, or constant, GDP.

The factor used to convert GDP from current to constant values in this way is called the *GDP deflator.* Unlike the Consumer price index, which measures inflation (or deflation—rarely!) in the price of household consumer goods, the GDP deflator measures changes in the prices all domestically produced goods and services in an economy—including investment goods and government services, as well as household consumption goods.

Constant-GDP figures allow us to calculate a GDP growth rate, which tells us how much a country's production has increased (or decreased, if the growth rate is negative) compared to the previous year.

Real GDP growth rate for year n = [(Real GDP in year n) - (Real GDP in year n - 1)]/ (Real GDP in year n - 1)

Another thing that it may be desirable to compensate for is population growth. If a country's GDP doubled over some period but its population tripled, the increase in GDP may not be deemed such a great accomplishment: the average person in the country is producing less than they were before. *Per-capita GDP* is the measure compensated for population growth.

Cross-border comparison

The level of GDP in different countries may be compared by converting their value in national currency according to *either* the current currency exchange rate, or the purchase power parity exchange rate.

- **Current currency exchange rate** is the exchange rate in the international currency market.
- **Purchasing power parity exchange rate** is the exchange rate based on the purchasing power parity (PPP) of a currency relative to a selected standard (usually the United States dollar). This is a comparative (and theoretical) exchange rate, the only way to directly realize this rate is to sell an entire CPI basket in one country, convert the cash at the currency market rate & then rebuy that same basket of goods in the other country (with the converted cash). Going from country to country, the distribution of prices within the basket will vary; typically, non-tradable purchases will consume a greater proportion of the basket's total cost in the higher GDP country, per the Balassa-Samuelson effect.

The ranking of countries may differ significantly based on which method is used.

- The *current exchange rate method* converts the value of goods and services using global currency exchange rates. The method can offer better indications of a country's international purchasing power and relative economic strength. For instance, if 10% of GDP is being spent on buying hi-tech foreign arms, the number of weapons purchased is entirely governed by *current exchange rates*, since arms are a traded product bought on the international market. There is no meaningful 'local' price distinct from the international price for high technology goods.
- The *purchasing power parity method* accounts for the relative effective domestic purchasing power of the average producer or consumer within an economy. The method can provide a better indicator of the living standards of less developed countries, because it compensates for the weakness of local currencies in the international markets. For example, India ranks 11th by nominal GDP, but fourth by PPP. The PPP method of GDP conversion is more relevant to non-traded goods and services.

There is a clear pattern of the *purchasing power parity method* decreasing the disparity in GDP between high and low income (GDP) countries, as compared to the *current exchange rate method*. This finding is called the Penn effect.

For more information, see Measures of national income and output.

Standard of living and GDP

GDP per capita is not a measurement of the standard of living in an economy. However, it is often used as such an indicator, on the rationale that all citizens would benefit from their country's increased economic production. Similarly, GDP per capita is not a measure of personal income. GDP may increase while real incomes for the majority decline. For example, in the US from 1990 to 2006 the earnings (adjusted for inflation) of individual workers, in private industry and services, increased by less than 0.5% per year while GDP (adjusted for inflation) increased about 3.6% per year.

The major advantage of GDP per capita as an indicator of standard of living is that it is measured frequently, widely, and consistently. It is measured frequently in that most countries provide information on GDP on a quarterly basis, allowing trends to be seen quickly. It is measured widely in that some measure of GDP is available for almost every country in the world, allowing inter-country comparisons. It is measured consistently in that the technical definition of GDP is relatively consistent among countries.

The major disadvantage is that it is not a measure of standard of living. GDP is intended to be a measure of total national economic activity— a separate concept.

The argument for using GDP as a standard-of-living proxy is not that it is a good indicator of the absolute level of standard of living, but that living standards tend to move with per-capita GDP, so that *changes* in living standards are readily detected through changes in GDP.

Limitations of GDP to judge the health of an economy

GDP is widely used by economists to gauge the health of an economy, as its variations are relatively quickly identified. However, its value as an indicator for the standard of living is considered to be limited. Not only that, but if the aim of economic activity is to produce ecologically sustainable increases in the overall human standard of living, GDP is a perverse measurement; it treats loss of ecosystem services as a benefit instead of a cost. Other criticisms of how the GDP is used include:

- **Wealth distribution**–GDP does not take disparity in incomes between the rich and poor into account. See income inequality metrics for discussion of a variety of inequality-based economic measures.
- **Non-market transactions**–GDP excludes activities that are not provided through the market, such as household production and volunteer or unpaid services. As a result, GDP is understated. Unpaid work conducted on Free and Open Source Software (such as Linux) contribute nothing to GDP, but it was estimated that it would have cost more than a billion US dollars for a commercial company to develop. Also, if Free and Open Source Software became identical to its proprietary software counterparts, and the nation producing the propriety software stops buying proprietary software and switches to Free and Open Source Software, then the GDP of this nation would reduce, however there would be no reduction in economic production or standard of living. The work of New Zealand economist Marilyn Waring has highlighted that if a concerted attempt to factor in unpaid work were made, then it would in part undo the injustices of unpaid (and in some cases, slave) labour, and also provide the political transparency and accountability necessary for democracy. Shedding some doubt on this claim, however, is the theory that won economist Douglass North the Nobel Prize in 1993. North argued that the creation and strengthening of the patent system, by encouraging private invention and enterprise, became the fundamental catalyst behind the Industrial Revolution in England.

- **Underground economy**–Official GDP estimates may not take into account the underground economy, in which transactions contributing to production, such as illegal trade and tax-avoiding activities, are unreported, causing GDP to be underestimated.
- **Non-monetary economy**–GDP omits economies where no money comes into play at all, resulting in inaccurate or abnormally low GDP figures. For example, in countries with major business transactions occurring informally, portions of local economy are not easily registered. Bartering may be more prominent than the use of money, even extending to services (I helped you build your house ten years ago, so now you help me).
- GDP also ignores subsistence production.
- **Quality improvements and inclusion of new products**–By not adjusting for quality improvements and new products, GDP understates true economic growth. For instance, although computers today are less expensive and more powerful than computers from the past, GDP treats them as the same products by only accounting for the monetary value. The introduction of new products is also difficult to measure accurately and is not reflected in GDP despite the fact that it may increase the standard of living. For example, even the richest person from 1900 could not purchase standard products, such as antibiotics and cell phones, that an average consumer can buy today, since such modern conveniences did not exist back then.
- **What is being produced**–GDP counts work that produces no net change or that results from repairing harm. For example, rebuilding after a natural disaster or war may produce a considerable amount of economic activity and thus boost GDP. The economic value of health care is another classic example—it may raise GDP if many people are sick and they are receiving expensive treatment, but it is not a desirable situation. Alternative economic estimates, such as the standard of living or discretionary income per capita try to measure the human utility of economic activity. See uneconomic growth.
- **Externalities**–GDP ignores externalities or economic bads such as damage to the environment. By counting goods which increase utility but not deducting bads or accounting for the negative effects of higher production, such as more pollution, GDP is overstating economic welfare. The Genuine Progress Indicator is thus proposed by ecological economists and green economists as a substitute for GDP, supposing a consensus on relevant data to measure "progress". In countries highly dependent on resource extraction or with high ecological footprints the disparities between GDP and GPI can be very large, indicating ecological overshoot. Some environmental costs, such as cleaning up oil spills are included in GDP.
- **Sustainability of growth**–GDP is not a tool of economic projections, which would make it subjective, it is just a measurement of economic activity. That is why it does not measure what is considered the sustainability of growth. A country may achieve a temporarily high GDP by over-exploiting natural resources or by misallocating investment. For example, the large deposits of phosphates gave the people of Nauru one of the highest per capita incomes on earth, but since 1989 their standard of living has declined sharply as the supply has run out. Oil-rich states can sustain

high GDPs without industrializing, but this high level would no longer be sustainable if the oil runs out. Economies experiencing an economic bubble, such as a housing bubble or stock bubble, or a low private-saving rate tend to appear to grow faster owing to higher consumption, mortgaging their futures for present growth. Economic growth at the expense of environmental degradation can end up costing dearly to clean up.

- One main problem in estimating GDP growth over time is that the purchasing power of money varies in different proportion for different goods, so when the GDP figure is deflated over time, GDP growth can vary greatly depending on the basket of goods used and the relative proportions used to deflate the GDP figure. For example, in the past 80 years the GDP per capita of the United States if measured by purchasing power of potatoes, did not grow significantly. But if it is measured by the purchasing power of eggs, it grew several times. For this reason, economists comparing multiple countries usually use a varied basket of goods.

- Cross-border comparisons of GDP can be inaccurate as they do not take into account local differences in the quality of goods, even when adjusted for purchasing power parity. This type of adjustment to an exchange rate is controversial because of the difficulties of finding comparable baskets of goods to compare purchasing power across countries. For instance, people in country A may consume the same number of locally produced apples as in country B, but apples in country A are of a more tasty variety. This difference in material well being will not show up in GDP statistics. This is especially true for goods that are not traded globally, such as housing.

- Transfer pricing on cross-border trades between associated companies may distort import and export measures[citation needed].

- As a measure of actual sale prices, GDP does not capture the economic surplus between the price paid and subjective value received, and can therefore underestimate aggregate utility.

Simon Kuznets in his very first report to the US Congress in 1934 said:

> ...the welfare of a nation can, therefore, scarcely be inferred from a measure of national income...

In 1962, Kuznets stated:

> Distinctions must be kept in mind between quantity and quality of growth, between costs and returns, and between the short and long run. Goals for more growth should specify more growth of what and for what.

Alternatives to GDP

- Human development index (HDI) - HDI uses GDP as a part of its calculation and then factors in indicators of life expectancy and education levels.
- Genuine progress indicator (GPI) or Index of Sustainable Economic Welfare (ISEW) - The GPI and the ISEW attempt to address many of the above criticisms by taking the same raw information supplied for GDP and then adjust for income distribution, add for the value of household and volunteer work, and subtract for crime and pollution.
- Gross national happiness (GNH) - GNH measures quality of life or social progress in more holistic and psychological terms than GDP.
- Gini coefficient - The Gini coefficient measures the disparity of income within a nation.
- Wealth estimates - The World Bank has developed a system for combining monetary wealth with intangible wealth (institutions and human capital) and environmental capital.
- Private Product Remaining - Murray Newton Rothbard and other Austrian economists argue as if government spending is taken from productive sectors and produces goods that consumers do not want, it is a burden on the economy and thus should be deducted. In his book, **America's Great Depression**, Rothbard argues that even government surpluses from taxation should be deducted to create an estimate of PPR.

Some people have looked beyond standard of living at a broader sense of quality of life or well-being:

- European Quality of Life Survey - The survey, first published in 2005, assessed quality of life across European countries through a series of questions on overall subjective life satisfaction, satisfaction with different aspects of life, and sets of questions used to calculate deficits of time, loving, being and having.
- Gross national happiness - The Centre for Bhutanese Studies in Bhutan is working on a complex set of subjective and objective indicators to measure 'national happiness' in various domains (living standards, health, education, eco-system diversity and resilience, cultural vitality and diversity, time use and balance, good governance, community vitality and psychological well-being). This set of indicators would be used to assess progress towards gross national happiness, which they have already identified as being the nation's priority, above GDP.
- Happy Planet Index - The happy planet index (HPI) is an index of human well-being and environmental impact, introduced by the New Economics Foundation (NEF) in 2006. It measures the environmental efficiency with which human well-being is achieved within a given country or group. Human well-being is defined in terms of subjective life satisfaction and life expectancy while environmental impact is defined by the Ecological Footprint.

Lists of countries by their GDP

- Lists of countries by GDP
- List of countries by GDP (nominal), (per capita)
- List of countries by GDP (PPP), (per capita), (per hour)
- List of countries by GDP growth
- List of countries by GDP (real) growth rate, (per capita)
- List of countries by GDP sector composition
- List of countries by future GDP estimates (PPP), (per capita), (nominal)

See also

- Chained volume series
- Eco-sufficiency
- Green gross domestic product
- Gross domestic product per barrel
- Gross output
- Gross regional domestic product

- Gross state product
- Gross value added
- Gross world product
- Intermediate consumption
- Inventory investment
- List of countries by average wage

- List of countries by household income
- List of economic reports by U.S. government agencies
- Misery index (economics)
- National average salary
- Potential output Natural gross domestic product
- Real gross domestic product

Bibliography

Australian Bureau for Statistics, *Australian National Accounts: Concepts, Sources and Mathods* [3], 2000. Retrieved November 2009. In depth explanations of how GDP and other national accounts items are determined.

United States Department of Commerce, Bureau of Economic Analysis, *Concepts and Methods of the United States National Income and Product Accounts* [4]PDF. Retrieved November 2009. In depth explanations of how GDP and other national accounts items are determined.

External links

Global

- World GDP Chart (since 1960) [5]
- Australian Bureau of Statistics Manual on GDP measurement [6]
- GDP-indexed bonds [7]
- GDP scaled maps [8]
- Euro area GDP growth rate (since 1996) as compared to the Bank Rate (since 2000) [9]
- World Development Indicators (WDI) [10]
- Economist Country Briefings [11]
- UN Statistical Databases [12]
- Is Life Getting Better : What is GDP? [13] Pamphlet describing the basic idea of GDP, from OECD's Measuring Progress project.

Data

- Thermal Maps of the World Nominal GDP in US$ purchasing power parity from the EIU 2007-2010 [14]
- Bureau of Economic Analysis: Official United States GDP data [15]
- Graphs of Historical Real U.S. GDP [16]
- Historicalstatistics.org: Links to historical statistics on GDP for different countries and regions [17]
- Complete listing of countries by GDP: Current Exchange Rate Method [18] Purchasing Power Parity Method [19]
- Historical US GDP (yearly data) [20], 1790–present
- Historical US GDP (quarterly data) [21], 1947–present
- OECD Statistics [22]
- Google - public data [23]: GDP and Personal Income of the U.S. (annual): Nominal Gross Domestic Product

Articles and books

- What's wrong with the GDP? [24]
- Limitations of GDP Statistics by Schenk, Robert. [25]
- whether output and CPI inflation are mismeasured, by Nouriel Roubini and David Backus, in Lectures in Macroeconomics [26]
- "Measurement of the Aggregate Economy" [27], chapter 22 of Dr. Roger A. McCain's Essential Principles of Economics: A Hypermedia Text [28]
- Salvatore Monni and Alessandro Spaventa "Shifting the Focus from Paradigms to Goals: A New Approach Towards Defining and Assessing Wellbeing", Working paper n. 114, Department of

Economics, Roma Tre University, April 2010 [29]

- Rodney Edvinsson, Growth, Accumulation, Crisis: With New Macroeconomic Data for Sweden 1800-2000 [30]PDF
- Clifford Cobb, Ted Halstead and Jonathan Rowe. "If the GDP is up, why is America down?" The Atlantic Monthly, vol. 276, no. 4, October 1995, pages 59–78.
- Jerorn C.J.M. van den Bergh, "Abolishing GDP [31]"

krc:Бютеулюк ич продукт

Gross national income

Gross national income (GNI) comprises the total value produced within a country (i.e. its gross domestic product), together with its income received from other countries (notably interest and dividends), less similar payments made to other countries.

The GNI consists of: the personal consumption expenditures, the gross private investment, the government consumption expenditures, the net income from assets abroad (net income receipts), and the gross exports of goods and services, after deducting two components: the gross imports of goods and services, and the indirect business taxes. The GNI is similar to the gross national product (GNP), except that in measuring the GNP one does not deduct the indirect business taxes.

For example, the profits of a US-owned company operating in the UK will count towards US GNI and UK GDP, but will not count towards UK GNI or US GDP. Similarly, if a country becomes increasingly in debt, and spends large amounts of income servicing this debt this will be reflected in a decreased GNI but not a decreased GDP. Similarly, if a country sells off its resources to entities outside their country this will also be reflected over time in decreased GNI, but not decreased GDP. This would make the use of GDP more attractive for politicians in countries with increasing national debt and decreasing assets.

See also

- Net national income
- Measures of national income and output
- Gross national income in the European Union
- List of countries by GNI per capita
- Low-Income Countries Under Stress (LICUS) (World Bank program)
- National average salary

Developed market

In investing, **developed markets** are those countries that are thought to be the most developed and therefore less risky.

FTSE Group's list

FTSE Group, a provider of economic and financial data, assigns the market status of countries as Developed, Advanced Emerging, Secondary Emerging or Frontier on the basis of their economic size, wealth, quality of markets, depth of markets, breadth of markets. According to the FTSE Group the following countries are classified as developed markets:

- Australia
- Austria
- Belgium
- Canada
- Denmark
- Finland
- France
- Germany
- Greece
- Hong Kong
- Ireland
- Israel
- Italy
- Japan
- Luxembourg
- Netherlands
- New Zealand
- Norway
- Portugal
- Singapore
- South Korea
- Spain
- Sweden
- Switzerland
- United Kingdom
- United States

FTSE Criteria

Developed countries all have met criteria under the following categories

1. They are high income economies (as measured by the World Bank GNI Per capita Rating, 2008)
2. Market and Regulatory Environment EMG EMG

    1. Formal stock market regulatory authorities actively monitor market (e.g., SEC, FSA, SFC)
    2. Fair and non-prejudicial treatment of minority shareholders
    3. Non or selective incidence of foreign ownership restrictions
    4. No objections or significant restrictions or penalties applied on the repatriation of capital
    5. Free and well-developed equity market
    6. Free and well-developed foreign exchange market
    7. Non or simple registration process for foreign investors
3. Custody and Settlement

    1. Settlement - Rare incidence of failed trades
    2. Custody-Sufficient competition to ensure high quality custodian services
    3. Clearing & settlement - T +3 or shorter, T+7 or shorter for Frontier
    4. Stock Lending is permitted

     5. Settlement - Free delivery available

     6. Custody - Omnibus account facilities available to international investors

4. Dealing Landscape

     1. Brokerage - Sufficient competition to ensure high quality broker services

     2. Liquidity - Sufficient broad market liquidity to support sizeable global investment

     3. Transaction costs - implicit and explicit costs to be reasonable and competitive

     4. Short sales permitted

     5. Off-exchange transactions permitted

     6. Efficient trading mechanism

     7. Transparency - market depth information / visibility and timely trade reporting process

5. Derivatives

     1. Developed derivatives markets

6. Size of Market

     1. Market Capitalisation

     2. Total Number of Listed Companies (as at 31st Dec 2008)

MSCI list

As of May 2010, MSCI Barra classified the following 27 countries as developed markets:

- Australia
- Austria
- Belgium
- Canada
- Cyprus
- Denmark
- Finland
- France
- Germany
- Greece
- Hong Kong
- Iceland
- Ireland
- Israel
- Italy
- Japan
- Luxembourg
- Netherlands
- New Zealand
- Norway
- Portugal
- Singapore
- Spain
- Sweden
- Switzerland
- United Kingdom
- United States

Dow-Jones list

As of May 2010, Dow Jones classified the following 30 countries as developed markets:

- 🇦🇺 Australia
- 🇦🇹 Austria
- 🇧🇪 Belgium
- 🇨🇦 Canada
- 🇨🇾 Cyprus
- 🇩🇰 Denmark
- 🇫🇮 Finland
- 🇫🇷 France
- Germany
- 🇬🇷 Greece
- 🇭🇰 Hong Kong
- 🇮🇸 Iceland
- 🇮🇪 Ireland
- 🇮🇱 Israel
- 🇮🇹 Italy
- Japan
- 🇲🇹 Malta
- 🇳🇱 Netherlands
- 🇳🇿 New Zealand
- 🇳🇴 Norway
- 🇵🇹 Portugal
- Singapore
- 🇸🇮 Slovenia
- South Korea
- 🇪🇸 Spain
- 🇸🇪 Sweden
- 🇨🇭 Switzerland
- 🇹🇼 Taiwan
- 🇬🇧 United Kingdom
- 🇺🇸 United States

Russell Global list

As of June 2009, Russell Investments classified the following 26 countries as developed markets:

- 🇦🇺 Australia
- 🇦🇹 Austria
- 🇧🇪 Belgium
- 🇨🇦 Canada
- 🇩🇰 Denmark
- 🇫🇮 Finland
- 🇫🇷 France
- Germany
- 🇬🇷 Greece
- 🇭🇰 Hong Kong
- 🇮🇸 Iceland
- 🇮🇪 Ireland
- 🇮🇱 Israel
- 🇮🇹 Italy
- Japan
- Luxembourg
- 🇳🇱 Netherlands
- 🇳🇿 New Zealand
- 🇳🇴 Norway
- 🇵🇹 Portugal
- Singapore
- 🇪🇸 Spain
- 🇸🇪 Sweden
- 🇨🇭 Switzerland
- 🇬🇧 United Kingdom
- 🇺🇸 United States

See also

- Developed country
- Emerging markets
- First World
- Frontier markets
- North-South divide

Measures of national income and output

A variety of **measures of national income and output** are used in economics to estimate total economic activity in a country or region, including gross domestic product (**GDP**), gross national product (**GNP**), and net national income (**NNI**). All are specially concerned with counting the total amount of goods and services produced within some "boundary". The boundary may be defined geographically, or by citizenship; and limits on the type of activity also form part of the conceptual boundary; for instance, these measures are for the most part limited to counting goods and services that are exchanged for money: production not for sale but for barter, for one's own personal use, or for one's family, is largely left out of these measures, although some attempts are made to include some of those kinds of production by *imputing* monetary values to them. Mr Ian Davies defines development as 'Simply how happy and free the citizens of that country feel.'

National accounts

Main article: National accounts

Arriving at a figure for the total production of goods and services in a large region like a country entails a large amount of data-collection and calculation. Although some attempts were made to estimate national incomes as long ago as the 17th century, the systematic keeping of national accounts, of which these figures are a part, only began in the 1930s, in the United States and some European countries. The impetus for that major statistical effort was the Great Depression and the rise of Keynesian economics, which prescribed a greater role for the government in managing an economy, and made it necessary for governments to obtain accurate information so that their interventions into the economy could proceed as much as possible from a basis of fact.

Market value

Main article: Market value

In order to count a good or service it is necessary to assign some value to it. The value that the measures of national income and output assign to a good or service is its market value – the price it fetches when bought or sold. The actual usefulness of a product (its use-value) is not measured – assuming the use-value to be any different from its market value.

Three strategies have been used to obtain the market values of all the goods and services produced: the product (or output) method, the expenditure method, and the income method. The product method looks at the economy on an industry-by-industry basis. The total output of the economy is the sum of the outputs of every industry. However, since an output of one industry may be used by another industry and become part of the output of that second industry, to avoid counting the item twice we use, not the value output by each industry, but the value-added; that is, the difference between the value of what it puts out and what it takes in. The total value produced by the economy is the sum of the values-added by every industry.

The expenditure method is based on the idea that all products are bought by somebody or some organisation. Therefore we sum up the total amount of money people and organisations spend in buying things. This amount must equal the value of everything produced. Usually expenditures by private individuals, expenditures by businesses, and expenditures by government are calculated separately and then summed to give the total expenditure. Also, a correction term must be introduced to account for imports and exports outside the boundary.

The income method works by summing the incomes of all producers within the boundary. Since what they are paid is just the market value of their product, their total income must be the total value of the product. Wages, proprieter's incomes, and corporate profits are the major subdivisions of income.

The output approach The output approach focuses on finding the total output of a nation by directly finding the total value of all goods and services a nation produces.

Because of the complication of the multiple stages in the production of a good or service, only the final value of a good or service is included in total output. This avoids an issue often called 'double counting', wherein the total value of a good is included several times in national output, by counting it repeatedly in several stages of production. In the example of meat production, the value of the good from the farm may be $10, then $30 from the butchers, and then $60 from the supermarket. The value that should be included in final national output should be $60, not the sum of all those numbers, $100. The values added at each stage of production over the previous stage are respectively $10, $20, and $30. Their sum gives an alternative way of calculating the value of final output.

Formulae:

GDP(gross domestic product) at market price = value of output in an economy in a particular year - intermediate consumption

NNP at factor cost = GDP at market price - depreciation + NFIA *(net factor income from abroad)* - net indirect taxes

The income approach

The income approach focuses on finding the total output of a nation by finding the total income received by the factors of production owned by that nation.

The main types of income that are inclhose who provide the natural resources), interest (the money paid for the use of man-made resources, such as machines used in production), and profit (the money gained by the entrepreneur - the businessman who combines these resources to produce a good or service).

Formulae:

NDP at factor cost = compensation of employee + operating surplus + mixed income of self employee

National income = NDP at factor cost + NFIA (net factor income from abroad) - Depreciation

The expenditure approach

The expenditure approach is basically an output accounting method. It focuses on finding the total output of a nation by finding the total amount of money spent. This is acceptable, because like income, the total value of all goods is equal to the total amount of money spent on goods. The basic formula for domestic output combines all the different areas in which money is spent within the region, and then combining them to find the total output.

$$GDP = C + I + G + (X - M)$$

Where:

C = household consumption expenditures / personal consumption expenditures

I = gross private domestic investment

G = government consumption and gross investment expenditures

X = gross exports of goods and services

M = gross imports of goods and services

Note: (**X - M**) is often written as X_N, which stands for "net exports"

Names

The names of the measures consist of one of the words "Gross" or "Net", followed by one of the words "National" or "Domestic", followed by one of the words "Product", "Income", or "Expenditure". All of these terms can be explained separately.

"Gross" means total product, regardless of the use to which it is subsequently put.

"Net" means "Gross" minus the amount that must be used to offset depreciation — ie., wear-and-tear or obsolescence of the nation's fixed capital assets. "Net" gives an indication of how much product is actually available for consumption or new investment.

"Domestic" means the boundary is geographical: we are counting all goods and services produced within the country's borders, regardless of by whom.

"National" means the boundary is defined by citizenship (nationality). We count all goods and services produced by the nationals of the country (or businesses owned by them) regardless of where that production physically takes place.

The output of a French-owned cotton factory in Senegal counts as part of the Domestic figures for Senegal, but the National figures of France.

"Product", "Income", and "Expenditure" refer to the three counting methodologies explained earlier: the product, income, and expenditure approaches. However the terms are used loosely.

"Product" is the general term, often used when any of the three approaches was actually used. Sometimes the word "Product" is used and then some additional symbol or phrase to indicate the methodology; so, for instance, we get "Gross Domestic Product by income", "GDP (income)", "GDP(I)", and similar constructions.

"Income" specifically means that the income approach was used.

"Expenditure" specifically means that the expenditure approach was used.

Note that all three counting methods should in theory give the same final figure. However, in practice minor differences are obtained from the three methods for several reasons, including changes in inventory levels and errors in the statistics. One problem for instance is that goods in inventory have been produced (therefore included in Product), but not yet sold (therefore not yet included in Expenditure). Similar timing issues can also cause a slight discrepancy between the value of goods produced (Product) and the payments to the factors that produced the goods (Income), particularly if inputs are purchased on credit, and also because wages are collected often after a period of production.

GDP and GNP

Main articles: GDP and GNP

Gross domestic product (GDP) is defined as "the value of all final goods and services produced in a country in 1 year".

Gross National Product (GNP) is defined as "the market value of all goods and services produced in one year by labour and property supplied by the residents of a country."

As an example, the table below shows some GDP and GNP, and NNI data for the United States:

National income and output (Billions of dollars)

Period Ending	2003
Gross national product	11,063.3
Net U.S. income receipts from rest of the world	55.2
U.S. income receipts	329.1
U.S. income payments	-273.9
Gross domestic product	11,008.1
Private consumption of fixed capital	1,135.9
Government consumption of fixed capital	218.1
Statistical discrepancy	25.6
National Income	9,679.7

- **NDP**: Net domestic product is defined as "gross domestic product (GDP) minus depreciation of capital", similar to NNP.
- **GDP per capita**: Gross domestic product per capita is the mean value of the output produced per person, which is also the mean income.

National income and welfare

GDP per capita (per person) is often used as a measure of a person's welfare. Countries with higher GDP may be more likely to also score highly on other measures of welfare, such as life expectancy. However, there are serious limitations to the usefulness of GDP as a measure of welfare:

- Measures of GDP typically exclude unpaid economic activity, most importantly domestic work such as childcare. This leads to distortions; for example, a paid nanny's income contributes to GDP, but an unpaid parent's time spent caring for children will not, even though they are both carrying out the same economic activity.
- GDP takes no account of the inputs used to produce the output. For example, if everyone worked for twice the number of hours, then GDP might roughly double, but this does not necessarily mean that workers are better off as they would have less leisure time. Similarly, the impact of economic activity on the environment is not measured in calculating GDP.
- Comparison of GDP from one country to another may be distorted by movements in exchange rates. Measuring national income at purchasing power parity may overcome this problem at the risk of overvaluing basic goods and services, for example subsistence farming.
- GDP does not measure factors that affect quality of life, such as the quality of the environment (as distinct from the input value) and security from crime. This leads to distortions - for example, spending on cleaning up an oil spill is included in GDP, but the negative impact of the spill on well-being (e.g. loss of clean beaches) is not measured.
- GDP is the mean (average) wealth rather than median (middle-point) wealth. Countries with a skewed income distribution may have a relatively high per-capita GDP while the majority of its citizens have a relatively low level of income, due to concentration of wealth in the hands of a small fraction of the population. See Gini coefficient.

Because of this, other measures of welfare such as the Human Development Index (HDI), Index of Sustainable Economic Welfare (ISEW), Genuine Progress Indicator (GPI), gross national happiness (GNH), and sustainable national income (SNI) are used.

See also

- Chained volume series
- Compensation of employees
- European System of Accounts
- Green National Product
- Gross domestic product
- Gross national happiness (GNH)
- Gross national income in the European Union
- Gross output
- Input-output model
- Intermediate consumption
- National accounts
- National Income and Product Accounts
- Net output
- Penn World Table
- United Nations System of National Accounts (UNSNA)
- Wealth (economics)
- Capital formation

Bibliography

Australian Bureau of Statistics, *Australian National Accounts: Concepts, Sources and Methods* [1], 2000. This fairly large document has a wealth of information on the meaning of the national income and output measures and how they are obtained.

External links

- Historicalstatistics.org: Links to historical national accounts and statistics for different countries and regions [17]
- World Bank's Development and Education Program Website [2]

Income inequality metrics

The concept of inequality is distinct from that of poverty and fairness. **Income inequality metrics** or **income distribution metrics** are used by social scientists to measure the distribution of income, and economic inequality among the participants in a particular economy, such as that of a specific country or of the world in general. While different theories may try to explain how income inequality comes about, income inequality metrics simply provide a system of measurement used to determine the dispersion of incomes.

Income distribution has always been a central concern of economic theory and economic policy. Classical economists such as Adam Smith, Thomas Malthus and David Ricardo were mainly concerned with factor income distribution, that is, the distribution of income between the main factors of production, land, labour and capital.

Modern economists have also addressed this issue, but have been more concerned with the distribution of income across individuals and households. Important theoretical and policy concerns include the relationship between income inequality and economic growth. The article Economic inequality discusses the social and policy aspects of income distribution questions.

Defining income

All of the metrics described below are applicable to evaluating the distributional inequality of various kinds of resources. Here the focus is on income as a resource. As there are various forms of "income", the investigated kind of income has to be clearly described.

One form of income is the total amount of goods and services that a person receives, and thus there is not necessarily money or cash involved. If a subsistence farmer in Uganda grows his own grain it will count as income. Services like public health and education are also counted in. Often expenditure or consumption (which is the same in an economic sense) is used to measure income. The World Bank uses the so-called "living standard measurement surveys" to measure income. These consist of questionnaires with more than 200 questions. Surveys have been completed in most developing countries.

Applied to the analysis of income inequality within countries, "income" often stands for the taxed income per individual or per household. Here income inequality measures also can be used to compare the income distributions before and after taxation in order to measure the effects of progressive tax rates.

Properties of inequality metrics

In the economic literature on inequality four properties are generally postulated that any measure of inequality should satisfy:

Anonymity

This assumption states that an inequality metric does not depend on the "labeling" of individuals in an economy and all that matters is the distribution of income. For example, in an economy composed of two people, Mr. Smith and Mrs. Jones, where one of them has 60% of the income and the other 40%, the inequality metric should be the same whether it is Mr. Smith or Mrs. Jones who has the 40% share. This property distinguishes the concept of inequality from that of fairness where who owns a particular level of income and how it has been acquired is of central importance. An inequality metric is a statement simply about how income is distributed, not about who the particular people in the economy are or what kind of income they "deserve".

Scale independence

This property says that richer economies should not be automatically considered more unequal by construction. In other words, if every person's income in an economy is doubled (or multiplied by any positive constant) then the overall metric of inequality should not change. Of course the same thing applies to poorer economies. The inequality income metric should be independent of the aggregate level of income.

Population independence

Similarly, the income inequality metric should not depend on whether an economy has a large or small population. An economy with only a few people should not be automatically judged by the metric as being more equal than a large economy with lots of people. This means that the metric should be independent of the level of population.

Transfer principle

Pigou–Dalton, or the transfer principle - this is the assumption that makes an inequality metric actually a measure of inequality. In its weak form it says that if some income is transferred from a rich person to a poor person, while still preserving the order of income ranks, then the measured inequality should not increase. In its strong form, the measured level of inequality should decrease.

Common income inequality metrics

Among the most common metrics used to measure inequality are the Gini index (also known as Gini coefficient), the Theil index, and the Hoover index. They have all four properties described above.

An additional property of an inequality metric that may be desirable from an empirical point of view is that of 'decomposability'. This means that if a particular economy is broken down into sub-regions, and an inequality metric is computed for each sub region separately, then the measure of inequality for the economy as a whole should be a weighted average of the regional inequalities (in a weaker form, it means that it should be an explicit function of sub-regional inequalities, though not necessarily linear). Of the above indexes, only the Theil index has this property.

Because these income inequality metrics are summary statistics that seek to aggregate an entire distribution of incomes into a single index, the information on the measured inequality is reduced. This information reduction of course is the goal of computing inequality measures, as it reduces complexity.

A weaker reduction of complexity is achieved if income distributions are described by shares of total income. Rather than to indicate a single measure, the society under investigation is split into segments, e.g. into quintiles (or any other percentage of population). Usually each segment contains the same share of income earners. In case of an unequal income distribution, the shares of income available in each segment are different. In many cases the inequality indices mentioned above are computed from such segment data without evaluating the inequalities within the segments. The higher the amount of segments (e.g. deciles instead of quintiles), the closer the measured inequality of distribution gets to the real inequality. (If the inequality within the segments is known, the total inequality can be determined by those inequality metrics which have the property of being "decomposable".)

Quintile measures of inequality satisfy the transfer principle only in its weak form because any changes in income distribution outside the relevant quintiles are not picked up by this measures; only the distribution of income between the very rich and the very poor matters while inequality in the middle plays no role.

Details of the three inequality measures are described in the respective Wikipedia articles. The following subsections cover them only briefly.

Gini index

Main article: Gini coefficient

The range of the Gini index is between 0 and 1 (0% and 100%), where 0 indicates perfect equality and 1 (100%) indicates maximum inequality.

The Gini index is the most frequently used inequality index. The reason for its popularity is that it is easy to understand how to compute the Gini index as a ratio of two areas in Lorenz curve diagrams. As a disadvantage, the Gini index only maps a number to the properties of a diagram, but the diagram itself is not based on any model of a distribution process. The "meaning" of the Gini index only can be understood empirically. Additionally the Gini does not capture where in the distribution the inequality occurs. As a result two very different distributions of income can have the same Gini index.

Hoover index

Main article: Hoover index

The Hoover index is the simplest of all inequality measures to calculate: It is the proportion of all income which would have to be redistributed to achieve a state of perfect equality.

In a perfectly equal world, no resources would need to be redistributed to achieve equal distribution: a Hoover index of 0. In a world in which all income was received by just one family, almost 100% of that income would need to be redistributed (i.e., taken and given to other families) in order to achieve equality. The Hoover index then ranges between 0 and 1 (0% and 100%), where 0 indicates perfect equality and 1 (100%) indicates maximum inequality.

Theil index

Main article: Theil index

A Theil index of 0 indicates perfect equality. A Theil index of 1 indicates that the distributional entropy of the system under investigation is almost similar to a system with an 82:18 distribution. This is slightly more inequal than the inequality in a system to which the "80:20 Pareto principle" applies. The Theil index can be transformed into an Atkinson index, which has a range between 0 and 1 (0% and 100%), where 0 indicates perfect equality and 1 (100%) indicates maximum inequality.

The Theil index is an entropy measure. As for any resource distribution and with reference to information theory, "maximum entropy" occurs once income earners cannot be distinguished by their resources, i.e. when there is perfect equality. In real societies people can be distinguished by their different resources, with the resources being incomes. The more "distinguishable" they are, the lower is the "actual entropy" of a system consisting of income and income earners. Also based on information theory, the gap between these two entropies can be called "redundancy". It behaves like a negative entropy.

For the Theil index also the term "Theil entropy" had been used. This caused confusion. As an example, Amartya Sen commented on the Theil index, "given the association of doom with entropy in the context of thermodynamics, it may take a little time to get used to entropy as a good thing." It is important to understand that an increasing Theil index *does not* indicate an increasing entropy, instead it indicates an increasing redundancy (decreasing entropy).

High inequality yields high Theil redundancies. High redundancy means low entropy. But this does not necessarily imply that a very high inequality is "good", because very low entropies also can lead to explosive compensation processes. Neither does using the Theil index necessarily imply that a very low inequality (low redundancy, high entropy) is "good", because high entropy is associated with slow, weak and inefficient resource allocation processes.

There are three variants of the Theil index. When applied to income distributions, the first Theil index relates to systems within which incomes are stochastically distributed to income earners, whereas the second Theil index relates to systems within which income earners are stochastically distributed to incomes.

A third "symmetrized" Theil index is the arithmetic average of the two previous indices. Interestingly, the formula of the third Theil index has some similarity with the Hoover index (as explained in the related articles). As in case of the Hoover index, the symmetrized Theil index does not change when swapping the incomes with the income earners. How to generate that third Theil index by means of a spreadsheet computation directly from distribution data is shown below.

An important property of the Theil index which makes its application popular is its decomposability into the between-group and within-group component. For example, the Theil index of overall income inequality can be decomposed in the between-region and within region components of inequality, while the relative share attributable to the between-region component suggests the relative importance of spatial dimension of income inequality.

Comparison of the Theil index and the Hoover index

The Theil index indicates the distributional redundancy of a system, within which incomes are assigned to income earners in a stochastic process. In comparison, the Hoover index indicates the minimum size of the income share of a society, which would have to be redistributed in order to reach maximum entropy. Not to exceed that minimum size would require a perfectly planned redistribution. Therefore the Hoover index is the "non-stochastic" counterpart to the "stochastic" Theil index.

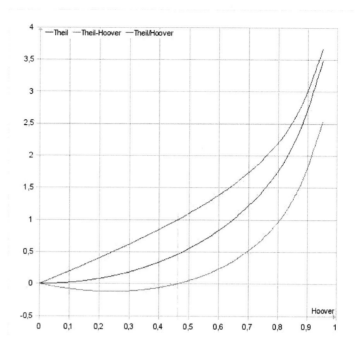

Illustration of the relation between Theil index T and the Hoover index H for societies divides into two quantiles ("a-fractiles"). Here the Hoover index and the Theil are equal at a value of around 0.46. The red curve shows the difference between the Theil index and the Hoover index as a function of the Hoover index. The green curve shows the Theil index divided by the Hoover index as a function of the Hoover index.

Applying the Theil index to allocation processes in the real world does *not* imply that these processes are stochastic: the Theil yields the *distance* between an ordered resource distribution in an observed system to the final stage of stochastic resource distribution in a closed system. Similarly, applying the Hoover index does *not* imply that allocation processes occur in a perfectly planned economy: the Hoover index yields the *distance* between the resource distribution in an observed system to the final stage of a planned "equalization" of resource distribution. For both indices, such an equalization only serves as a reference, not as a goal.

For a given distribution the Theil index can be larger than the Hoover index or smaller than the Hoover index:

- For *high* inequalities the Theil index is larger than the Hoover index.
  This means for achieving equilibrium (maximum entropy) in a closed system, more resources would have to be reallocated than in case of a planned and optimized reallocation process, where only the necessary minimum share of resources would have to be reallocated. For an open system the export of entropy (import of redundancy) would allow to maintain the distribution dynamics driven by high inequality.

- For *low* inequalities the Theil index is smaller than the Hoover index.

  Here, on the path to reaching equilibrium, a planned and optimized reallocation of resources would contribute more to the dynamics of redistribution than stochastic redistribution. This also is intuitively understandable, as low inequalities also weaken the urge to redistribute resources. People in such a system may tolerate or even foster an increase the inequality. As this is would be an increase of redundancy (an decrease of entropy), redundancy would have to be imported into (entropy would have to be exported from) the society. In that case the society needs to be an open system.

In order to increase the redundancy in the distribution category of a society as a closed system, entropy needs to be exported from the subsystem operating in the that economic category to other subsystems with other entropy categories in the society. For example, social entropy may increase. However, in the real world, societies are open systems, but the openness is restricted by the entropy exchange capabilities of the interfaces between the society and the environment of that society. For societies with a resource distribution which entropywise is similar to the resource distribution of a reference society with a 73:27 split (73% of the resources belong to 27% of the population and vice versa), the point where the Hoover index and the Theil index are equal, is at a value of around 46% (0.46) for the Hoover index and the Theil index.

Ratios

Another common class of metrics is to take the ratio of the income of two different groups, generally "higher over lower". This compares two *parts* of the income distribution, rather than the distribution as a whole; equality between these parts corresponds to 1:1, while the more unequal the parts, the greater the ratio. These statistics are easy to interpret and communicate, because they are relative (this population earns twice as much as this population), but, since they do not fall on an absolute scale, do not provide an absolute measure of inequality.

Ratio of percentiles

Particularly common to compare a given percentile to the median, as in the chart at right; compare seven-number summary, which summarizes a distribution by certain percentiles. While such ratios do not represent the *overall level* of inequality in the population as a whole, they provide measures of the *shape* of income distribution. For example, the attached graph shows that in the period 1967–2003, US income ratio between median and 10th and 20th percentile did not

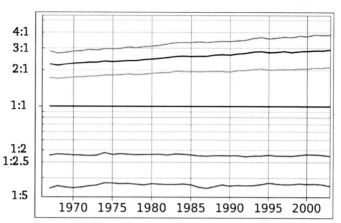

This graph shows income of a given percentage as a ratio to median, for 10th, 20th, 50th, 80th, 90th, and 95th percentile, for 1967–2003.
(50th percentile is 1:1 by definition.)

change significantly, while the ratio between the median and 80th, 90th, and 95th percentile increased. This reflects that the increase in the Gini coefficient of the US in this time period is due to gains by upper income earners (relative to the median), rather than by losses by lower income earners (relative to the median).

Share of income

A related class of ratios is "income share" – what percentage of national income a subpopulation accounts for. Taking the ration of income share to subpopulation size corresponds to a ratio of *mean* subpopulation income relative to *mean* income. Because income distribution is generally positively skewed, mean is higher than median, so ratios to mean are lower than ratios to median. This is particularly used to measure that fraction of income accruing to top earners – top 10%, 1%, .1%, .01% (1 in 10, in 100, in 1,000, in 10,000), and also "top 100" earners or the like; in the US top 400 earners is .0002% of earners (2 in 1,000,0000) – to study concentration of income – wealth condensation, or rather income condensation. For example, in the chart at right, US income share of top earners was approximately constant from the mid 1950s to the mid 1980s, then increased from the mid-1980s through 2000s; this increased inequality was reflected in the Gini coefficient.

For example, in 2007 the top decile (10%) of US earners accounted for 49.7% of total wages ($4.97 \approx 5$ times fraction under equality), and the top 0.01% of US earners accounted for 6% of total wages (600 times fraction under equality).

Spreadsheet computations

The Gini coefficient, the Hoover index and the Theil index as well as the related welfare functions can be computed together in a spreadsheet. The welfare functions serve as alternatives to the median income.

Group	Members per Group	Income per Group	Income per Individual	Relative Deviation	Accumulated Income	Gini	Hoover	Theil
1	A_1	E_1	$\bar{E}_1 = E_1/A_1$	$D_1 = E_1/\Sigma E - A_1/\Sigma A$	$K_1 = E_1$	$G_1 = (2 * K_1 - E_1) * A_1$	$H_1 = abs(D_1)$	$T_1 = \ln(\bar{E}_1) * D_1$
2	A_2	E_2	$\bar{E}_2 = E_2/A_2$	$D_2 = E_2/\Sigma E - A_2/\Sigma A$	$K_2 = E_2 + K_1$	$G_2 = (2 * K_2 - E_2) * A_2$	$H_2 = abs(D_2)$	$T_2 = \ln(\bar{E}_2) * D_2$
3	A_3	E_3	$\bar{E}_3 = E_3/A_3$	$D_3 = E_3/\Sigma E - A_3/\Sigma A$	$K_3 = E_3 + K_2$	$G_3 = (2 * K_3 - E_3) * A_3$	$H_3 = abs(D_3)$	$T_3 = \ln(\bar{E}_3) * D_3$
4	A_4	E_4	$\bar{E}_4 = E_4/A_4$	$D_4 = E_4/\Sigma E - A_4/\Sigma A$	$K_4 = E_4 + K_3$	$G_4 = (2 * K_4 - E_4) * A_4$	$H_4 = abs(D_4)$	$T_4 = \ln(\bar{E}_4) * D_4$
Totals	ΣA	ΣE	$\bar{E} = \Sigma E/\Sigma A$			ΣG	ΣH	ΣT
Inequality Measures						Gini $= 1 - \Sigma G/\Sigma A/\Sigma E$	Hoover $= \Sigma H / 2$	Theil $= \Sigma T / 2$
Welfare Function						$W_G = \bar{E} * (1 - Gini)$	$W_H = \bar{E} * (1 - Hoover)$	$W_T = \bar{E} * (1 - Theil)$

In the table, fields with a yellow background are used for data input. From these data inequality measures as well as the related welfare functions are computed and displayed in fields with green background.

In the example given here, "Theil index" stands for the arithmetic mean of a Theil index computed for the distribution of income within a society to the individuals (or households) in that society and a Theil index computed for the distribution of the individuals (or households) in the society to the income of that society. The difference between the Theil index and the Hoover index is the weighting of the relative deviation D. For the Hoover index the relative deviation D per group is weighted with its own sign. For the Theil index the relative deviation D per group is weighted with the information size provided by the income per individual in that group.

For the computation the society usually is divided into income groups. Often there are four or five groups consisting of a similar amount of individuals in each group. In other cases the groups are created based on income ranges which leads to having different amounts of individuals in the different groups. The table above shows a computation of inequality indices for four groups. For each group the amount of individuals (or households) per group A and the total income in that group E is specified.

The parameter pairs A and E need to be sorted for the computation of the Gini coefficient. (For the Theil index and the Hoover index no sorting is required.) A and E has the be sorted so that the values in the column "Income per individual" are lined up in ascending order.

Proper use of income inequality metrics

1. When using income metrics, it has to be made clear how income should be defined. Should it include capital gains, imputed house rents from home ownership, and gifts? If these income sources or alleged income sources (in the case of "imputed rent") are ignored (as they often are), how might this bias the analysis? How should non-paid work (such as parental childcare or doing ones own cooking instead of hiring a chef for every meal) be handled? Wealth or consumption may be more appropriate measures in some situations. Broader quality of life metrics might be useful.

2. The comparison of inequality measures requires that the segmentation of compared groups (societies etc.) into quintiles should be similar.

3. Distinguish properly, whether the basic unit of measurement is households or individuals. The Gini value for households is always lower than for individuals because of income pooling and intra-family transfers. And households have a varying amount of members. The metrics will be influenced either upward or downward depending on which unit of measurement is used.

4. Consider life cycle effects. In most Western societies, an individual tends to start life with little or no income, gradually increase income till about age 50, after which incomes will decline, eventually becoming negative. This affects the conclusions which can be drawn from a measured inequality. It has been estimated (by A.S. Blinder in *The Decomposition of Inequality*, MIT press) that 30% of measured income inequality is due to the inequality an individual experiences as they go through the various stages of life.

5. Clarify whether real or nominal income distributions should be used. What effect will inflation have on absolute measures? Do some groups (eg., pensioners) feel the effect of inflation more than others?

6. When drawing conclusion from inequality measurements, consider how we should allocate the benefits of government spending? How does the existence of a social security safety net influence the definition of absolute measures of poverty? Do government programs support some income groups more than others?

7. Inequality metrics measure inequality. They do not measure possible causes of income inequality. Some alleged causes include: life cycle effects (age), inherited characteristics (IQ, talent), willingness to take chances (risk aversion), the leisure/industriousness choice, inherited wealth, economic circumstances, education and training, discrimination, and market imperfections.

Keeping these points in mind helps to understand the problems caused by the improper use of inequality measures. However, they do not render inequality coefficients invalid. If inequality measures are computed in a well explained and *consistent* way, they can provide a good tool for quantitative comparisons of inequalities.

Inequality, growth, and progress

There is evidence from a broad panel of recent academic studies shows that there is a nonlinear relation between income inequality and the rate of growth and investment. Very high inequality slows growth; moderate inequality encourages growth. Studies differ on the effect of very low inequality.

Robert J. Barro, Harvard University found in his study "Inequality and Growth in a Panel of Countries" that higher inequality tends to retard growth in poor countries and encourage growth in well developed regions.. Income inequality diminishes growth potential through the erosion of social cohesion, increasing social unrest and social conflict causing uncertainty of property rights. Extreme inequality can effectively reduce access to productivity enhancement measures, or cause such measures to be allocated inefficiently toward those who already have, or can no longer absorb such measures.

In their study for the World Institute for Development Economics Research, Giovanni Andrea Cornia and Julius Court (2001) reach slightly different conclusions. The authors therefore recommend to pursue moderation also as to the distribution of wealth and particularly to avoid the extremes. Both very high egalitarianism and very high inequality cause slow growth. Considering the inequalities in economically well developed countries, public policy should target an 'efficient inequality range'. The authors claim that such efficiency range roughly lies between the values of the Gini coefficients of 25 (the inequality value of a typical Northern European country) and 40 (that of countries such as the USA, France, Germany and the UK).

Another researcher (W.Kitterer) has shown that in perfect markets inequality does not influence growth.

The precise shape of the inequality-growth curve obviously varies across countries depending upon their resource endowment, history, remaining levels of absolute poverty and available stock of social programs, as well as on the distribution of physical and human capital.

See also

- List of countries by income equality
- Economic inequality
- Income inequality in the United States
- Human Development Index
- International inequality
- Kuznets curve
- Poverty line
- United Nations Millennium Development Goals
- Socioeconomics
- "The rich get richer and the poor get poorer"
- Socialism - political system or objective dedicated to income equality

Literature

- A.B. Atkinson and F. Bourguignon, ed. (2000). *Handbook of Income Distribution*, v. 1. Elsevier.table of contents [1]
- _____," International Encyclopedia of the Social & Behavioral Sciences (2001), pp. 7265-7271. Abstract. [2]
- Yoram Amiel (Author), Frank A. Cowell: *Thinking about Inequality: Personal Judgment and Income Distributions*, 2000
- Philip B. Coulter: *Measuring Inequality*, 1989

External links

- Travis Hale, University of Texas Inequality Project: *The Theoretical Basics of Popular Inequality Measures* [3]; online computation of examples: 1A [4], 1B [5]
- Samuel Murray Matheson: *Distributive Fairness Measures for Sustainable Project Selection* [6], 1997
- Survey data from the government of Sri Lanka [7]
- Luxembourg Income Study [8] conducts comparative income inequality research
- Two Americas: One Rich, One Poor? Understanding Income Inequality in the United States [9]
- Has US Income Inequality *Really* Increased? [10]
- The Big Picture: Shifting Incomes from 1995 to 2005 [11]
- Inequality and Growth: What Can the Data Say? [12] - By Abhijit V. Banerjee and Esther Duflo
- World Bank: World Development Report 2000/2001, chapter 3 [13] - Income inequality contribution to growth (box 3.5)
- Inequality Worsens across Asia [14] from Dollars & Sense magazine, Nov/Dec 2007
- Software:
  - Free Online Calculator [15] computes the Gini Coefficient, plots the Lorenz curve, and computes many other measures of concentration for any dataset
  - Free Calculator: Online [16] (example for processing data from Table HINC-06 [17], U.S. Census Bureau, 2007: Income Distribution to $250,000 or More for Households) and downloadable scripts [18] (Python and Lua) for Atkinson, Gini, and Hoover inequalities
  - Python script [19] using Formulas in Amartya Sen's *On Economic Inequality*
  - Users of the R [20] data analysis software can install the "ineq" package which allows for computation of a variety of inequality indices including Gini, Atkinson, Theil.
  - A MATLAB Inequality Package [21], including code for computing Gini, Atkinson, Theil indexes and for plotting the Lorenz Curve. Many examples are available.

High income economy

A **high-income economy** is defined by the World Bank as a country with a Gross National Income per capita of $12,196 or more in 2009. While the term "high income" may be used interchangeably with "First World" and "developed country", the technical definitions of these terms differ. The term "first world" commonly refers to those prosperous countries that aligned themselves with the U.S. and NATO during the cold war. Several institutions, such as the Central Intelligence Agency (CIA) or International Monetary Fund (IMF), take factors other than high per capita income into account when classifying countries as "developed" or "advanced economies". According to the United Nations, for example, some high income countries may also be developing countries. The GCC (Persian Gulf States) countries, for example, are classified as developing high income countries. Thus, a high income country may be classified as either developed or developing. The Holy See, which is often considered a sovereign state, is not classified by the World Bank under this definition.

List of high income economies

According to the World Bank the following 69 countries (including territories) are classified as "high-income economies":

- Andorra
- Antigua & Barbuda
- Aruba
- Australia
- Austria
- The Bahamas
- Bahrain
- Barbados
- Belgium
- Bermuda
- Brunei
- Canada
- Cayman Islands
- Channel Islands

- Croatia
- Cyprus
- Czech Republic
- Denmark
- Equatorial Guinea
- Estonia
- Faroe Islands
- Finland
- France
- French Polynesia
- Germany
- Greece
- Greenland
- Guam

- Hong Kong
- Hungary
- Iceland
- Ireland
- Isle of Man
- Israel
- Italy
- Japan
- Kuwait
- Latvia
- Liechtenstein
- Luxembourg
- Macau
- Malta

- Monaco
- Netherlands
- Netherlands Antilles
- New Caledonia
- New Zealand
- Northern Mariana Islands
- Norway
- Oman
- Poland
- Portugal
- Puerto Rico
- Qatar
- San Marino
- Saudi Arabia

- Singapore
- Slovakia
- Slovenia
- South Korea
- Spain
- Sweden
- Switzerland
- Taiwan
- Trinidad and Tobago
- United Arab Emirates
- United Kingdom
- United States
- U.S. Virgin Islands

Subsistence economy

Part of a series on

Economic systems

Ideological systems

Anarchist · Capitalist
Communist · Corporatist
Fascist · Georgist
Islamic · Laissez-faire
Market socialist · (Neo-) Mercantilist
Participatory
Protectionist · Socialist
Syndicalist

Systems

Closed (Autarky) · Digital
Dual · Gift · Informal
Market · Mixed · Natural
Open · Planned · Subsistence
Underground · Virtual

Sectors

State Sector · Private sector
Voluntary sector · Nationalization
Privatization · Municipalization
Liberalization · Corporatization
Deregulation · Socialization
Collectivization · Common
ownership
Marketization · Expropriation
Financialization

Other types of economies

Anglo-Saxon · Feudal
Global · Hunter-gatherer
Information
Newly industrialized country
Palace · Plantation
Post-capitalist · Post-industrial
Social market · Socialist market
Token · Traditional
Transition · Barter
State capitalist · State-directed

Business and
economics portal

A **subsistence economy** is an economy which refers simply to the gathering or amassment of objects of value; the increase in wealth; or the creation of wealth. Capital can be generally defined as assets invested with the expectation that their value will increase, usually because there is the expectation of profit, rent, interest, royalties, capital gain or some other kind of return.

See also

- Hunter gatherer
- Subsistence farming

References

Chief Seattle to President Pierce regarding sale of land [1]

External links

- Appropriate Economic Systems in Asia, Africa & Latin America [2]

Black market

Part of a series on

Economic systems

Ideological systems

Anarchist · Capitalist
Communist · Corporatist
Fascist · Georgist
Islamic · Laissez-faire
Market socialist · (Neo-) Mercantilist
Participatory
Protectionist · Socialist
Syndicalist

Systems

Closed (Autarky) · Digital
Dual · Gift · Informal
Market · Mixed · Natural
Open · Planned · Subsistence
Underground · Virtual

Sectors

State Sector · Private sector
Voluntary sector · Nationalization
Privatization · Municipalization
Liberalization · Corporatization
Deregulation · Socialization
Collectivization · Common
ownership
Marketization · Expropriation
Financialization

Other types of economies

Anglo-Saxon · Feudal
Global · Hunter-gatherer
Information
Newly industrialized country
Palace · Plantation
Post-capitalist · Post-industrial
Social market · Socialist market
Token · Traditional
Transition · Barter
State capitalist · State-directed

**Business and
economics portal**

The **black market**(: (sometimes known as **underground** or **black economy**) is trade, goods and services that are not part of the official economy of a country; this may be legal activities where taxes are not paid, or illegal activities, such as drug dealing and prostitution.

In modern societies, the underground economy covers a vast array of activities. It is generally smaller in countries where economic freedom is greater, and it becomes progressively larger in those areas where corruption, regulation, or legal monopolies restrict economic activity in various goods, services, or trading groups.[citation needed]

Pricing

Goods acquired illegally take one of two price levels:

- They may be cheaper than legal market prices. The supplier does not have to pay for production costs or taxes. This is usually the case in the underground economy. Criminals steal goods and sell them below the legal market price, but there is no receipt, guarantee, and so forth.
- They may be more expensive than legal market prices. The product is difficult to acquire or produce, dangerous to handle or not easily available legally, if at all. If goods are illegal, such as some drugs, their prices can be vastly inflated over the costs of production.

Black markets can form part of border trade near the borders of neighboring jurisdictions with little or no border control if there are substantially different tax rates, or where goods are legal on one side of the border but not on the other. Products that are commonly smuggled like this include alcohol and tobacco. However, not all border trade is illegal.

Consumer issues

Even when the underground market offers lower prices, most consumers still buy on the legal market when possible, because:

- They may prefer legal suppliers, as they are easier to contact and can be held accountable for faults;
- In some jurisdictions, customers may be charged with a criminal offence if they knowingly participate in the black economy, even as a consumer;
- They may feel in danger of being hurt while making the deal;
- They may have a moral dislike of black marketing;
- In some jurisdictions (such as England and Wales), consumers in possession of stolen goods will have them taken away if they are traced, even if they did not know they were stolen. Though they themselves commit no offence, they are still left with no goods and no money back. This risk makes some averse to buying goods that they think may be from the underground market, even if in fact they are legitimate (for example, items sold at a car boot sale).

But some actively prefer the underground market, particularly when government regulations and monopolies hinder what would otherwise be a legitimate competitive service. For example:

- Unlicensed taxicabs. In Baltimore, it has been reported that many consumers actively prefer illegal taxis, citing that they are more available, convenient, and priced fairly.

Traded goods and services

Largest black markets	Estimated annual market value (Billion USD)
Total	1,100 or 1,400
Marijuana	142
Prostitution	108
Counterfeit technology products	100
Counterfeit pharmaceutical drugs	75
Prescription drugs	73
Cocaine	70
Opium and heroin	65
Web Video piracy	60
Software piracy	53
Cigarette smuggling	50

In developed countries, some examples of underground economic activities include:

Transportation providers

Where taxicabs, buses, and other transportation providers are strictly regulated or monopolised by government, a black market typically flourishes to provide transportation to poorly served or overpriced communities. In the United States, some cities restrict entry to the taxicab market with a medallion system— that is, taxicabs must get a special license and display it on a medallion in the vehicle. This has led to a market in Carpooling/illegal taxicab operation, although in most jurisdictions it is not illegal to sell the medallions themselves.[citation needed]

Illegal drugs

Main article: Illegal drug trade

From the late 19th and early 20th centuries, many countries began to ban the keeping or using of some recreational drugs, such as the United States' war on drugs. Many people nonetheless continue to use illegal drugs, and a black market exists to supply them. Despite law enforcement efforts to intercept them, demand remains high, providing a large profit motive for organized criminal groups to keep drugs supplied. The United Nations has reported that the retail market value of illegal drugs is $321.6 billion USD.

Although law enforcement officers do capture a small proportion of the illegal drugs, the high and very stable demand for such drugs ensures that black market prices will simply rise in response to the decrease in supply—encouraging new distributors to enter the market. Many drug legalisation activists draw parallels between the illegal drug trade and the Prohibition of alcohol in the United States in the 1920s.

In the United Kingdom, it is not illegal to take drugs, but it is illegal to possess them. This can lead to the unintended consequence that those in possession may swallow the evidence; once in the body they are committing no crime.

Prostitution

Prostitution is illegal or highly regulated in most countries across the world. These places form a classic study of the underground economy, because of consistent high demand from customers, relatively high pay, but labor intensive and low skilled work, which attracts a continual supply of workers. While prostitution exists in almost every country, studies show that it tends to flourish more in poorer countries, and in areas with large numbers of unattached men, such as around military bases.

Prostitutes in the black market generally operate with some degree of secrecy, sometimes negotiating prices and activities through codewords and subtle gestures. In countries such as the Netherlands, where prostitution is legal but regulated, illegal prostitutes exist whose services are offered cheaper without regard for the legal requirements or procedures— health checks, standards of accommodation, and so on.

In other countries such as Nicaragua where legal prostitution is regulated, hotels may require both parties to identify themselves, to prevent the rise of child prostitution.

Weaponry

The legislatures of many countries forbid or restrict the personal ownership of weapons. These restrictions can range from small knives to firearms, either altogether or by classification (e.g. caliber, automation, etc.), to explosives. The black market supplies the demands for weaponry that can not be obtained legally, or may only be obtained legally after obtaining permits and paying fees. This may be by smuggling the arms from countries where they were bought legally or stolen, or by stealing from arms manufacturers within the country itself, using insiders. In cases where the underground economy is unable to smuggle firearms, they can also satisfy requests by gunsmithing their own firearms. Those who may buy this way include criminals, those who wish to use them for illegal activities, and collectors.

In England and Wales some kinds of arms designed for shooting animals may be kept at home but must be registered with the local police force and kept in a locked cabinet. Some people buy on the black market if they would not meet the conditions for registration— for example if they have a record of committing a criminal offense, however minor.

In some jurisdictions, collectors may legally keep antique weapons. Sometimes they must be disarmed (incapable of being fired); but sometimes they are so ineffective by modern standards that they are allowed to be kept intact. For example a blunderbuss or cannon is hardly likely to be used for a drive-by shooting.

Alcohol and tobacco

It has been reported that smuggling one truckload of cigarettes from a low-tax US state to a high-tax state can lead to a profit of up to $2 million. The low-tax states are generally the major tobacco producers, and have come under enormous criticism for their reluctance to increase taxes. North Carolina eventually agreed to raise its taxes from 5 cents to 35 cents per pack of 20 cigarettes, although this remains far below the national average. But South Carolina has so far refused to follow suit and raise taxes from seven cents per pack (the lowest in the USA).

In the UK it has been reported that "27% of cigarettes and 68% of roll your own tobacco [is] purchased on the black market".

Booze Cruise

Main article: Booze cruise

In the UK, the **Booze Cruise**— a day-trip ferry to continental Europe simply to get alcohol and tobacco at lower tax rates— is still very popular. Its popularity varies on the Euro to Sterling exchange rate, and the relative tax rates between the different countries. Some people do not even bother to get off the boat, they buy their stock on board and sail straight back. Ferry companies offer extremely low fares, in the expectation that they will make the money up in sales on the boat. The same system exists for boats between Liverpool and Dublin, Ireland.

Providing the goods are for personal consumption, "Booze Cruises" are entirely legal. Because there are no customs restrictions between European Union countries it is not strictly a black market, but closer to a grey market. The UK and Ireland are both European Union members and are both in a Common Travel Area so there are neither customs nor passport checks between the two countries.

Copyrighted media

Street vendors in countries where there is scant enforcement of copyright law, particularly in Asia, often sell deeply discounted copies of films, music CDs, and computer software such as video games, sometimes even before the official release of the title. A determined counterfeiter with a few hundred dollars can make copies that are digitally identical to an original and suffer no loss in quality; innovations in consumer DVD and CD writers and the widespread availability of cracks on the Internet for most forms of copy protection technology make this cheap and easy to do.

This has proved very difficult for copyright holders to combat through the law courts, because the operations are distributed and widespread— there is no "Mr. Big"[citation needed]. Since digital information can be duplicated repeatedly with no loss of quality, and distributed electronically at little to no cost, the effective underground market value of media is zero, differentiating it from nearly all other forms of underground economic activity. The issue is compounded by widespread indifference to enforcing copyright law, both with governments and the public at large. To steal a car is seen as a crime in most people's eyes, but to obtain illicit copies of music or a game is not.

See also: Copyright infringement

Currency

Main article: Fixed exchange rate

Money itself is traded on the black market. This may happen for one or more of several reasons:

- The government sets ("pegs") the local currency at some arbitrary level to another currency that does not reflect its true market value.
- A government makes it difficult or illegal for its citizens to own much or any foreign currency.
- The government taxes exchanging the local currency with other currencies, either in one direction or both (e.g. foreigners are taxed to buy local currency, or residents are taxed to buy foreign currency)
- The currency is counterfeit.
- The currency has been acquired illegally and need to be laundered before the money can be used.

A government may officially set the rate of exchange of its currency with that of other currencies—typically the US dollar. When it does, it is often pegged at an exchange rate that is artificially low—that is, below what would be the market value if it were a floating currency. Others in possession of the foreign currency, for example expatriate workers, will sell the foreign currency to buy local currency at higher exchange rates than they can get officially.

More rarely, a government may peg its currency too high. This tends to make the foreign currency become a de facto currency for the country, since it is easier for everyone to deal in the tradable foreign currency than the local one. Tourists and occasional visitors tend to deal solely in a major hard currency instead of the local currency. The whole country is essentially then trading on the black market. Some countries, such as Ecuador, abandoned their local currency and now use US dollars, essentially for this reason, a process known as dollarization. See also the example of the Ghanaian cedi from the 1970s and 1980s.

The Cuban convertible peso and US Continental dollar both have had black market rates significantly different from their face value.

If foreign currency is difficult or illegal for local citizens to acquire, they will pay a premium to acquire it. Taxation is generally less important but, if it is high enough, can still encourage a black market simply for tax avoidance even if currency trading is generally legal.

Fuel

In the EU it is not illegal for a person or business to buy fuel in one EU state for their own use in another, but as with other goods the tax will generally be payable by the final customer at the physical place of making the purchase.

Between the Republic of Ireland and Northern Ireland there has often been a black market in petrol and diesel. The direction of smuggling can change depending on the variation of the taxes and the exchange rate between the Euro and Pound Sterling; indeed sometimes diesel will be smuggled in one direction and petrol the other.

In some countries diesel fuel for agricultural vehicles or domestic use is taxed at a much lower rate than that for other vehicles. This is known as dyed fuel, because a coloured dye is added so it can be detected if used in other vehicles (e.g. a red dye in the UK, a green dye in Ireland). Nevertheless, the saving is attractive enough to make a black market in agricultural diesel. In 2007 it was estimated that £350 million was not gained in potential revenue this way in the UK.

Appearance and disappearance

If an economic good is illegal but not seen by many in society as particularly harmful, such as alcohol under prohibition in the United States, the black market prospers. Black marketeers can reinvest profits in diverse legal or illegal activities, well beyond the original source of profit.

Some, for example in the marijuana-trade debate, argue for removing the underground markets by making illegal products legal. This would, in their view:

- decrease the illegal cashflow, thus making the performance of other, potentially more harmful, activities financially harder
- allow quality and safety controls on the traded goods, thus reducing harm to consumers
- let the goods be taxed, providing a source of revenue
- free up court time and prison space and save taxpayer money.

Modern examples

Wars

Black markets flourish in most countries during wartime. States that are engaged in total war or other large-scale, extended wars must necessarily impose restrictions on home use of critical resources that are needed for the war effort, such as food, gasoline, rubber, metal, etc., typically through rationing. In most cases, a black market develops to supply rationed goods at exorbitant prices. The rationing and price controls enforced in many countries during World War II encouraged widespread black market activity. One source of black-market meat under wartime rationing was by farmers declaring fewer domestic animal births to the Ministry of Food than actually happened. Another in Britain was supplies from the USA, intended only for use in USA army bases on British land, but leaked into the local native British black market.

During the Vietnam war, soldiers would spend Military Payment Certificates on maid service and sexual entertainment,[citation needed] thus supporting their partners and their families. If the Vietnamese civilian wanted something that was hard to get, he would purchase it at double the price from one of the soldiers, who had a monthly ration card and thus had access to the military stores.[citation needed] The transactions ran through the on-base maids to the local populace. Despite the fact that these activities were illegal, only flagrant or large-scale black marketeers were prosecuted by the military.[citation needed]

Prohibition in the United States

Main article: Prohibition in the United States

Alcohol

See also: Legal drinking age

A classic example of creating a black market is the Prohibition of alcohol during the 1920s in the United States. Many organized crime syndicates took advantage of the lucrative opportunities in the resulting black market in banned alcohol production and sale. Most people did not think drinking alcohol was particularly harmful nor that its buyers and sellers should be treated like common criminals. So illegal speakeasies prospered, and organizations such as the Mafia grew tremendously more powerful through their black market activities distributing alcohol. This lasted until repeal of Prohibition.

Although Prohibition ended in 1933, there are still some parallels today with evasion of the drinking age of 21 in the United States, which is high compared to other industrialized countries and three years above the age of majority in nearly all states. Like Prohibition, this law is widely (but more covertly) disobeyed as well. Though social sources of supply predominate for underage drinkers, some bars and stores knowingly serve and sell to those who are underage, and some may even make deals with local police. Many college towns especially have a vast network of fraternities and sororities (and others) that run what can be considered modern-day speakeasies in their houses, in which age is irrelevant. Since the substance in question, alcohol, is legal for those over 21, it can be considered more of a gray market than a black market.

Smoking

This effect is seen similarly today, when jurisdictions pass bans on smoking in bars and restaurants. In these jurisdictions, smokeasies arise which allow smoking despite the legal prohibition. In a sense the owner is not a black marketeer since he is not necessarily selling tobacco, but he profits by the sale of other goods on his premises (typically alcohol).

This phenomenon is very prevalent in many US state jurisdictions with smoking bans, including California, Philadelphia, Utah, Seattle, Ohio, and Washington, D.C..

Comparison with regular economy

Country	Estimated size of shadow economy in percent of GDP, average over 1990-93
Developing economies	
Africa	
Nigeria and Egypt	68-76%
Tunisia and Morocco	39-45%
Central and South America	
Guatemala, Mexico, Peru and Panama	40-60%
Chile, Costa Rica, Venezuela, Brazil, Paraguay and Colombia	25-35%
Asia	
Thailand	70%
Philippines, Sri Lanka and Malaysia	38-50%
Hong Kong and Singapore	13%
Transition economies	
Central Europe	
Hungary, Bulgaria and Poland	20-28%
Romania, Slovakia and Czech Republic	7-16%
Former Soviet Union	
Georgia, Azerbaijan, Ukraine and Belarus	28-43%

Russia, Lithuania, Latvia and Estonia	20-27%
Developed economies	
Greece, Italy, Spain, Portugal and Belgium	24-30%
Sweden, Norway, Denmark, Ireland, France, The Netherlands, Germany and Great Britain	13-23%
Japan, United States, Austria and Switzerland	8-10%

Market economy

Agorists and some other proponents of the free market argue that the black market is the most free market. Other regulated markets, they claim, suffer one way or another from undue interference in the general working of a free market.

Others[citation needed] argue that black markets are often controlled by other parties — such as a gang that aggressively regulates the drug trade in its territory — in a similar fashion to the government control of white markets, and are therefore not truly free markets. Agorists, however, use the term "red market" to distinguish between black markets in general and those based on violence and theft.

See also

- Agorism
- Counter-economics
- Informal economy
- Grey market
- Business ethics
- Wide boy
- Household electricity approach
- Unreported employment

Further reading

- Schneider, Friedrich; Enste, Dominik H. (2000). "Shadow Economies: Size, Causes, and Consequences" [1]. *Journal of Economic Literature* (American Economic Association) **38** (1): 77–114..

External links

- Official March 2000 French Parliamentary Report on the obstacles on the control and repression of financial criminal activity and of money-laundering in Europe [2] by French MPs Vincent Peillon and Arnaud Montebourg, third section on "Luxembourg's political dependency toward the financial sector: the Clearstream affair" (pp. 83–111 on PDF version)

- *The Underground Economy* from National Center for Policy Analysis [3] (1998)
- *Going Underground: America's Shadow Economy* by Jim McTague [4] (2005)
- *The Underground Economy: Global Evidence of Its Size and Impact* [5] (1997)
- The Effects of a Black Market Using Supply and Demand [6]
- Information on Black Market products [7]
- Economist, Aug 11th 2010, A lengthening shadow: Shadow economies have grown since the financial crisis began [8]

Standard of living

Standard of living is generally measured by standards such as real (i.e. inflation adjusted) income per person and poverty rate. Other measures such as access and quality of health care, income growth inequality and educational standards are also used. Examples are access to certain goods (such as number of refrigerators per 1000 people), or measures of health such as life expectancy. It is the ease by which people living in a time or place are able to satisfy their needs and/or wants.

The idea of a 'standard' may be contrasted with the quality of life, which takes into account not only the material standard of living, but also other more intangible aspects that make up human life, such as leisure, safety, cultural resources, social life, physical health, environmental quality issues etc. More complex means of measuring well-being must be employed to make such judgments, and these are very often political, thus controversial. Even between two nations or societies that have similar material standards of living, quality of life factors may in fact make one of these places more attractive to a given individual or group.

However, there can be problems even with just using numerical averages to compare material standards of living, as opposed to, for instance, a Pareto index (a measure of the breadth of income or wealth distribution). Standards of living are perhaps inherently subjective. As an example, countries with a very small, very rich upper class and a very large, very poor lower class may have a high mean level of income, even though the majority of people have a low "standard of living". This mirrors the problem of poverty measurement, which also tends towards the relative. This illustrates how distribution of income can disguise the actual standard of living.

Likewise Country A, a perfectly socialist country with a planned economy with very low average per capita income would receive a higher score for having lower income inequality than Country B with a higher income inequality, even if the bottom of Country B's population distribution had a higher per capita income than Country A. Real examples of this include former East Germany compared to former West Germany or North Korea compared to South Korea. In each case, the socialist country has a low income discrepancy (and therefore would score high in that regard), but lower per capita incomes than a large majority of their neighboring counterpart. This can be avoided by using the measure of income at various percentiles of the population rather than a highly relative and controversial overall income inequality measure.

External links

- *Industrial Revolution and the Standard of Living* [1] by Freddy Madero

mhr:Илышын кӱкшыт

Disposable and discretionary income

Disposable income is total personal income minus personal current taxes. In national accounts definitions, personal income, minus personal current taxes equals disposable personal income. Subtracting personal outlays (which includes the major category of personal (or, private) consumption expenditure) yields personal (or, private) savings.

Restated, consumption expenditure plus savings equals disposable income after accounting for transfers such as payments to children in school or elderly parents' living arrangements.

The marginal propensity to consume (MPC) is the fraction of a change in disposable income that is consumed. For example, if disposable income rises by $100, and $65 of that $100 is consumed, the MPC is 65%. Restated, the marginal propensity to save is 35%.

Discretionary income is income after subtracting taxes and normal expenses (such as rent or mortgage, utilities, insurance, medical, transportation, property maintenance, child support, inflation, food and sundries, &c.) to maintain a certain standard of living. It is the amount of an individual's income available for spending after the essentials (such as food, clothing, and shelter) have been taken care of:

Discretionary income = Gross income - taxes - necessities

Despite the formal definitions above, disposable income is commonly used to denote **discretionary income**. The meaning should therefore be interpreted from context. Commonly, disposable income is the amount of "play money" left to spend or save. The Consumer Leverage Ratio is the expression of the ratio of Total Household Debt to Disposable Income.

Use of discretionary income in high-income loan applications

When applying for a loan (mortgage, consumer loan), lenders may take into consideration a high-income applicant's discretionary income in order to assess the loan repayment capacity of the applicant. Discretionary income provides the lender with more information on the applicant's capacity to repay than the debt-to-income ratio in the case where the applicant has a lot of debt, but also a lot of income, such that the percent of available income may be smaller than normal standards would allow, but the actual amount of money is still large.

External links

- A simple discretionary income calculator [1] -- even though this says it's measuring "disposable income," using the economist's language, it's discretionary income.
- US Bureau of Economic Analysis - Chart of American Disposable Income [2]
- Eurostat, News Release No. 60/2010, Household Savings and Disposable Income [3], 30 April 2010
- Eurostat, Statistics Explained, Glossary article: National Disposable Income [4]
- OECD Disposable income statistics [5]
- Google - public data [6]: GDP and Personal Income of the U.S. (annual): Disposal Personal Income
- Google - public data [7]: GDP and Personal Income of the U.S. (annual): Disposal Personal Income per capita

Sustainable development

Environmental law
Pollution control and remediation
Air Hazardous substances Waste Water
Resource conservation and management
Fisheries Forests Historic sites Minerals Oil and gas Parks Species Water
Planning, land use, and infrastructure
Impact review Municipal planning Land use Transportation infrastructure Energy infrastructure Environmental justice
Related topics
Administrative law Bankruptcy law Energy law Insurance law International law

See also: Sustainability

Sustainable development is a pattern of resource use that aims to meet human needs while preserving the environment so that these needs can be met not only in the present, but also for generations to come. The term was used by the Brundtland Commission which coined what has become the most often-quoted definition of sustainable development as development that "meets the needs of the present without compromising the ability of future generations to meet their own needs."

Sustainable development ties together concern for the carrying capacity of natural systems with the social challenges facing humanity. As early as the 1970s "sustainability" was employed to describe an economy "in equilibrium with basic ecological support systems." Ecologists have pointed to The Limits to Growth,[citation needed] and presented the alternative of a "steady state economy" in order to address environmental concerns.

The field of sustainable development can be conceptually broken into three constituent parts: environmental sustainability, economic sustainability and sociopolitical sustainability.

Scope and definitions

The concept has included notions of weak sustainability, strong sustainability and deep ecology. Sustainable development does not focus solely on environmental issues.

In 1987, the United Nations released the Brundtland Report, which defines sustainable development as 'development which meets the needs of the present without compromising the ability of future generations to meet their own needs.'

The United Nations 2005 World Summit Outcome Document refers to the "interdependent and mutually

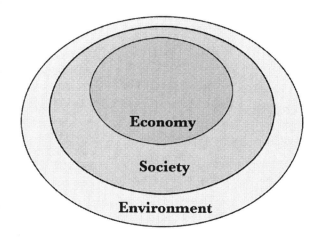

A representation of sustainability showing how both economy and society are constrained by environmental limits (2003)

reinforcing pillars" of sustainable development as economic development, social development, and environmental protection.

Indigenous peoples have argued, through various international forums such as the United Nations Permanent Forum on Indigenous Issues and the Convention on Biological Diversity, that there are *four* pillars of sustainable development, the fourth being cultural. *The Universal Declaration on Cultural Diversity* (UNESCO, 2001) further elaborates the concept by stating that "...cultural diversity is as necessary for humankind as biodiversity is for nature"; it becomes "one of the roots of development understood not simply in terms of economic growth, but also as a means to achieve a more satisfactory intellectual, emotional, moral and spiritual existence". In this vision, cultural diversity is the fourth policy area of sustainable development.

Economic Sustainability: Agenda 21 clearly identified information, integration, and participation as key building blocks to help countries achieve development that recognises

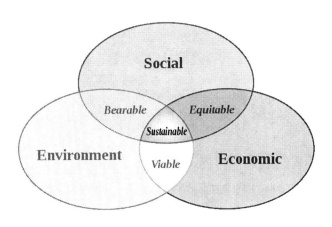

Scheme of sustainable development: at the confluence of three constituent parts.(2006)<ref name=Adams2006>Adams, W.M. (2006). "The Future of Sustainability: Re-thinking Environment and Development in the Twenty-first Century." [1] Report of the IUCN Renowned Thinkers Meeting, 29–31 January 2006. Retrieved on: 2009-02-16.</ref><ref>UCN. 2006. The Future of Sustainability: Re-thinking Environment and Development in the Twenty-first Century. Report of the IUCN Renowned Thinkers Meeting, 29–31 January 2006 http://cmsdata.iucn.org/downloads/iucn_future_of_sustanability. pdf</ref>

these interdependent pillars. It emphasises that in sustainable development everyone is a user and provider of information. It stresses the need to change from old sector-centred ways of doing business to new approaches that involve cross-sectoral co-ordination and the integration of environmental and social concerns into all development processes. Furthermore, Agenda 21 emphasises that broad public participation in decision making is a fundamental prerequisite for achieving sustainable development.

The natural resource of wind powers these 5MW wind turbines on this wind farm 28 km off the coast of Belgium.

According to Hasna Vancock, sustainability is a process which tells of a development of all aspects of human life affecting sustenance. It means resolving the conflict between the various competing goals, and involves the simultaneous pursuit of economic prosperity, environmental quality and social equity famously known as three dimensions (triple bottom line) with is the resultant vector being technology, hence it is a continually evolving process; the 'journey' (the process of achieving sustainability) is of course vitally important, but only as a means of getting to the destination (the desired future state). However, the 'destination' of sustainability is not a fixed place in the normal sense that we understand destination. Instead, it is a set of wishful characteristics of a future system.

Green development is generally differentiated from sustainable development in that Green development prioritizes what its proponents consider to be environmental sustainability over economic and cultural considerations. Proponents of Sustainable Development argue that it provides a context in which to improve overall sustainability where cutting edge Green development is unattainable. For example, a cutting edge treatment plant with extremely high

Solar towers utilize the natural resource of the sun, and are a renewable energy source. From left: PS10 and PS20 solar towers.

maintenance costs may not be sustainable in regions of the world with fewer financial resources. An environmentally ideal plant that is shut down due to bankruptcy is obviously less sustainable than one that is maintainable by the community, even if it is somewhat less effective from an environmental standpoint.

Some research activities start from this definition to argue that the environment is a combination of nature and culture. The Network of Excellence "Sustainable Development in a Diverse World", sponsored by the European Union, integrates multidisciplinary capacities and interprets cultural diversity as a key element of a new strategy for sustainable development.

Still other researchers view environmental and social challenges as opportunities for development action. This is particularly true in the concept of sustainable enterprise that frames these global needs as opportunities for private enterprise to provide innovative and entrepreneurial solutions. This view is now being taught at many business schools including the Center for Sustainable Global Enterprise at Cornell University and the Erb Institute for Global Sustainable Enterprise at the University of Michigan.

The United Nations Division for Sustainable Development lists the following areas as coming within the scope of sustainable development:

Sustainable development is an eclectic concept, as a wide array of views fall under its umbrella. The concept has included notions of weak sustainability, strong sustainability and deep ecology. Different conceptions also reveal a strong tension between ecocentrism and anthropocentrism. Many definitions and images (Visualizing Sustainability) [2] of sustainable development coexist. Broadly defined, the sustainable development mantra enjoins current generations to take a systems approach to growth and development and to manage natural, produced, and social capital for the welfare of their own and future generations.

During the last ten years, different organizations have tried to measure and monitor the proximity to what they consider sustainability by implementing what has been called sustainability metrics and indices.

Sustainable development is said to set limits on the developing world. While current first world countries polluted significantly during their development, the same countries encourage third world countries to reduce pollution, which sometimes impedes growth. Some consider that the implementation of sustainable development would mean a reversion to pre-modern lifestyles.

Others have criticized the overuse of the term:

> "[The] word sustainable has been used in too many situations today, and ecological sustainability is one of those terms that confuse a lot of people. You hear about sustainable development, sustainable growth, sustainable economies, sustainable societies, sustainable agriculture. Everything is sustainable (Temple, 1992)."

Environmental sustainability

Environmental sustainability is the process of making sure current processes of interaction with the environment are pursued with the idea of keeping the environment as pristine as naturally possible based on ideal-seeking behavior.

Water is an important natural resource that covers 71% of the Earth's surface. Image is the Earth photographed from Apollo 17.

An "unsustainable situation" occurs when natural capital (the sum total of nature's resources) is used up faster than it can be replenished. Sustainability requires that human activity only uses nature's resources at a rate at which they can be replenished naturally. Inherently the concept of sustainable development is intertwined with the concept of carrying capacity. Theoretically, the long-term result of environmental degradation is the inability to sustain human life. Such degradation on a global scale could imply extinction for humanity.

Consumption of renewable resources	State of environment	Sustainability
More than nature's ability to replenish	Environmental degradation	Not sustainable
Equal to nature's ability to replenish	Environmental equilibrium	Steady state economy
Less than nature's ability to replenish	Environmental renewal	Environmentally sustainable

The notion of capital in sustainable development

Deforestation of native rain forest in Rio de Janeiro City for extraction of clay for civil engineering (2009 picture).

The sustainable development debate is based on the assumption that societies need to manage three types of capital (economic, social, and natural), which may be non-substitutable and whose consumption might be irreversible. Daly (1991), for example, points to the fact that natural capital can not necessarily be substituted by economic capital. While it is possible that we can find ways to replace some natural resources, it is much more unlikely that they will ever be able to replace eco-system services, such as the protection provided by the ozone layer, or the climate stabilizing function of the Amazonian forest. In fact natural capital, social capital and economic capital are often complementarities. A further obstacle to substitutability lies also in the multi-functionality of many natural resources. Forests, for example, not only provide the raw material for paper (which can be substituted quite easily), but they also maintain biodiversity, regulate water flow, and absorb CO_2.

Another problem of natural and social capital deterioration lies in their partial irreversibility. The loss in biodiversity, for example, is often definite. The same can be true for cultural diversity. For example with globalisation advancing quickly the number of indigenous languages is dropping at alarming rates. Moreover, the depletion of natural and social capital may have non-linear consequences. Consumption of natural and social capital may have no observable impact until a certain threshold is reached. A lake can, for example, absorb nutrients for a long time while actually increasing its productivity. However, once a certain level of algae is reached lack of oxygen causes the lake's ecosystem to break down suddenly.

Market failure

If the degradation of natural and social capital has such important consequence the question arises why action is not taken more systematically to alleviate it. Cohen and Winn (2007) point to four types of market failure as possible explanations: First, while the benefits of natural or social capital depletion can usually be privatized the costs are often externalized (i.e. they are borne not by the party responsible but by society in general). Second, natural capital is often undervalued by society since we are not fully aware of the real cost of the depletion of natural capital. Information asymmetry is a third reason—often the link between cause and effect is obscured, making it difficult for actors to make informed choices. Cohen and Winn close with the realization that contrary to economic theory many firms are not perfect optimizers. They postulate that firms often do not optimize resource allocation because they are caught in a "business as usual" mentality.

Before flue gas desulfurization was installed, the air-polluting emissions from this power plant in New Mexico contained excessive amounts of sulfur dioxide.

The business case for sustainable development

The most broadly accepted criterion for corporate sustainability constitutes a firm's efficient use of natural capital. This eco-efficiency is usually calculated as the economic value added by a firm in relation to its aggregated ecological impact. This idea has been popularised by the World Business Council for Sustainable Development (WBCSD) under the following definition: "Eco-efficiency is achieved by the delivery of competitively priced goods and services that satisfy human needs and bring quality of life, while progressively reducing ecological impacts and resource intensity throughout the life-cycle to a level at least in line with the earth's carrying capacity." (DeSimone and Popoff, 1997: 47)

Similar to the eco-efficiency concept but so far less explored is the second criterion for corporate sustainability. Socio-efficiency describes the relation between a firm's value added and its social impact. Whereas, it can be assumed that most corporate impacts on the environment are negative (apart from rare exceptions such as the planting of trees) this is not true for social impacts. These can be either positive (e.g. corporate giving, creation of employment) or negative (e.g. work accidents, mobbing of employees, human rights abuses). Depending on the type of impact socio-efficiency thus either tries to minimize negative social impacts (i.e. accidents per value added) or maximise positive social impacts (i.e. donations per value added) in relation to the value added.

Both eco-efficiency and socio-efficiency are concerned primarily with increasing economic sustainability. In this process they instrumentalize both natural and social capital aiming to benefit from win-win situations. However, as Dyllick and Hockerts point out the business case alone will not be sufficient to realise sustainable development. They point towards eco-effectiveness, socio-effectiveness, sufficiency, and eco-equity as four criteria that need to be met if sustainable development is to be reached.

Critique of the concept of sustainable development

The concept of "Sustainable Development" raises several critiques at different levels.

Purpose

Various writers have commented on the population control agenda that seems to underlie the concept of sustainable development. Maria Sophia Aguirre writes:

Deforestation and increased road-building in the Amazon Rainforest are a significant concern because of increased human encroachment upon wilderness areas, increased resource extraction and further threats to biodiversity.

> "Sustainable development is a policy approach that has gained quite a lot of popularity in recent years, especially in international circles. By attaching a specific interpretation to sustainability, population control policies have become the overriding approach to development, thus becoming the primary tool used to "promote" economic development in developing countries and to protect the environment."

Mary Jo Anderson suggests that the real purpose of sustainable development is to contain and limit economic development in developing countries, and in so doing control population growth. It is suggested that this is the reason the main focus of most programs is still on low-income agriculture. Joan Veon, a businesswoman and international reporter, who covered 64 global meetings on sustainable development posits that:

> "Sustainable development has continued to evolve as that of protecting the world's resources while its true agenda is to control the world's resources. It should be noted that Agenda 21 sets up the global infrastructure needed to manage, count, and control all of the world's assets."

Consequences

John Baden views the notion of sustainable development as dangerous because the consequences have unknown effects. He writes: "In economy like in ecology, the interdependence rule applies. Isolated actions are impossible. A policy which is not carefully enough thought will carry along various perverse and adverse effects for the ecology as much as for the economy. Many suggestions to save our environment and to promote a model of

The retreat of Aletsch Glacier in the Swiss Alps (situation in 1979, 1991 and 2002), due to global warming.

'sustainable development' risk indeed leading to reverse effects." Moreover, he evokes the bounds of public action which are underlined by the public choice theory: the quest by politicians of their own interests, lobby pressure, partial disclosure etc. He develops his critique by noting the vagueness of the expression, which can cover anything : . It is a gateway to interventionist proceedings which can be against the principle of freedom and without proven efficacy. Against this notion, he is a proponent of private property to impel the producers and the consumers to save the natural resources. According to Baden, "the improvement of environment quality depends on the market economy and the existence of legitimate and protected property rights." They enable the effective practice of personal responsibility and the development of mechanisms to protect the environment. The State can in this context "create conditions which encourage the people to save the environment."

Vagueness of the term

Some criticize the term "sustainable development", stating that the term is too vague. For example, both Jean-Marc Jancovici or the philosopher Luc Ferry express this view. The latter writes about sustainable development: "I know that this term is obligatory, but I find it also absurd, or rather so vague that it says nothing." Luc Ferry adds that the term is trivial by a proof of contradiction: "who would like to be a proponent of an "untenable development! Of course no one! [..] The term is more charming than meaningful. [..] Everything must

A sewage treatment plant that uses environmentally friendly solar energy, located at Santuari de Lluc monastery.

be done so that it does not turn into Russian-type administrative planning with ill effects."

Basis

Sylvie Brunel, French geographer and specialist of the Third World, develops in *A qui profite le développement durable* (Who benefits from sustainable development?) (2008) a critique of the basis of sustainable development, with its binary vision of the world, can be compared to the Christian vision of Good and Evil, a idealized nature where the human being is an animal like the others or even an alien. Nature – as Rousseau thought – is better than the human being. It is a parasite, harmful for the nature. But the human is the one who protects the biodiversity, where normally only the strong survive.

Moreover, she thinks that the ideas of sustainable development can hide a will to protectionism from the developed country to impede the development of the other countries. For Sylvie Brunel, the sustainable development serves as a pretext for the protectionism and "I have the feeling about sustainable development that it is perfectly helping out the capitalism".

"De-growth"

The proponents of the de-growth reckon that the term of sustainable development is an oxymoron. According to them, on a planet where 20% of the population consumes 80% of the natural resources, a sustainable development cannot be possible for this 20%: "According to the origin of the concept of sustainable development, a development which meets the needs of the present without compromising the ability of future generations to meet their own needs, the right term for the developed countries should be a sustainable de-growth".

Sustainable development in economics

The Venn diagram of sustainable development shown above has many versions, but was first used by economist Edward Barbier (1987). However, Pearce, Barbier and Markandya (1989) criticized the Venn approach due to the intractability of operationalizing separate indices of economic, environmental, and social sustainability and somehow combining them. They also noted that the Venn approach was inconsistent with the Brundtland Commission Report, which emphasized the interlinkages between economic development, environmental degradation, and population pressure instead of three objectives. Economists have since focused on viewing the economy and the environment as a single interlinked system with a unified valuation methodology (Hamilton 1999, Dasgupta 2007). Intergenerational equity can be incorporated into this approach, as has become common in economic valuations of climate change economics (Heal,2009). Ruling out discrimination against future generations and allowing for the possibility of renewable alternatives to petro-chemicals and other non-renewable resources, efficient policies are compatible with increasing human welfare, eventually reaching a golden-rule steady state (Ayong le Kama, 2001 and Endress et al.2005). Thus the three pillars of sustainable development are interlinkages, intergenerational equity, and dynamic efficiency (Stavins, et al. 2003).

Arrow et al. (2004) and other economists (e.g. Asheim,1999 and Pezzey, 1989 and 1997) have advocated a form of the weak criterion for sustainable development – the requirement than the wealth of a society, including human-capital, knowledge-capital and natural-capital (as well as produced capital) not decline over time. Others, including Barbier 2007, continue to contend that strong sustainability – non-depletion of essential forms of natural capital – may be appropriate.

See also

- Applied Sustainability
- Bright green environmentalism
- C. Arden Pope
- Carrying capacity
- Centre for Development and Population Activities
- Civilization
- Clean tech law
- Cleaner Production
- Conservation biology
- Conservation development
- Conservation ethic
- Cultural landscape
- Ecological economics
- Ecologically sustainable development
- Environmental issue
- Green building
- Green Globe
- Hydroelectricity
- Industrial Ecology
- Living Planet Index
- Limits to growth
- Geothermal energy
- Maximum sustainable yield
- Micro-Sustainability
- Natural environment
- Natural landscape
- Nature
- Outline of sustainability
- List of sustainability topics

- Passive solar building design
- Renewable energy
- Residential cluster development
- Solar energy
- Strategic Sustainable Development
- Sustainable forest management
- Sustainable living
- Sustainable yield
- Sustainopreneurship
- World Cities Summit
- Zero carbon city

Organizations and research

- 2010 International Year of Biodiversity
- 2010 Biodiversity Indicators Partnership
- Afrique verte
- Agronomy for Sustainable Development
- Appropedia
- Dashboard of Sustainability
- Earth Charter
- Fondazione Eni Enrico Mattei
- Greenhouse Development Rights
- Institute for Environment and Sustainability (IES)
- Institute for Trade, Standards and Sustainable Development (ITSSD)
- International Institute for Environment and Development
- International Institute for Sustainable Development
- International Mountain Day - Dec. 11
- International Organization for Sustainable Development
- National Center for Appropriate Technology
- National Strategy for a Sustainable America
- Sovereignty International
- Stakeholder Forum for a Sustainable Future
- Sustainable Tourism CRC
- The Earth Institute
- The Venus Project
- United Nations Decade of Education for Sustainable Development
- World Cities Summit

Further reading

- Book Review [3] on *An Introduction to Sustainable Development* by Peter Rogers, Kazi Jalal, & John Boyd Sustainability: Science, Practice, & Policy [4], Published online June 18, 2008
- Pezzey, J; M. Toman (January 2002). "The Economics of Sustainability:A Review of Journal Articles" [5]. *Resources for the Future DP 02-03*: 1–36. Retrieved 2009-06-16.
- Mark Jarzombek, "Sustainability - Architecture: between Fuzzy Systems and Wicked Problems," Blueprints 21/1 (Winter 2003), pp. 6–9.
- Wallace, Bill (2005). *Becoming part of the solution : the engineer's guide to sustainable development*. Washington, DC: American Council of Engineering Companies. ISBN 0910090378.

External links

- Globe Awards-the Leading Sustainability Awards [6]
- CII - ITC Centre of Excellence for Sustainable Development [7]
- The Sustainable Development Research Program of the Fondazione Eni Enrico Mattei [8]
- European Sustainable Development Network - ESDN [9] - Sustainable development policies and strategies in Europe
- World Bank [10] website on sustainable development.
- Erb Institute for Global Sustainable Enterprise at the University of Michigan [11]
- World Creative Youth Forum (WCYF) 2009 [12] - Upcoming international youth forum on Education for Sustainable Development in May 2009 in the Philippines
- WWW-Virtual Library Sustainable development [13] - Links to sustainable development sources
- World Business Council for Sustainable Development [14]
- The Center for Sustainable Global Enterprise [15] at Cornell University views environmental and social needs as business opportunities.
- U.K. Sustainable Development Commission [16]
- Appropedia - a Wiki focused on sustainable international development and poverty reduction
- Citizens Network for Sustainable Development [17]
- Sustainable Development Law & Policy [18]
- Stakeholder Forum for a Sustainable Future [19]
- Sustainable Development Policy Institute, Pakistan [20]
- Consilience: The Journal of Sustainable Development, based at Columbia University [21]
- Peter Ainsworth on degrowth and sustainable development [22] Published on La Clé des langues

Purchasing power parity

Purchasing power parity (PPP) is a theory of long-term equilibrium exchange rates based on relative price levels of two countries. The idea originated with the School of Salamanca in the 16th century and was developed in its modern form by Gustav Cassel in 1918. The concept is founded on the law of one price; the idea that in absence of transaction costs, identical goods will have the same price in different markets.

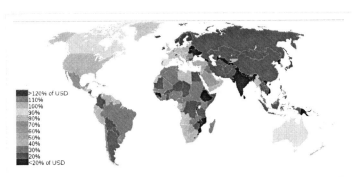

Purchasing Power Parity (PPP) of Gross Domestic Product for the countries of the world as of 2003. The economy of the United States is used as a reference, so that country is set at 100. Bermuda has the highest index value, 154, thus goods sold in Bermuda are 54% more expensive than in the United States.

In its "absolute" version, the purchasing power of different currencies is equalized for a given basket of goods. In the "relative" version, the difference in the rate of change in prices at home and abroad—the difference in the inflation rates—is equal to the percentage depreciation or appreciation of the exchange rate.

The best-known and most-used purchasing power parity exchange rate is the Geary-Khamis dollar (the "international dollar").

PPP exchange rate (the "real exchange rate") fluctuations are mostly due to different rates of inflation between the two economies. Aside from this volatility, consistent deviations of the market and PPP exchange rates are observed, for example (market exchange rate) prices of non-traded goods and services are usually lower where incomes are lower. (A U.S. dollar exchanged and spent in India will buy more haircuts than a dollar spent in the United States). Basically, PPP deduces exchange rates between currencies by finding goods available for purchase in both currencies and comparing the total cost for those goods in each currency.

There can be marked differences between PPP and market exchange rates. For example, the World Bank's *World Development Indicators 2005* estimated that in 2003, one Geary-Khamis dollar was equivalent to about 1.8 Chinese yuan by purchasing power parity—considerably different from the nominal exchange rate. This discrepancy has large implications; for instance, GDP per capita in the People's Republic of China is about US$1,800 while on a PPP basis it is about US$7,204. This is frequently used to assert that China is the world's second-largest economy, but such a calculation would only be valid under the PPP theory. At the other extreme, Denmark's nominal GDP per capita is around

US$62,100, but its PPP figure is only US$37,304.

PPP measurement

The PPP exchange-rate calculation is controversial because of the difficulties of finding comparable baskets of goods to compare purchasing power across countries.

Estimation of purchasing power parity is complicated by the fact that countries do not simply differ in a uniform price level; rather, the difference in food prices may be greater than the difference in housing prices, while also less than the difference in entertainment prices. People in different countries typically consume different baskets of goods. It is necessary to compare the cost of baskets of goods and services using a price index. This is a difficult task because purchasing patterns and even the goods available to purchase differ across countries. Thus, it is necessary to make adjustments for differences in the quality of goods and services. Additional statistical difficulties arise with multilateral comparisons when (as is usually the case) more than two countries are to be compared.

When PPP comparisons are to be made over some interval of time, proper account needs to be made of inflationary effects.

Big Mac Index

Main article: Big Mac Index

An example of one measure of PPP is the Big Mac Index popularized by *The Economist*, which looks at the prices of a Big Mac burger in McDonald's restaurants in different countries. If a Big Mac costs US$4 in the United States and GBP£3 in the United Kingdom, the PPP exchange rate would be £3 for $4. The Big Mac Index is presumably useful because it is based on a well-known good whose final price, easily tracked in many countries, includes input costs from a wide range of sectors in the local economy, such as

Big Mac hamburgers, like this one from Japan, are similar worldwide.

agricultural commodities (beef, bread, lettuce, cheese), labor (blue and white collar), advertising, rent and real estate costs, transportation, etc. However, in some emerging economies, western fast food represents an expensive niche product price well above the price of traditional staples—i.e. the Big Mac is not a mainstream 'cheap' meal as it is in the west but a luxury import for the middle classes and foreigners. Although it is not perfect, the index still offers significant insight and an easy example to the understanding of PPP.

Need for PPP adjustments to GDP

The exchange rate reflects transaction values for traded goods *among* countries in contrast to non-traded goods, that is, goods produced for home-country use. Also, currencies are traded for purposes other than trade in goods and services, *e.g.*, to buy capital assets whose prices vary more than those of physical goods. Also, different interest rates, speculation, hedging or interventions by central banks can influence the foreign-exchange market.

The PPP method is used as an alternative to correct for possible statistical bias. The Penn World Table is a widely cited source of PPP adjustments, and the so-called Penn effect reflects such a systematic bias in using exchange rates to outputs among countries.

For example, if the value of the Mexican peso falls by half compared to the U.S. dollar, the Mexican Gross Domestic Product measured in dollars will also halve. However, this exchange rate results from international trade and financial markets. It does not necessarily mean that Mexicans are poorer by a half; if incomes and prices measured in pesos stay the same, they will be no worse off assuming that imported goods are not essential to the quality of life of individuals. Measuring income in different countries using PPP exchange rates helps to avoid this problem.

PPP exchange rates are especially useful when official exchange rates are artificially manipulated by governments. Countries with strong government control of the economy sometimes enforce official exchange rates that make their own currency artificially strong. By contrast, the currency's black market exchange rate is artificially weak. In such cases a PPP exchange rate is likely the most realistic basis for economic comparison.

Difficulties

The main reasons why different measures do not perfectly reflect standards of living are

- PPP numbers can vary with the specific basket of goods used, making it a rough estimate.
- Differences in quality of goods are hard to measure and thereby reflect in PPP.

PPP calculations are often used to measure poverty rates.

Range and quality of goods

The goods that the currency has the "power" to purchase are a basket of goods of different types:

1. Local, non-tradable goods and services (like electric power) that are produced and sold domestically.
2. Tradable goods such as non-perishable commodities that can be sold on the international market (e.g. diamonds).

The more a product falls into category 1 the further its price will be from the currency exchange rate. (Moving towards the PPP exchange rate.) Conversely, category 2 products tend to trade close to the currency exchange rate. (For more details of why, see: Penn effect).

More processed and expensive products are likely to be tradable, falling into the second category, and drifting from the PPP exchange rate to the currency exchange rate. Even if the PPP "value" of the Chinese currency is five times stronger than the currency exchange rate, it won't buy five times as much of internationally traded goods like steel, cars and microchips, but non-traded goods like housing, services ("haircuts"), and domestically produced crops. The relative price differential between tradables and non-tradables from high-income to low-income countries is a consequence of the Balassa-Samuelson effect, and gives a big cost advantage to labour intensive production of tradable goods in low income countries (like China), as against high income countries (like Switzerland). The corporate cost advantage is nothing more sophisticated than access to cheaper workers, but because the pay of those workers goes further in low-income countries than high, the relative pay differentials (inter-country) can be sustained for longer than would be the case otherwise. (This is another way of saying that the wage rate is based on average local productivity, and that this is below the per capita productivity that factories selling tradable goods to international markets can achieve.) An equivalent cost benefit comes from non-traded goods that can be sourced locally (nearer the PPP-exchange rate than the nominal exchange rate in which receipts are paid). These act as a cheaper factor of production than is available to factories in richer countries.

PPP calculations tend to overemphasise the primary sectoral contribution, and underemphasise the industrial and service sectoral contributions to the economy of a nation.

Additional Issues

In addition to methodological issues presented by the selection of a basket of goods, PPP estimates can also vary based on the statistical capacity of participating countries. The International Comparison Program, which PPP estimates are based off, require the disaggregation of national accounts into production, expenditure or (in some cases) income, and not all participating countries routinely disaggregate their data into such categories.

Some aspects of PPP comparison are theoretically impossible or unclear. For example, there is no basis for comparison between the Ethiopian laborer who lives on teff with the Thai laborer who lives on rice, because teff is impossible to find in Thailand and vice versa, so the price of rice in Ethiopia or teff in Thailand cannot be determined. As a general rule, the more similar the price structure between countries, the more valid the PPP comparison.

PPP levels will also vary based on the formula used to calculate price matrices. Different possible formulas include GEKS-Fisher, Geary-Khamis, IDB, and the superlative method. Each has advantages and disadvantages.

Linking regions presents another methodological difficulty. In the 2005 ICP round, regions were compared by using a list of some 1,000 identical items for which a price could be found for 18 countries, selected so that at least two countries would be in each region. While this was superior to earlier "bridging" methods, which is not fully take into account differing quality between goods, it may serve to overstate the PPP basis of poorer countries, because the price indexing on which PPP is based will assign to poorer countries the greater weight of goods consumed in greater shares in richer countries.

2005 ICP

The 2005 ICP round resulted in large downward adjustments of PPP (or upward adjustments of price level) for several Asian countries, including China (-40%), India (-36%), Bangladesh (-42%) and the Philippines (-43%). Surjit Bhalla has argued that these adjustments are unrealistic. For example, in the case of China, backward extrapolation of 2005 ICP PPP based on Chinese annual growth rates would yield a 1952 PPP per capita of $153 1985 International dollars, but Pritchett has persuasively argued that $250 1985 dollars is the minimum required to sustain a population, or has ever been observed for more than a short period. Therefore, both the 2005 ICP PPP for China and China's growth rates cannot both be correct. Angus Maddison has calculated somewhat slower growth rates for China than official figures, but even under his calculations, the 1952 PPP per capita comes to only $229.

Deaton Heston has suggested that the discrepancy can be explained by the fact that the 2005 ICP examined only urban prices, which overstate the national price level for Asian countries, and also the fact that Asian countries adjusted for productivity across noncomparable goods such as government services, whereas non-Asian countries did not make such an adjustment. Each of these two factors, according to him, would lead to an underestimation of GDP by PPP of about 12%.

Clarification to PPP Numbers of the IMF

The GDP number for all reporting areas are **one** number in the reporting areas local currency. Therefore, in the local currency the PPP and market (or government) exchange rate is always 1.0 to its own currency, so the PPP and market exchange rate GDP number is always per definition the same for any duration of time, anytime, in that area's currency. The only time the PPP exchange rate and the market exchange rate can differ is when the GDP number is converted into another currency.

Only because of different base numbers (because of for example "current" or "constant" prices, or an annualized or averaged number) are the USD to USD PPP exchange rate not 1.0, see the IMF data here: [1]. The PPP exchange rate is 1.023 from 1980 to 2002, and the "constant" and "current" price is the same in 2000, because that's the base year for the "constant" (inflation adjusted) currency.

See also

- Big Mac Index
- International dollar
- Relative Purchasing Power Parity
- List of cities by GDP
- List of countries by GDP (PPP)
- List of countries by GDP (PPP) per capita
- List of countries by future GDP (PPP) estimates
- List of countries by future GDP (PPP) per capita estimates
- Measures of national income and output
- Penn effect
- Karl Gustav Cassel
- Geary-Khamis dollar

External links

- Penn World Table [2]
- Explanations from the U. of British Columbia [3] (also provides daily updated PPP charts)
- OECD Purchasing Power Parity estimates [4] updated annually by the Organization for Economic Co-Operation and Development (OECD)
- World Bank International Comparison Project [5] provides PPP estimates for a large number of countries
- UBS's "Prices and Earnings" Report 2006 [6] Good report on purchasing power containing a Big Mac index as well as for staples such as bread and rice for 71 world cities.
- "Understanding PPPs and PPP based national accounts" [7] provides an overview of methodological issues in calculating PPP and in designing the ICP under which the main PPP tables (Maddison, Penn World Tables, and World Bank WDI) are based

Industrialisation

Industrialisation (British English) or **Industrialization** (Canadian & American English) is the process of social and economic change that transforms a human group from a pre-industrial society into an industrial one. It is a part of a wider modernisation process, where social change and economic development are closely related with technological innovation, particularly with the development of large-scale energy and metallurgy production. It is the extensive organisation of an economy for the purpose of manufacturing.

Industrialisation also introduces a form of philosophical change where people obtain a different attitude towards their perception of nature, and a sociological process of ubiquitous rationalisation.

There is considerable literature on the factors facilitating industrial modernisation and enterprise development. Key positive factors identified by researchers have ranged from favourable political-legal environments for industry and commerce, through abundant natural resources of various kinds, to plentiful supplies of relatively low-cost, skilled and adaptable labour.

One survey[citation needed] of countries in Africa, Latin America, the Caribbean, and the Middle East and the rest of Asia in the late 20th century found that high levels of structural differentiation, functional specialisation, and autonomy of economic systems from government were likely to contribute greatly to industrial-commercial growth and prosperity. Amongst other things, relatively open trading systems with zero or low duties on imported goods tended to stimulate industrial cost-efficiency and innovation across the board. Free and flexible labour and other markets also helped raise general business-economic performance levels, as did rapid popular learning capabilities.

Positive work ethics in populations at large combined with skills in quickly utilising new technologies and scientific discoveries were likely to boost production and income levels — and as the latter rose, markets for consumer goods and services of all kinds tended to expand and provide a further stimulus to industrial investment and economic growth. By the end of the century, East Asia was one of the most economically successful regions of the world — with free market countries such as Hong Kong being widely seen as models for other, less developed countries around the world to emulate. The first country to industrialise was Great Britain during the Industrial Revolution.

Description

According to the original sector classification of Jean Fourastié, an economy consists of a "Primary sector" of commodity production (farming, livestock breeding, exploitation of mineral resources), a "secondary sector" of manufacturing and processing, and a "Tertiary Sector" of service industries. The industrialisation process is historically based on the expansion of the secondary sector in an economy dominated by primary activities.

The first ever transformation to an industrial economy from an agrarian one was called the Industrial Revolution and this took place in the late 18th and early 19th centuries in a few countries of Western Europe and North America, beginning in Great Britain. This was the first industrialization in the world's history.

The Second Industrial Revolution describes a later, somewhat less dramatic change that came about in the late 19th century with the widespread availability of electric power, internal combustion engines, and assembly lines to the already industrialised nations.

The lack of an industrial sector in a country is widely seen as a major handicap in improving a country's economy, and power, pushing many governments to encourage or enforce industrialisation.

History of industrialisation

Main article: Pre-industrial society

Most pre-industrial economies had standards of living not much above subsistence, aming that the majority of the population were focused on producing their means of survival. For example, in medieval Europe, 80% of the labour force was employed in subsistence agriculture.

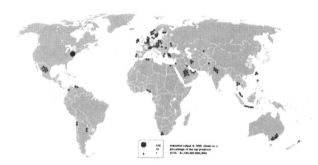

Map showing the global distribution of industrial output in 2005, based on a percentage of the top producer, which is the United States

Some pre-industrial economies, such as classical Athens, had trade and commerce as significant factors, so native Greeks could enjoy wealth far beyond a sustenance standard of living through the use of slavery. Famines were frequent in most pre-industrial societies, although some, such as the Netherlands and England of the seventeenth and eighteenth centuries, the Italian city states of the fifteenth century, the medieval Islamic Caliphate, and the ancient Greek and Roman civilisations were able to escape the famine cycle through increasing trade and commercialisation of the agricultural sector. It is estimated that during the seventeenth century Netherlands imported nearly 70% of its grain supply and in the fifth century BC Athens imported three quarters of its total food supply.

Industrialisation through innovation in manufacturing processes first started with the Industrial Revolution in the north-west and Midlands of England in the eighteenth century. It spread to Europe and North America in the nineteenth century, and to the rest of the world in the twentieth.

Industrial revolution in Western Europe

Main article: Industrial Revolution

In the eighteenth and nineteenth centuries, Great Britain experienced a massive increase in agricultural productivity known as the British Agricultural Revolution, which enabled an unprecedented population growth, freeing a significant percentage of the workforce from farming, and helping to drive the Industrial Revolution.

Due to the limited amount of arable land and the overwhelming efficiency of mechanised farming, the increased population could not be dedicated to agriculture. New agricultural techniques allowed a single peasant to feed more workers than previously; however, these

A Watt steam engine, the steam engine fuelled primarily by coal that propelled the Industrial Revolution in Great Britain and the world.

techniques also increased the demand for machines and other hardwares, which had traditionally been provided by the urban artisans. Artisans, collectively called bourgeoisie, employed rural exodus workers to increase their output and meet the country's needs.

The growth of their business coupled with the lack of experience of the new workers pushed a rationalisation and standardisation of the duties the in workshops, thus leading to a division of labour, that is, a primitive form of Fordism. The process of creating a good was divided into simple tasks, each one of them being gradually mechanized in order to boost productivity and thus increase income.

The accumulation of capital allowed investments in the conception and application of new technologies, enabling the industrialisation process to continue to evolve. The industrialisation process formed a class of industrial workers who had more money to spend than their agricultural cousins. They spent this on items such as tobacco and sugar, creating new mass markets that stimulated more investment as merchants sought to exploit them.

The mechanisation of production spread to the countries surrounding England in western and northern Europe and to British settler colonies, helping to make those areas the wealthiest, and shaping what is now known as the Western world.

Some economic historians argue that the possession of so-called 'exploitation colonies' eased the accumulation of capital to the countries that possessed them, speeding up their development. The consequence was that the subject country integrated a bigger economic system in a subaltern position, emulating the countryside, which demands manufactured goods and offers raw materials, while the colonial power stressed its urban posture, providing goods and importing food. A classical example of this mechanism is said to be the triangular trade, which involved England, southern United States and western

The Crystal Palace Great Exhibition. The United Kingdom was the first country in the world to industrialize.

Africa. Critics argue that this polarity still affects the world, and has deeply retarded industrialisation of what is now known as the Third World.

Some have stressed the importance of natural or financial resources that Britain received from its many overseas colonies or that profits from the British slave trade between Africa and the Caribbean helped fuel industrial investment.

Early industrialisation in other countries

After the Convention of Kanagawa issued by Commodore Matthew C. Perry forced Japan to open the ports of Shimoda and Hakodate to American trade, the Japanese government realised that drastic reforms were necessary to stave off Western influence. The Tokugawa shogunate abolished the feudal system. The government instituted military reforms to modernise the Japanese army and also constructed the base for industrialisation. In the 1870s, the Meiji government vigorously promoted technological and industrial development that eventually changed Japan to a powerful modern country.

In a similar way, Russia suffered during the Allied intervention in the Russian Civil War. The Soviet Union's centrally controlled economy decided to invest a big part of its resources to enhance its industrial production and infrastructures to assure its survival, thus becoming a world superpower.

During the Cold war, the other European socialist countries, organised under the Comecon framework, followed the same developing scheme, albeit with a less emphasis on heavy industry.

Southern European countries saw a moderate industrialisation during the 1950s-1970s, caused by a healthy integration of the European economy, though their level of development, as well as those of eastern countries, doesn't match the western standards.

The Third World

Main article: Third World

A similar state-led developing programme was pursued in virtually all the Third World countries during the Cold War, including the socialist ones, but especially in Sub-Saharan Africa after the decolonisation period.[citation needed] The primary scope of those projects was to achieve self-sufficiency through the local production of previously imported goods, the mechanisation of agriculture and the spread of education and health care. However, all those experiences failed bitterly due to a lack of realism: most countries didn't have a pre-industrial bourgeoisie able to carry on a capitalistic development or even a stable and peaceful state. Those aborted experiences left huge debts toward western countries and fuelled public corruption.

Petrol producing countries

Oil-rich countries saw similar failures in their economic choices. An EIA report stated that OPEC member nations were projected to earn a net amount of $1.251 trillion in 2008 from their oil exports. Because oil is both important and expensive, regions that had big reserves of oil had huge liquidity incomes. However, this was rarely followed by economic development. Experience shows that local elites were unable to re-invest the petrodollars obtained through oil export, and currency is wasted in luxury goods.

This is particularly evident in the Persian Gulf states, where the per capita income is comparable to those of western nations, but where no industrialisation has started. Apart from two little countries (Bahrain and the United Arab Emirates), Arab states have not diversified their economies, and no replacement for the upcoming end of oil reserves is envisaged.

Industrialisation in Asia

Apart from Japan, where industrialisation began in the late 19th century, a different pattern of industrialisation followed in East Asia. One of the fastest rates of industrialisation occurred in the late 20th century across four countries known as the Asian tigers thanks to the existence of stable governments and well structured societies, strategic locations, heavy foreign investments, a low cost skilled and motivated workforce, a competitive exchange rate, and low custom duties.

In the case of South Korea, the largest of the four Asian tigers, a very fast paced industrialisation took place as it quickly moved away from the manufacturing of value added goods in the 1950s and 60s into the more advanced steel, shipbuilding and automobile industry in the 1970s and 80s, focusing on the high-tech and service industry in the 1990s and 2000s. As a result, South Korea became a major economic power and today is one of the wealthiest countries in Asia.

This starting model was afterwards successfully copied in other larger Eastern and Southern Asian countries, including communist ones. The success of this phenomenon led to a huge wave of offshoring

– i.e., Western factories or Tertiary Sector corporations choosing to move their activities to countries where the workforce was less expensive and less collectively organised.

China and India, while roughly following this development pattern, made adaptations in line with their own histories and cultures, their major size and importance in the world, and the geo-political ambitions of their governments (etc.).

Currently, China's government is actively investing in expanding its own infrastructures and securing the required energy and raw materials supply channels, is supporting its exports by financing the United States balance payment deficit through the purchase of US treasury bonds, and is strengthening its military in order to endorse a major geopolitical role.

Meanwhile, India's government is investing in specific vanguard economic sectors such as bioengineering, nuclear technology, pharmaceutics, informatics, and technologically-oriented higher education, openly overpassing its needs, with the goal of creating several specialisation poles able to conquer foreign markets.

Both Chinese and Indian corporations have also started to make huge investments in Third World countries, making them significant players in today's world economy.

Newly industrialised countries

Main article: Newly industrialised country

In recent decades, a few countries in Latin America, Asia, and Africa, such as Turkey, South Africa, Malaysia, Philippines and Mexico have experienced substantial industrial growth, fuelled by exportations going to countries that have bigger economies: the United States, Japan, China, India and the EU. They are sometimes called newly-industrialised countries.[citation needed]

The countries in green are considered to be newly industrialising nations. China and India (in dark green) are a special case.

Despite this trend being artificially influenced by the oil price increases since 2003, the phenomenon is not entirely new nor totally speculative (for instance see: Maquiladora). Most analysts conclude in the next few decades the whole world will experience industrialisation, and international inequality will be replaced with worldwide social inequality.[citation needed]

Other outcomes

Urbanisation

Main article: Urbanisation

The concentration of labour into factories has brought about the rise of large towns to serve and house the working population.

Exploitation

Main articles: Exploitation and Exploitation of natural resources

Workers have to leave their family in order to come to work in the towns and cities where the industries are found..

Change to family structure

The family structure changes with industrialisation. The sociologist Talcott Parsons noted that in pre-industrial societies there is an extended family structure spanning many generations who robably remained in the same location for generations. In industrialised societies the nuclear family, consisting of only of parents and their growing children, predominates. Families and children reaching adulthood are more mobile and tend to relocate to where jobs exist. Extended family bonds become more tenuous.

Environment

Industrialisation has spawned its own health problems. Modern stressors include noise, air, water pollution, poor nutrition, dangerous machinery, impersonal work, isolation, poverty, homelessness, and substance abuse. Health problems in industrial nations are as much caused by economic, social, political, and cultural factors as by pathogens. Industrialisation has become a major medical issue world wide. *[citation needed]*

Current situation

In 2005, the USA was the largest producer of industrial output followed by Japan and China, according to International Monetary Fund.[*citation needed*]

Currently the "international development community" (World Bank, OECD, many United Nations departments, and some other organisations)[*citation needed*] endorses development policies like water purification or primary education.[*citation needed*] The community does not recognise traditional industrialisation policies as being adequate to the Third World or beneficial in the longer term, with the perception that it could only create inefficient local industries unable to compete in a free-trade dominated world.

GDP composition of sector and labour fore by occupation. The green, red, and blue components of the colours of the countries represent the percentages for the agriculture, industry, and services sectors, respectively.

See also

- Division of labour
- Deindustrialisation
- Newly industrialising country
- Urbanisation
- Myth of Progress

Further reading

- Hewitt, T., Johnson, H. and Wield, D. (Eds) (1992) *industrialisation and Development*, Oxford University Press: Oxford.
- Hobsbawm, Eric (1962): *The Age of Revolution.* Abacus.
- Kiely, R (1998) *industrialisation and Development: A comparative analysis*, UCL Press:London.
- Pomeranz, Ken (2001)*The Great Divergence: China, Europe and the Making of the Modern World Economy* (Princeton Economic History of the Western World) by (Princeton University Press; New Ed edition, 2001)
- Kemp, Tom (1993) *Historical Patterns of Industrialization*, Longman: London. ISBN 0-582-09547-6

Alternatives to GDP for Measurement

Human Development Index

The **Human Development Index** (**HDI**) is a composite statistic used to rank countries by level of "human development" and separate developed (high development), developing (middle development), and underdeveloped (low development) countries. The statistic is composed from data on life expectancy, education and per-capita GDP (as an indicator of standard of living) collected at the national level using the formula given in the Methodology section below.

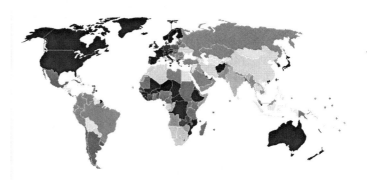

World map indicating the Human Development Index (based on 2007 data, published on October 5, 2009)[Wikipedia:Citation neededcitation needed](Color-blind compliant map) For red-green color vision problems.

Origins of the HDI

The origins of the HDI are to be found in the United Nations Development Programme's (UNDP) Human Development Reports (HDRs). These were devised and launched by a group of economists in 1990 and had the explicit purpose: "to shift the focus of development economics from national income accounting to people centered policies". To produce the HDRs, they brought together a group of well known development economists including: Paul Streeten, vaishnav, Frances Stewart, Gustav Ranis, Keith Griffin, Sudhir Anand and Meghnad Desai. But it was Amartya Sen's work on capabilities and functionings that provided the underlying conceptual framework. Haq was sure that a simple composite measure of human development was needed in order to convince the public, academics, and policy-makers that they can and should evaluate development not only by economic advances but also improvements in human well-being. Sen initially opposed this idea, but he went on to help Haq develop the Human Development Index (HDI). Sen was worried that it was difficult to capture the full complexity of human capabilities in a single index but Haq persuaded him that only a single number would shift the attention of policy-makers from concentration on economic to human well-being.

The HDI has been used since 1990 by the United Nations Development Programme for its annual Human Development Reports.

Three dimensions in the HDI

The HDI combines three dimensions:

- Life expectancy at birth, as an index of population health and longevity
- Knowledge and education, as measured by the adult literacy rate (with two-thirds weighting) and the combined primary, secondary, and tertiary gross enrollment ratio (with one-third weighting).
- Standard of living, as indicated by the natural logarithm of gross domestic product per capita at purchasing power parity.

Methodology

The formula defining the HDI is promulgated by the United Nations Development Programme (UNDP) In general, to transform a raw variable, say x, into a unit-free index between 0 and 1 (which allows different indices to be added together), the following formula is used:

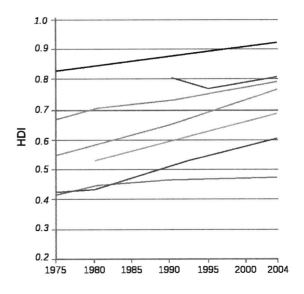

HDI trends between 1975 and 2004

- $$x\text{-index} = \frac{x - \min(x)}{\max(x) - \min(x)}$$

where $\min(x)$ and $\max(x)$ are the lowest and highest values the variable x can attain, respectively.

The Human Development Index (HDI) then represents the uniformly weighted sum with ⅓ contributed by each of the following factor indices:

- Life Expectancy Index = $\dfrac{LE - 25}{85 - 25}$

- Education Index = $\dfrac{2}{3} \times ALI + \dfrac{1}{3} \times GEI$

  - Adult Literacy Index (ALI) = $\dfrac{ALR - 0}{100 - 0}$

  - Gross Enrollment Index (GEI) = $\dfrac{CGER - 0}{100 - 0}$

- GDP = $\dfrac{\log(GDPpc) - \log(100)}{\log(40000) - \log(100)}$

2009 report

Main article: List of countries by Human Development Index

The 2009 report was released on October 5, 2009, and covers the period up to 2007. It was titled "Overcoming barriers: Human mobility and development". The top countries by HDI were grouped in a new category called "Very High Human Development". The report refers to these countries as **developed countries**. They are:

- Norway 0.971 (▲ 1)
- Australia 0.970 (▲ 2)
- Iceland 0.969 (▼ 2)
- Canada 0.966 (▼ 1)
- Ireland 0.965 (➡)
- Netherlands 0.964 (➡)
- Sweden 0.963 (➡)
- France 0.961 (▲ 3)
- Switzerland 0.960 (▲ 1)

- Japan 0.960 (▼ 2)
- Luxembourg 0.960 (▼ 2)
- Finland 0.959 (➡)
- United States 0.956 (▲ 2)

- Austria 0.955 (➡)
- Spain 0.955 (▲ 1)
- Denmark 0.955 (▼ 3)
- Belgium 0.953 (➡)
- Italy 0.951 (▲ 1)
- Liechtenstein 0.951 (▼ 1)
- New Zealand 0.950 (➡)
- United Kingdom 0.947 (➡)
- Germany 0.947 (➡)

- Singapore 0.944 (▲ 1)
- Hong Kong 0.944 (▼ 1)
- Greece 0.942 (➡)
- South Korea 0.937 (➡)

- Israel 0.935 (▲ 1)
- Andorra 0.934 (▼ 1)
- Slovenia 0.929 (➡)
- Brunei 0.920 (➡)
- Kuwait 0.916 (➡)
- Cyprus 0.914 (➡)
- Qatar 0.910 (▲ 1)
- Portugal 0.909 (▼ 1)
- United Arab Emirates 0.903 (▲ 2)

- Czech Republic 0.903 (➡)
- Barbados 0.903 (▲ 2)
- Malta 0.902 (▼ 3)

In this report, Peru was promoted from the "medium" category to the "high development" category.

Countries not included

The following nations are not ranked in the 2009 Human Development Index, for being a non-UN member, unable, or unwilling to provide the necessary data at the time of publication.

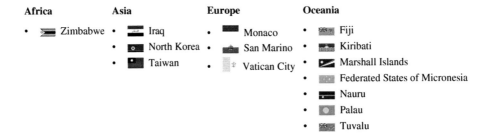

Africa	Asia	Europe	Oceania
• ⬛ Zimbabwe	• ⬛ Iraq	• ⬛ Monaco	• ⬛ Fiji
	• ⬛ North Korea	• ⬛ San Marino	• ⬛ Kiribati
	• ⬛ Taiwan	• ⬛ Vatican City	• ⬛ Marshall Islands
			• ⬛ Federated States of Micronesia
			• ⬛ Nauru
			• ⬛ Palau
			• ⬛ Tuvalu

2008 statistical update

Main article: List of countries by Human Development Index

A new index was released on December 18, 2008. This so-called "statistical update" covers the period up to 2006 and was published without an accompanying report on human development. The update is relevant due to newly released estimates of purchasing power parities (PPP), implying substantial adjustments for many countries, resulting in changes in HDI values and, in many cases, HDI ranks.

- Iceland 0.968 (═)
- Norway 0.968 (═)
- Canada 0.967 (▲ 1)
- Australia 0.965 (▼ 1)
- Ireland 0.960 (═)
- Netherlands 0.958 (▲ 3)
- Sweden 0.958 (▼ 1)
- Japan 0.956 (═)
- Luxembourg 0.956 (▲ 9)
- Switzerland 0.955 (▼ 3)
- France 0.954 (▼ 1)

- Finland 0.954 (▼ 1)
- Denmark 0.952 (▲ 1)
- Austria 0.951 (▲ 1)
- United States 0.950 (▼ 3)
- Spain 0.949 (▼ 3)
- Belgium 0.948 (▼ 1)
- Greece 0.947 (▲ 6)
- Italy 0.945 (▲ 1)
- New Zealand 0.944 (▼ 1)
- United Kingdom 0.942 (▼ 4)
- Hong Kong 0.942 (▼ 1)

- Germany 0.940 (▼ 1)
- Israel 0.930 (▼ 1)
- South Korea 0.928 (▲ 1)
- Slovenia 0.923 (▲ 1)
- Brunei 0.919 (▲ 3)
- Singapore 0.918 (▼ 3)
- Kuwait 0.912 (▲ 4)
- Cyprus 0.912 (▼ 2)
- United Arab Emirates 0.903 (▲ 8)
- Bahrain 0.902 (▲ 9)
- Portugal 0.900 (▼ 4)

Countries not included

The following nations are not ranked in the 2008 Human Development Index, for being non-UN member, unable, or unwilling to provide the necessary data at the time of publication.

Africa	**Asia**	**Europe**	**Oceania**
• Somalia	• Taiwan	• Andorra	• Kiribati
• Zimbabwe		• Liechtenstein	• Marshall Islands
		• Monaco	• Federated States of Micronesia
		• San Marino	• Nauru
		• Vatican City	• Palau
			• Tuvalu

2007/2008 report

The report for 2007/2008 was launched in Brasilia, Brazil, on November 27, 2007. Its focus was on "Fighting climate change: Human solidarity in a divided world." Most of the data used for the report are derived largely from 2005 or earlier, thus indicating an HDI for 2005. Not all UN member states choose to or are able to provide the necessary statistics.

The report showed a small increase in world HDI in comparison with last year's report. This rise was fueled by a general improvement in the developing world, especially of the least developed countries group. This marked improvement at the bottom was offset with a decrease in HDI of high income countries.

A HDI below 0.5 is considered to represent "low development". All 22 countries in that category are located in Africa. The highest-scoring Sub-Saharan countries, Gabon and South Africa, are ranked 119th and 121st, respectively. Nine countries departed from this category this year and joined the "medium development" group.

A HDI of 0.8 or more is considered to represent "high development". This includes all developed countries, such as those in North America, Western Europe, Oceania, and Eastern Asia, as well as some developing countries in Eastern Europe, Central and South America, Southeast Asia, the Caribbean, and the oil-rich Arabian Peninsula. Seven countries were promoted to this category this year, leaving the "medium development" group: Albania, Belarus, Brazil, Libya, Macedonia, Russia and Saudi Arabia.

On the following table, green arrows (▲) represent an increase in ranking over the previous study, while red arrows (▼) represent a decrease in ranking. They are followed by the number of spaces they moved. Blue dashes (━) represent a nation that did not move in the rankings since the previous study.

- Iceland 0.968 (▲ 1)
- Norway 0.968 (▼ 1)
- Australia 0.962 (▬)
- Canada 0.961 (▲ 2)
- Ireland 0.959 (▼ 1)
- Sweden 0.956 (▼ 1)
- Switzerland 0.955 (▲ 2)
- Japan 0.953 (▼ 1)
- Netherlands 0.953 (▲ 1)
- France 0.952 (▲ 6)

- Finland 0.952 (▬)
- United States 0.951 (▼ 4)
- Spain 0.949 (▲ 6)
- Denmark 0.949 (▲ 1)
- Austria 0.948 (▼ 1)
- Belgium 0.946 (▼ 4)
- United Kingdom 0.946 (▲ 1)
- Luxembourg 0.944 (▼ 6)
- New Zealand 0.943 (▲ 1)
- Italy 0.941 (▼ 3)

- Hong Kong 0.937 (▲ 1)
- Germany 0.935 (▲ 1)
- Israel 0.932 (▬)
- Greece 0.926 (▬)
- Singapore 0.922 (▬)
- South Korea 0.921 (▬)
- Slovenia 0.917 (▬)
- Cyprus 0.903 (▲ 1)
- Portugal 0.897 (▼ 1)
- Brunei 0.894 (▲ 4)

Past top countries

The list below displays the top-ranked country from each year of the index. Canada has been ranked the highest eight times, followed by Norway at seven times. Japan has been ranked highest three times and Iceland twice.

In each original report

The year represents when the report was published. In parentheses is the year for which the index was calculated.

- 2009 (2007)– Norway
- 2008 (2006)– Iceland
- 2007 (2005)– Iceland
- 2006 (2004)– Norway
- 2005 (2003)– Norway
- 2004 (2002)– Norway
- 2003 (2001)– Norway

- 2002 (2000)– Norway
- 2001 (1999)– Norway
- 2000 (1998)– Canada
- 1999 (1997)– Canada
- 1998 (1995)– Canada
- 1997 (1994)– Canada
- 1996 (1993)– Canada

- 1995 (1992)– Canada
- 1994 (????)– Canada
- 1993 (????)– Japan
- 1992 (1990)– Canada
- 1991 (1990)– Japan
- 1990 (????)– Japan

2009 revision

The 2009 Report calculated HDIs for past years using a consistent methodology and data series. They are not strictly comparable with those in earlier Human Development Reports. The index was calculated using data pertaining to the year shown.

- 2007– Norway
- 2006– Norway
- 2005– Norway
- 2000– Canada

- 1995– Canada
- 1990– Canada
- 1985– Canada
- 1980– Canada

Criticisms

The Human Development Index has been criticised on a number of grounds, including failure to include any ecological considerations, focusing exclusively on national performance and ranking, and not paying much attention to development from a global perspective. Two authors claimed that the human development reports "have lost touch with their original vision and the index fails to capture the essence of the world it seeks to portray". The index has also been criticized as "redundant" and a "reinvention of the wheel", measuring aspects of development that have already been exhaustively studied. The index has further been criticised for having an inappropriate treatment of income, lacking year-to-year comparability, and assessing development differently in different groups of countries.

Economist Bryan Caplan has criticised the way HDI scores are produced; each of the three components are bounded between zero and one. As a result of that, rich countries effectively cannot improve their ranking in certain categories, even though there is a lot of scope for economic growth and longevity left. "This effectively means that a country of immortals with infinite per-capita GDP would get a score of .666 (lower than South Africa and Tajikistan) if its population were illiterate and never went to school." He argues, "Scandinavia comes out on top according to the HDI because the HDI is basically a measure of how Scandinavian your country is."

The following are common criticisms directed at the HDI: that it is a redundant measure that adds little to the value of the individual measures composing it; that it is a means to provide legitimacy to arbitrary weightings of a few aspects of social development; that it is a number producing a relative ranking which is useless for inter-temporal comparisons, and difficult to compare a country's progress or regression since the HDI for a country in a given year depends on the levels of, say, life expectancy or GDP per capita of other countries in that year. However, each year, UN member states are listed and ranked according to the computed HDI. If high, the rank in the list can be easily used as a means of national aggrandizement; alternatively, if low, it can be used to highlight national insufficiencies. Using the HDI as an absolute index of social welfare, some authors have used panel HDI data to measure the impact of economic policies on quality of life.

Ratan Lal Basu criticises the HDI concept from a completely different angle. According to him the Amartya Sen-Mahbub ul Haq concept of HDI considers that provision of material amenities alone would bring about Human Development, but Basu opines that Human Development in the true sense should embrace both material and moral development. According to him human development based on HDI alone, is similar to dairy farm economics to improve dairy farm output. To quote: 'So human development effort should not end up in amelioration of material deprivations alone: it must undertake to bring about spiritual and moral development to assist the biped to become truly human.' For example, a high suicide rate would bring the index down.

A few authors have proposed alternative indices to address some of the index's shortcomings. However, of those proposed alternatives to the HDI, few have produced alternatives covering so many countries, and that no development index (other than, perhaps, Gross Domestic Product per capita) has been used so extensively – or effectively, in discussions and developmental planning as the HDI.

However, there has been one lament about the HDI that has resulted in an alternative index: David Hastings, of the United Nations Economic and Social Commission for Asia and the Pacific published a report geographically extending the HDI to 230+ economies, where the UNDP HDI for 2009 enumerates 182 economies.

See also

- Education Index
- Democracy Index
- Freedom House
- Legatum Prosperity Index
- Gini coefficient
- Gender Parity Index
- Gender-related Development Index
- Gender Empowerment Measure
- Global Peace Index
- Living Planet Index
- Gross national happiness
- Happy Planet Index
- Physical quality-of-life index
- Human development (humanity)
- American Human Development Report
- Child Development Index
- Satisfaction with Life Index

- Genuine progress indicator

Lists:

- List of countries by Human Development Index
- List of African countries by Human Development Index
- List of Australian states and territories by HDI
- List of Argentine provinces by Human Development Index
- List of Brazilian states by Human Development Index
- List of Canadian provinces and territories by HDI
- List of Chilean provinces by Human Development Index
- List of Chinese administrative divisions by Human Development Index
- List of European countries by Human Development Index
- List of Indian states by Human Development Index
- List of Latin American countries by Human Development Index
- List of Mexican states by Human Development Index
- List of Pakistani Districts by Human Development Index
- List of Philippine provinces by Human Development Index
- List of Russian federal subjects by HDI
- List of South African provinces by HDI
- List of US states by HDI
- List of Venezuelan states by Human Development Index

External links

- Human Development Report [1]
- Human Development Index – Updated Country Rankings (Dec. 2008) [2]
- Technical note explaining the definition of the HDI [3]PDF (5.54 MB)
- List of countries by HDI at NationMaster.com [4]
- Human Development Map [5]
- America Is # ... 15? [6] by Dalton Conley, *The Nation*, March 4, 2009

Genuine progress indicator

The **genuine progress indicator** (GPI) is a concept in green economics and welfare economics that has been suggested to replace, or supplement, gross domestic product (GDP) as a metric of economic growth.

GPI is an attempt to measure whether a country's growth, increased production of goods, and expanding services have actually resulted in the improvement of the welfare (or well-being) of the people in the country. GPI advocates claim that it can more reliably measure economic progress, as it distinguishes between worthwhile growth and uneconomic growth.

The GDP vs the GPI is analogous to the difference between the gross profit of a company and the net profit; the Net Profit is the Gross Profit minus the costs incurred. Accordingly, the GPI will be zero if the financial costs of crime and pollution equal the financial gains in production of goods and services, all other factors being constant.

Motivation

Most economists assess the progress in welfare of the people by comparing the gross domestic product over time, that is, by adding up the annual dollar value of all goods and services produced within a country over successive years. However, GDP was never intended to be used for such purpose. It is prone to productivism or consumerism, over-valuing production and consumption of goods, and not reflecting improvement in human well-being. It also fails to distinguish between money spent for new production and money spent to repair negative outcomes from previous expenditure. For example, one million dollars spent to build new homes may be an indication of progress but one million dollars spent in aid relief to those whose homes have been destroyed is not the same kind of progress. This becomes important especially when considering the true costs of development that destroys wetlands and hence exacerbate flood damages. Simon Kuznets, the inventor of the concept of the GDP, notes in his very first report to the US Congress in 1934:

> ...the welfare of a nation [can] scarcely be inferred from a measure of national income...

An adequate measure must also take into account ecological yield and the ability of nature to provide services. These things are part of a more inclusive ideal of progress, which transcends the traditional focus on raw industrial production.

Theoretical foundation

The need for a **GPI** to supplement biased indicators such as GDP was highlighted by analyses of uneconomic growth in the 1980s notably that of Marilyn Waring who studied biases in the UN System of National Accounts.

By the early 1990s there was a consensus in human development theory and ecological economics that growth in money supply was actually reflective of a loss of well-being: that lacks of essential natural and social services were being paid for in cash and that this was expanding the economy but degrading life.

The matter remains controversial and is a main issue between advocates of green economics and neo-classical economics. Neoclassical economists understand the limitations of GDP for measuring human wellbeing but nevertheless regard GDP as an important, though imperfect measure of economic output and would be wary of too close an identification of GDP growth with aggregate human welfare. However GDP tends to be reported as synonymous with economic progress by journalists and politicians and the GPI seeks to correct this shorthand by providing a more encompassing measure.

Some economists, notably Herman Daly, John B. Cobb and Philip Lawn have asserted that a country's growth, increased goods production, and expanding services have both "costs" and "benefits"--not just the "benefits" that contribute to GDP. They assert that, in some situations, expanded production facilities damage the health, culture, and welfare of people. Growth that was in excess of sustainable norms (e.g. of ecological yield) had to be considered to be uneconomic. According to the "threshold hypothesis", developed by Manfred Max-Neef, the notion that *when macroeconomic systems expand beyond a certain size, the additional benefits of growth are exceeded by the attendant costs.* (Max-Neef 1995.)

According to Lawn's model, the "costs" of economic activity include the following potential harmful effects:

- Cost of resource depletion
- Cost of crime
- Cost of ozone depletion
- Cost of family breakdown
- Cost of air, water, and noise pollution
- Loss of farmland
- Loss of wetlands

Analysis by Robert Costanza also around 1995 of nature's services and their value showed that a great deal of degradation of nature's ability to clear waste, prevent erosion, pollinate crops, etc., was being done in the name of monetary profit opportunity: this was adding to GDP but causing a great deal of long term risk in the form of mudslides, reduced yields, lost species, water pollution, etc.. Such effects have been very marked in areas that suffered serious deforestation, notably Haiti, Indonesia, and some coastal mangrove regions of India and South America. Some of the worst land abuses for instance have been shrimp farming operations that destroyed mangroves, evicted families, left coastal lands salted and useless for agriculture, but generated a significant cash profit for those who were able to control the export market in shrimp: this has become a signal example to those who contest the idea that GDP growth is necessarily desirable.

GPI takes account of these problems by incorporating sustainability: whether a country's economic activity over a year has left the country with a better or worse future possibility of repeating at least the same level of economic activity in the long run. For example, agricultural activity that uses replenishing water resources, such as river runoff, will score a higher GPI than the same level of agricultural activity that drastically lowers the water table by pumping irrigation water from wells.

"Income" vs. "capital depletion"

Hicks (1946) pointed out that the practical purpose of calculating income is to indicate the maximum amount people can produce and consume without undermining their capacity to produce and consume the same amount in the future. From a national income perspective, it is necessary to answer the following question: "Can a nation's entire GDP be consumed without undermining its ability to produce and consume the same GDP in the future?" This question is however largely ignored in contemporary economics, but fits under the idea of sustainability.

"Enjoyment of life" vs. "production of goods"

Irving Fisher (1906) contended that "economic welfare depends on the psychic enjoyment of life," not just the production of goods.

Results

At least 11 countries (including Austria, England, Sweden and Germany) have recalculated their gross domestic product using the GPI. The data for European countries and the United States show a steady decline over the last 30 years

Applying the genuine progress indicator to legislative decisions

The best known attempts to apply the concepts of GPI to legislative decisions are probably the GPI Atlantic [1] indicator pioneered by Ronald Colman for Atlantic Canada, the Alberta GPI [2] pioneered by economist Mark Anielski to measure the long-term economic, social and environmental sustainability of the province of Alberta and the **environmental and sustainable development indicators** used by the Government of Canada to measure its own **progress** to achieving well-being goals: its Environment and Sustainable Development Indicators Initiative (Canada) [3] is a substantial effort to justify state services in **GPI** terms. It assigns the Commissioner for the Environment and

Sustainable Development (Canada) [4], an officer in the Auditor-General of Canada's office, to perform the analysis and report to the House of Commons. However, Canada continues to state its overall budgetary targets in terms of reducing its debt to GDP ratio, which implies that GDP increase and debt reduction in some combination are its main priorities.

In the EU the Metropole efforts and the London Health Observatory methods are equivalents focused mostly on urban lifestyle.

The EU and Canadian efforts are among the most advanced in any of the G8 or OECD nations, but there are parallel efforts to measure quality of life or standard of living in health (not strictly wealth) terms in all developed nations. This has also been a recent focus of the labour movement.

Supporting countries and groups

- Netherlands[citation needed]
- France[citation needed]
- Germany[citation needed]
- Canada planning applications [5]. GDP has functioned as an "income sheet." GPI will function as a "balance sheet," taking into consideration that some income sources are very costly and contribute a negative profit overall.
- Redefining Progress [6]. Reports and analyses. A non-profit organization with headquarters in Oakland, California. See also: Publications of Redefining Progress [7]
- Minnesota's Progress Indicator [8]

See also

- Ecological footprint
- Full cost accounting (FCA) (with relevance to the environment)
- Global Peace Index
- Green gross domestic product (Green GDP)
- Gross domestic product (GDP)
- Happy Planet Index (HPI)
- Human Development Index (HDI)
- ISEW (Index of sustainable economic welfare)
- Living planet index
- Quality-of-life index

Further reading

News articles

- "Advantage or Illusion: Is Alberta's Progress Sustainable?" by Mark Anielski. *Encompass* Vol. 5, No. 5, July/August 2001.
- "The Growth Consensus Unravels [9]" by Jonathan Rowe. *Dollars and Sense*, July-August 1999, pp. 15-18, 33.
- "Real Wealth: The Genuine Progress Indicator Could Provide an Environmental Measure of the Planet's Health [10]" by Linda Baker. *E Magazine*, May/June 1999, pp. 37-41.
- "The GDP Myth: Why 'Growth' Isn't Always a Good Thing" by Jonathan Rowe, and Judith Silverstein. *Washington Monthly*, March 1999, pp. 17-21.
- "Economic Issues" by Lusi Song, Troy Martin, and Timothy Polo. *4EM Taylor*, May 28, 2008, pp. 1-3.
- "Why Bigger Isn't Better: The Genuine Progress Indicator - 1999 Update [11]" by Clifford Cobb, Gary Sue Goodman, and Mathis Wackernagel, Redefining Progress, November 1999

Scientific articles and books

- A. Charles, C. Burbidge, H. Boyd and A. Lavers. 2009. Fisheries and the Marine Environment in Nova Scotia: Searching for Sustainability and Resilience. GPI Atlantic. Halifax, Nova Scotia. Web: http://www.gpiatlantic.org/pdf/fisheries/fisheries_2008.pdf
- Colman, Ronald. (2003). Economic Value of Civic and Voluntary Work. GPI Atlantic. Halifax, Nova Scotia. Web: http://www.gpiatlantic.org/publications/summaries/volsumm.pdf
- Anielski, M, M. Griffiths, D. Pollock, A. Taylor, J. Wilson, S. Wilson. 2001. Alberta Sustainability Trends 2000: Genuine Progress Indicators Report 1961 to 1999. Pembina Institute for Appropriate Development. April 2001.
- Anielski, M. 2001. The Alberta GPI Blueprint: The Genuine Progress Indicator (GPI) Sustainable Well-Being Accounting System. Pembina Institute for Appropriate Development. September 2001.
- Anielski, M. and C. Soskolne. 2001. "Genuine Progress Indicator (GPI) Accounting: Relating Ecological Integrity to Human Health and Well-Being." Paper in Just Ecological Integrity: The Ethics of Maintaining Planetary Life, eds. Peter Miller and Laura Westra. Lanham, Maryland: Rowman and Littlefield: pp. 83-97.
- Daly, H., 1996. *Beyond Growth: The Economics of Sustainable Development*. Beacon Press, Boston.
- Daly, H. & Cobb, J., 1989. *For the Common Good*. Beacon Press, Boston.
- Fisher, I., 1906. *Nature of Capital and Income*. A.M. Kelly, New York.
- Hicks, J., 1946. *Value and Capital*, Second Edition. Clarendon, London.
- Lawn, P.A. "A theoretical foundation to support the Index of Sustainable Economic Welfare (ISEW), Genuine Progress Indicator (GPI), and other related indexes". *Ecological Economics* **44**

(2003) 105-118.

- Max-Neef, M. "Economic growth and quality of life". *Ecological Economics '15* (1995) 115-118.
- *Redefining Progress*, 1995. "Gross production vs genuine progress". Excerpt from the Genuine Progress Indicator: Summary of Data and Methodology. Redefining Progress, San Francisco.
- L. Pannozzo, R. Colman, N. Ayer, T. Charles, C. Burbidge, D. Sawyer, S. Stiebert , A. Savelson, C. Dodds. (2009). The 2008 Nova Scotia GPI Accounts; Indicators of Genuine Progress . GPI Atlantic. Halifax, Nova Scotia. Web: http://www.gpiatlantic.org/pdf/integrated/gpi2008.pdf

External links

- Hansard record of Canadian House of Commons debate of June 2, 2003 [12]
- GPI Atlantic [13]
- GPI Pacific [14]
- GPI at Redefining Progress [15]
- Alberta GPI at Anielski Management Inc. [16]
- Alberta GPI at The Pembina Institute for Appropriate Development [17]
- Most recent Sustainable Development Indicators for Canada [18]
- http://www.gpiatlantic.org/publications/pubs.htm

Gross national happiness

The concept of **gross national happiness (GNH)** was developed in an attempt to define an indicator that measures quality of life or social progress in more holistic and psychological terms than gross domestic product (GDP).

The term was coined in 1972 by Bhutan's former King Jigme Singye Wangchuck, who has opened up Bhutan to the age of modernization, soon after the demise of his father, King Jigme

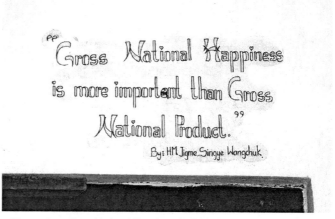

Slogan about Gross National Happiness in Thimphu's School of Traditional Arts

Dorji Wangchuck. He used the phrase to signal his commitment to building an economy that would serve Bhutan's unique culture based on Buddhist spiritual values. At first offered as a casual, offhand remark, the concept was taken seriously, as the Centre for Bhutan Studies, under the leadership of Karma Uru, developed a sophisticated survey instrument to measure the population's general level of well-being. The Canadian health epidemiologist Michael Pennock had a major role in the design of the instrument, and uses (what he calls) a "de-Bhutanized" version of the survey in his work in Victoria, British Columbia. Ura and Pennock have also collaborated on the development of policy screening tools which can be used to examine the potential impacts of projects or programs on GNH. These tools are available on the grossnationalhappiness.com website.

Like many psychological and social indicators, GNH is somewhat easier to state than to define with mathematical precision. Nonetheless, it serves as a unifying vision for Bhutan's five-year planning process and all the derived planning documents that guide the economic and development plans of the country. Proposed policies in Bhutan must pass a GNH review based on a GNH impact statement that is similar in nature to the Environmental Impact Statement required for development in the U.S.

The Bhutanese grounding in Buddhist ideals suggests that beneficial development of human society takes place when material and spiritual development occur side by side to complement and reinforce each other. The four pillars of GNH are the promotion of sustainable development, preservation and promotion of cultural values, conservation of the natural environment, and establishment of good governance. At this level of generality, the concept of GNH is transcultural—a nation need not be Buddhist in order to value sustainable development, cultural integrity, ecosystem conservation, and good governance. Through collaboration with an international group of scholars and empirical researchers the Centre for Bhutan Studies further defined these four pillars with greater specificity into eight general contributors to happiness- physical, mental and spiritual health; time-balance; social and community vitality; cultural vitality; education; living standards; good governance; and ecological vitality. Although the GNH framework reflects its Buddhist origins, it is solidly based upon the empirical research literature of happiness, positive psychology and wellbeing.

Weakness of GDP

As a chief economic indicator, GDP has numerous flaws long known to economists. GDP measures the amount of commerce in a country, but counts remedial and defensive expenditures (such as the costs of security, police, pollution clean up, etc.) as positive contributions to commerce. A better measure of economic well-being would deduct such costs, and add in other non-market benefits (such as volunteer work, unpaid domestic work, and unpriced ecosystem services) in arriving at an indicator of well-being. As economic development on the planet approaches or surpasses the limits of ecosystems to provide resources and absorb human effluents, calling into question the ability of the planet to continue to support civilization (per the arguments of Jared Diamond, among others), many people have called for getting "Beyond GDP" (the title of a recent EU conference) in order to measure progress not as the mere increase in commercial transactions, nor as an increase in specifically economic well-being, but as an increase in general well-being as people themselves subjectively report it. GNH is a strong contributor to this movement to discard measurements of commercial transactions as a key indicator and to instead directly assess changes in the social and psychological well-being of populations.

While conventional development models stress economic growth as the ultimate objective, the concept of GNH is based on the premise that some forms of economic development are "uneconomic", a concept that is advanced by the nascent field of ecological economics. Such development costs more in loss of ecosystem services, and in the imposition of "urban disamenities," than it produces as a positive contribution to well-being. (The difficulty, of course, is that for many forms of development, the gains are taken privately, while the costs the development imposes are born generally and publicly.)

Qualitative and quantitative indicators

There is no exact quantitative definition of GNH, but elements that contribute to GNH are subject to quantitative measurement. Low rates of infant mortality, for instance, correlate positively with subjective expressions of well-being or happiness within a country. (This makes sense; it is no large leap to assume that premature death causes sorrow.) The practice of social science has long been directed toward transforming subjective expression of large numbers of people into meaningful quantitative data; there is no major difference between asking people "how confident are you in the economy?" and "how satisfied are you with your job?"

GNH, like the Genuine Progress Indicator, refers to the concept of a quantitative measurement of well-being and happiness. The two measures are both motivated by the notion that subjective measures like well-being are more relevant and important than more objective measures like consumption. It is not measured directly, but only the factors which are believed to lead to it.

According to Daniel Kahneman, a Princeton University psychologist, happiness can be measured using the day reconstruction method, which consists in recollecting memories of the previous working day by writing a short diary.

A second-generation GNH concept, treating happiness as a socioeconomic development metric, was proposed in 2006 by Med Jones, the President of International Institute of Management. The metric measures socioeconomic development by tracking 7 development area including the nation's mental and emotional health. GNH value is proposed to be an index function of the total average per capita of the following measures:

1. Economic Wellness: Indicated via direct survey and statistical measurement of economic metrics such as consumer debt, average income to consumer price index ratio and income distribution
2. Environmental Wellness: Indicated via direct survey and statistical measurement of environmental metrics such as pollution, noise and traffic
3. Physical Wellness: Indicated via statistical measurement of physical health metrics such as severe illnesses

4. Mental Wellness: Indicated via direct survey and statistical measurement of mental health metrics such as usage of antidepressants and rise or decline of psychotherapy patients

5. Workplace Wellness: Indicated via direct survey and statistical measurement of labor metrics such as jobless claims, job change, workplace complaints and lawsuits

6. Social Wellness: Indicated via direct survey and statistical measurement of social metrics such as discrimination, safety, divorce rates, complaints of domestic conflicts and family lawsuits, public lawsuits, crime rates

7. Political Wellness: Indicated via direct survey and statistical measurement of political metrics such as the quality of local democracy, individual freedom, and foreign conflicts.

The above 7 metrics were incorporated into the first Global GNH Survey.

Ed Diener, a psychologist from the University of Illinois at Urbana-Champaign, has developed a scale referred to as *subjective well-being,* a concept related to happiness and quality of life, which has been used to compare nations to each other on this construct. This study found that "high income, individualism, human rights, and social equality correlated strongly with each other, and with SWB" (p. 851, abstract).

Adam Kramer, a psychologist from the University of Oregon, has developed a behavioral model of "Gross National Happiness" based on the use of positive and negative words in social network status updates, resulting in a quantitative GNH metric.

Conferences

In 2009, the 5th International Conference was held at Foz do Iguaçu, Brazil, with more than 800 participants. The conference was organised by Future Vision Ecological Institute and Itaipu Bi-national Hydroelectric Facility, in collaboration with the Centre for Bhutan Studies. The growing interest in GNH within Brazil has resulted from the work of Dr. Susan Andrews at the Instituto Visão Futuro which sponsored a series of events in São Paulo and Campinas in October 2008. Speakers included Karma Ura from Bhutan and Michael Pennock from Canada. A summary of the 5th Annual International Conference, along with MP3 audio recordings are available at http:/ / www. grossnationalhappiness.com/articlesongnh/gnh5.aspx

The 4th International Conference on Gross National Happiness was held in Bhutan with a focus on Practice and Measurement. Results of the Bhutanese survey were presented and a number of international contributors discussed different approaches and challenges to the measurement and application of the GNH framework. Conference proceedings are available at http:/ / www. bhutanstudies.org.bt/main/gnh4.php

The *3rd International Conference on Gross National Happiness Towards Global Transformation: WORLD VIEWS MAKE A DIFFERENCE* offered an opportunity to articulate Asian world views towards transformation in a 'message to the world'. It took place in Nong Khai and Bangkok, Thailand between 22 and 28 November 2007.

Implying the transition from a natural to modernized state, the 3rd International Conference on Gross National Happiness (GNH 3) took place in two locations: the first three days took place in rural north-eastern province of Nong Khai and the last three days in the urban campus of Chulalongkorn University in central Bangkok, Thailand. The organizers planned all activities so that participants were able to explore a large variety of venues, presentation and discussion formats and draw on the great variety and talents of the entire group of 800 participants who registered.

Main co-organizers were the Sathirakoses Nagapradipa Foundation (Thailand), Centre for Bhutan Studies, while local NGOs, progressive business group Social Venture Network and the government of Thailand in particular The Ministry of Social Development and Human Security, Thailand, have formed a support network together with research agencies and other government departments like the Thai Health Promotion Foundation.

"Rethinking Development: Local Pathways to Global Wellbeing", the *Second International Conference on Gross National Happiness* was held in Antigonish, Nova Scotia June 20–24, 2005, co-hosted by Genuine Progress Index Atlantic (proceedings online); the Coady International Institute; Shambhala; the Centre for Bhutan Studies; the Province of Nova Scotia; the Gorsebrook Research Institute at Saint Mary's University; and the University of New Brunswick.

The second regional Conference took place November 8–11, 2006 at Meiji Gakuin University in Yokohama. The conference examined Haida successes to apply non western economic and social modalities.

Happiness as understood by neo-classical economics

Under neo-classical economic theory happiness, subjectively defined, has long been the standard of measurement used interchangeably with utility as well as the general welfare.

Modern classical economics no longer attempts to quantify happiness or satisfaction through measurements in consumption and profits. Instead, modern neoclassical framework argue that individual's preference is revealed through choice. Therefore, if an individual decided to purchase an apple over orange, the satisfaction one derived from apple is revealed to be greater than an orange. Similarly, modern economics also consider that work/leisure balance is also matter of individual choice.

The idea that modern neoclassical economics define happiness on the basis of consumption is widely disputed. The basis of utility has been defined as revealed preference.

The assumption within neoclassic economics that satisfactions are highly subjective found expression in the work of Vilfredo Pareto, whose definition of optimal allocation in the nineteenth century was a crucial contribution that allowed further development of the mathematical precision of the discipline. Pareto argued that because satisfactions are subjective, we cannot know for certain that we have increased the amount of satisfaction in the system if we take a dollar from a billionaire and give it to a starving person to buy food; for all we know, the billionaire might have derived as much satisfaction from that dollar as the starving person does in spending it on food.

This counter-intuitive result is the cornerstone of Pareto Optimality: a system is in Pareto Optimality when no one can be made better off (in their own estimation) without making someone worse off (in their own estimation). In practice, "better off" and "worse off" are defined by consumption: by definition, it is always better to consume more. Thus, Pareto Optimality led to the bias in standard economics toward perpetual growth models—models that are increasingly being called into question, as being impractical (and dangerously destructive) in a finite world.[citation needed]

External studies

In a widely cited study, "A Global Projection of Subjective Well-being: A Challenge to Positive Psychology?" by Adrian G. White of the University of Leicester in 2007, Bhutan ranked 8th out of 178 countries in Subjective Well-Being, a metric that has been used by many psychologists since 1997. In fact, it is the only country in the top 20 "happiest" countries that has a very low GDP.

National happiness is also sometimes classified under empirically studied **"National Happyism;"** and psychologists, Drs. Ed Diener and Robert Biswas-Diener, have researched and analyzed what could be described as technological elements and characteristics of happiness for both individuals and societies.

Criticism

Critics allege that because GNH depends on a series of subjective judgments about well-being, governments may be able to define GNH in a way that suits their interests. In the case of Bhutan, for instance, they say that the government expelled about one hundred thousand people and stripped them of their Bhutanese citizenship on the grounds that the deportees were ethnic Nepalese who had settled in the country illegally, though Bhutan's policies in this regard have no direct or obvious relevance to its use of GNH as an indicator guiding policy. Other countries, notably Brazil, Italy, and parts of Canada, are exploring use of measurements derived from Bhutan's GNH as their primary indicator of well-being. Critics say that international comparison of well-being will be difficult on this model; proponents maintain that each country can define its own measure of GNH as it chooses, and that comparisons over time between nations will have validity. GDP provides a convenient, international scale; but (proponents of GNH say) to continue to use GDP for this reason in the face of its known flaws is to allow ease of measurement to define what it is we measure and value, an approach that is logically indefensible. Research demonstrates that markers of social and individual well-being are remarkably transcultural: people generally report greater subjective life satisfaction if they have strong and frequent social ties, live in healthy ecosystems, experience good governance, etc. Nevertheless, it remains true that reliance on national measures of GNH would render international comparisons of relative well-being more problematic, since there is not and is not likely ever to be a common scale as "portable" as GDP has been.

Alternative indicators of emotion as an analog to economic progress have also been supported by a number of NGOs such as the UK's New Economics Foundation, and are employed in some governments notably in Europe and Canada. [citation needed]. The Gallup poll system also collects data on wellbeing on a national and international scale.

See also

- Global Peace Index
- Happiness economics
- Happy Planet Index
- Legatum Prosperity Index
- Satisfaction with Life Index
- Operationalization
- Post-materialism
- Psychometrics
- Utilitarianism
- World Values Survey

References

- Adler Braun, Alejandro. *Gross National Happiness in Bhutan: A Living Example of an Alternative Approach to Progress,* September 24, 2009. http://www.grossnationalhappiness.com/OtherArticles/GNHPaperbyAlejandro.pdf
- Brooks, Arthur (2008), *Gross National Happiness*, Basic Books, ISBN 0-465-00278-1
- Diener, Ed and Robert-Biswas Diener. *Happiness — Unlocking the Mysteries of Psychological Wealth*. Oxford: Blackwell Publishing Ltd., 2008. 290 pages. ISBN 978-1-4051-4661-6.
- Eric Zencey, "GDP RIP," New York Times, August 9, 2009 [1]
- Eric Ezechieli, "Beyond Sustainable Development: Education for Gross National Happiness in Bhutan" http://suse-ice.stanford.edu/monographs/Ezechieli.pdf , Stanford University, 2003
- Kammann, R. "The Analysis and Measurement of Happiness as a Sense of Well-Being", Social Indicators Research, 15(2) (1984:Aug.) p. 91-115
- Layard, Richard (2005), *Happiness: Lessons from a new Science*, Penguin Press, ISBN 0-14-303701-3
- Powdyel, T.S. "Gross National Happiness, A Tribute," Gross National Happiness, Kinga, Sonam, et al. (eds) (1999), Thimphu: The Center for Bhutan Studies
- Priesner, Stefan (2004), Indigeneity and Unversality in Social Science: A South Asian Response, SAGE Publications, ISBN 0-7619-3215-1

- Thinley, L. (1998, October). Values and Development: "Gross National Happiness." Speech Presented at the Millenium Meeting for Asia and the Pacific, Seoul, Republic of Korea.

External links

- Gross National Happiness American Project [2]
- Official Bhutanese Gross National Happiness Website [3], Centre for Bhutan Studies
- Nadia Mustafa, "What About Gross National Happiness?" [4], Time, 10 January 2005
- Rajni Bakshi, "Gross National Happiness" [5], *Resurgence*, 25 January 2005
- International Institute of Management - US based GHN research, GNH policy white paper [6]
- Bhutan 2008 Paeans to the King [7]
- Gross National Happiness, Chapter 9 [8] Facts about Bhutan by Lily Wangchhuk
- GNH 2 Media Clips [9] tracks the appearance of the notion of "Gross National Happiness" in the media 2000-2005

Gini coefficient

The **Gini coefficient** is a measure of statistical dispersion developed by the Italian statistician Corrado Gini and published in his 1912 paper "Variability and Mutability" (Italian: *Variabilità e mutabilità*).

The Gini coefficient is a measure of the inequality of a distribution, a value of 0 expressing total equality and a value of 1 maximal

Gini-coefficient of national income distribution around the world (dark green: <0.25, red: >0.60)

inequality. It has found application in the study of inequalities in disciplines as diverse as economics, health science, ecology, chemistry and engineering.

It is commonly used as a measure of inequality of income or wealth. Worldwide, Gini coefficients for income range from approximately 0.23 (Sweden) to 0.70 (Namibia) although not every country has been assessed.

Definition

The Gini coefficient is usually defined mathematically based on the Lorenz curve, which plots the proportion of the total income of the population (y axis) that is cumulatively earned by the bottom x% of the population (see diagram). The line at 45 degrees thus represents perfect equality of incomes. The Gini coefficient can then be thought of as the ratio of the area that lies between the line of equality and the Lorenz curve (marked 'A' in the diagram) over the total area under the line of equality (marked 'A' and 'B' in the diagram); i.e., G=A/(A+B).

The Gini coefficient can range from 0 to 1; it is sometimes multiplied by 100 to range between 0 and 100. A low Gini coefficient indicates a more equal distribution, with 0 corresponding to complete equality, while higher Gini

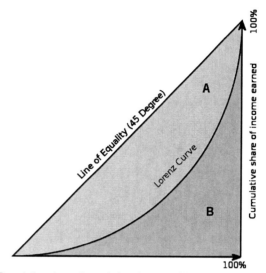

Graphical representation of the Gini coefficient.
The graph shows that the Gini is equal to the area marked 'A' divided by the sum of the areas marked 'A' and 'B' (that is, Gini = A/(A+B)). It is also equal to 2*A, as A+B = 0.5 (since the axes scale from 0 to 1).

coefficients indicate more unequal distribution, with 1 corresponding to complete inequality. To be validly computed, no negative goods can be distributed. Thus, if the Gini coefficient is being used to describe household income inequality, then no household can have a negative income. When used as a measure of income inequality, the most unequal society will be one in which a single person receives 100% of the total income and the remaining people receive none (G=1); and the most equal society will be one in which every person receives the same income (G=0).

Some find it more intuitive (and it is mathematically equivalent) to think of the Gini coefficient as half of the relative mean difference. The mean difference is the average absolute difference between two items selected randomly from a population, and the relative mean difference is the mean difference divided by the average, to normalize for scale.

Calculation

The Gini index is defined as a ratio of the areas on the Lorenz curve diagram. If the area between the line of perfect equality and the Lorenz curve is A, and the area under the Lorenz curve is B, then the Gini index is A/(A+B). Since A+B = 0.5, the Gini index, G = A/(0.5) = 2A = 1-2B. If the Lorenz curve is represented by the function Y = L(X), the value of B can be found with integration and:

$$G = 1 - 2 \int_0^1 L(X)dX.$$

In some cases, this equation can be applied to calculate the Gini coefficient without direct reference to the Lorenz curve. For example:

- For a population uniform on the values y_i, $i = 1$ to n, indexed in non-decreasing order ($y_i \leq y_{i+1}$):

$$G = \frac{1}{n}\left(n + 1 - 2\left(\frac{\sum_{i=1}^{n}(n+1-i)y_i}{\sum_{i=1}^{n}y_i}\right)\right)$$

  This may be simplified to:

$$G = \frac{2\sum_{i=1}^{n} iy_i}{n\sum_{i=1}^{n}y_i} - \frac{n+1}{n}$$

- For a discrete probability function f(y), where y_i, $i = 1$ to n, are the points with nonzero probabilities and which are indexed in increasing order ($y_i < y_{i+1}$):

$$G = 1 - \frac{\sum_{i=1}^{n} f(y_i)(S_{i-1} + S_i)}{S_n}$$

  where

$$S_i = \Sigma_{j=1}^{i} f(y_j)\, y_j \text{ and } S_0 = 0$$

- For a cumulative distribution function F(y) that is piecewise differentiable, has a mean μ, and is zero for all negative values of y:

$$G = 1 - \frac{1}{\mu}\int_0^{\infty}(1 - F(y))^2 dy = \frac{1}{\mu}\int_0^{\infty} F(y)(1 - F(y))dy$$

- Since the Gini coefficient is half the relative mean difference, it can also be calculated using formulas for the relative mean difference. For a random sample S consisting of values y_i, $i = 1$ to n, that are indexed in non-decreasing order ($y_i \leq y_{i+1}$), the statistic:

$$G(S) = \frac{1}{n-1}\left(n + 1 - 2\left(\frac{\sum_{i=1}^{n}(n+1-i)y_i}{\sum_{i=1}^{n}y_i}\right)\right)$$

  is a consistent estimator of the population Gini coefficient, but is not, in general, unbiased. Like, G, G(S) has a simpler form:

$$G(S) = 1 - \frac{2}{n-1}\left(n - \frac{\sum_{i=1}^{n} iy_i}{\sum_{i=1}^{n}y_i}\right).$$

There does not exist a sample statistic that is in general an unbiased estimator of the population Gini coefficient, like the relative mean difference.

Sometimes the entire Lorenz curve is not known, and only values at certain intervals are given. In that case, the Gini coefficient can be approximated by using various techniques for interpolating the missing values of the Lorenz curve. If (X_k, Y_k) are the known points on the Lorenz curve, with the X_k indexed in increasing order ($X_{k-1} < X_k$), so that:

- X_k is the cumulated proportion of the population variable, for k = 0,...,n, with $X_0 = 0$, $X_n = 1$.
- Y_k is the cumulated proportion of the income variable, for k = 0,...,n, with $Y_0 = 0$, $Y_n = 1$.
- Y_k should be indexed in non-decreasing order ($Y_k > Y_{k-1}$)

If the Lorenz curve is approximated on each interval as a line between consecutive points, then the area B can be approximated with trapezoids and:

$$G_1 = 1 - \sum_{k=1}^{n}(X_k - X_{k-1})(Y_k + Y_{k-1})$$

is the resulting approximation for G. More accurate results can be obtained using other methods to approximate the area B, such as approximating the Lorenz curve with a quadratic function across pairs of intervals, or building an appropriately smooth approximation to the underlying distribution function that matches the known data. If the population mean and boundary values for each interval are also known, these can also often be used to improve the accuracy of the approximation.

The Gini coefficient calculated from a sample is a statistic and its standard error, or confidence intervals for the population Gini coefficient, should be reported. These can be calculated using bootstrap techniques but those proposed have been mathematically complicated and computationally onerous even in an era of fast computers. Ogwang (2000) made the process more efficient by setting up a "trick regression model" in which the incomes in the sample are ranked with the lowest income being allocated rank 1. The model then expresses the rank (dependent variable) as the sum of a constant *A* and a normal error term whose variance is inversely proportional to y_k;

$$k = A + N(0, s^2/y_k)$$

Ogwang showed that *G* can be expressed as a function of the weighted least squares estimate of the constant *A* and that this can be used to speed up the calculation of the jackknife estimate for the standard error. Giles (2004) argued that the standard error of the estimate of *A* can be used to derive that of the estimate of *G* directly without using a jackknife at all. This method only requires the use of ordinary least squares regression after ordering the sample data. The results compare favorably with the estimates from the jackknife with agreement improving with increasing sample size. The paper describing this method can be found here: http://web.uvic.ca/econ/ewp0202.pdf

However it has since been argued that this is dependent on the model's assumptions about the error distributions (Ogwang 2004) and the independence of error terms (Reza & Gastwirth 2006) and that these assumptions are often not valid for real data sets. It may therefore be better to stick with jackknife methods such as those proposed by Yitzhaki (1991) and Karagiannis and Kovacevic (2000). The debate continues.

The Gini coefficient can be calculated if you know the mean of a distribution, the number of people (or percentiles), and the income of each person (or percentile). Princeton development economist Angus Deaton (1997, 139) simplified the Gini calculation to one easy formula:

$$G = \frac{N+1}{N-1} - \frac{2}{N(N-1)u}(\Sigma_{i=1}^{n} P_i X_i)$$

where u is mean income of the population, P_i is the income rank P of person i, with income X, such that the richest person receives a rank of 1 and the poorest a rank of N. This effectively gives higher weight to poorer people in the income distribution, which allows the Gini to meet the Transfer Principle.

Generalised inequality index

The Gini coefficient and other standard inequality indices reduce to a common form. Perfect equality—the absence of inequality—exists when and only when the inequality ratio, $r_j = x_j/\overline{x}$, equals 1 for all j units in some population; for example, there is perfect income equality when everyone's income x_j equals the mean income $\overline{x}$, so that $r_j = 1$ for everyone). Measures of inequality, then, are measures of the average deviations of the $r_j = 1$ from 1; the greater the average deviation, the greater the inequality. Based on these observations the inequality indices have this common form:

$$Inequality = \Sigma_j \, p_j \, f(r_j) \, ,$$

where p_j weights the units by their population share, and $f(r_j)$ is a function of the deviation of each unit's r_j from 1, the point of equality. The insight of this generalised inequality index is that inequality indices differ because they employ different functions of the distance of the inequality ratios (the r_j) from 1.

Gini coefficient of income distributions

While developed European nations and Canada tend to have Gini indices between 24 and 36, the United States' and Mexico's Gini indices are both above 40, indicating that the United States and Mexico have greater inequality. Using the Gini can help quantify differences in welfare and compensation policies and philosophies. However it should be borne in mind that the Gini coefficient can be misleading when used to make political comparisons between large and small countries (see criticisms section).

The Gini index for the entire world has been estimated by various parties to be between 56 and 66.

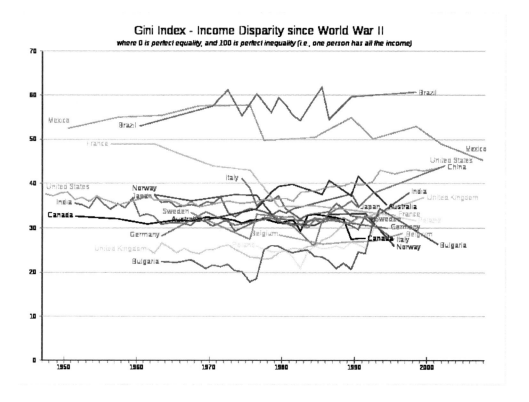

US income Gini indices over time

Gini indices for the United States at various times, according to the US Census Bureau:

- 1929: 45.0 (estimated)
- 1947: 37.6 (estimated)
- 1967: 39.7 (first year reported)
- 1968: 38.6 (lowest index reported)
- 1970: 39.4
- 1980: 40.3
- 1990: 42.8
- 2000: 46.2
- 2005: 46.9
- 2006: 47.0 (highest index reported)
- 2007: 46.3
- 2008: 46.69
- 2009: 46.8

EU Gini index

In 2005 the AVERAGE Gini index for the EU was estimated at 31.

Advantages of Gini coefficient as a measure of inequality

- The Gini coefficient's main advantage is that it is a measure of inequality by means of a ratio analysis, rather than a variable unrepresentative of most of the population, such as per capita income or gross domestic product.

- It can be used to compare income distributions across different population sectors as well as countries, for example the Gini coefficient for urban areas differs from that of rural areas in many countries (though the United States' urban and rural Gini coefficients are nearly identical).

- It is sufficiently simple that it can be compared across countries and be easily interpreted. GDP statistics are often criticized as they do not represent changes for the whole population; the Gini coefficient demonstrates how income has changed for poor and rich. If the Gini coefficient is rising as well as GDP, poverty may not be improving for the majority of the population.

- The Gini coefficient can be used to indicate how the distribution of income has changed within a country over a period of time, thus it is possible to see if inequality is increasing or decreasing.

- The Gini coefficient satisfies four important principles:
  - *Anonymity*: it does not matter who the high and low earners are.
  - *Scale independence*: the Gini coefficient does not consider the size of the economy, the way it is measured, or whether it is a rich or poor country on average.
  - *Population independence*: it does not matter how large the population of the country is.
  - *Transfer principle*: if income (less than half of the difference), is transferred from a rich person to a poor person the resulting distribution is more equal.

Disadvantages of Gini coefficient as a measure of inequality

- While the Gini coefficient measures inequality of *income*, it does not measure inequality of *opportunity*. For example, some countries may have a social class structure that may present barriers to upward mobility; this is not reflected in their Gini coefficients.

- The Gini coefficient of different sets of people cannot be averaged to obtain the Gini coefficient of all the people in the sets: if a Gini coefficient were to be calculated for each person it would always be zero. For a large, economically diverse country, a much higher coefficient will be calculated for the country as a whole than will be calculated for each of its regions. (The coefficient is usually applied to measurable nominal income rather than local purchasing power, tending to increase the calculated coefficient across larger areas.)

- The Lorenz curve may understate the actual amount of inequality if richer households are able to use income more efficiently than lower income households or vice versa. From another point of view, measured inequality may be the result of more or less efficient use of household incomes.

- Economies with similar incomes and Gini coefficients can still have very different income distributions. (This is true for any single measure of a distribution.) This is because the Lorenz curves can have different shapes and yet still yield the same Gini coefficient. For example, consider a society where half of individuals had no income and the other half shared all the income equally (i.e. whose Lorenz curve is linear from (0,0) to (0.5,0) and then linear to (1,1)). As is easily calculated, this society has Gini coefficient 0.5 -- the same as that of a society in which 75% of people equally shared 25% of income while the remaining 25% equally shared 75% (i.e. whose Lorenz curve is linear from (0,0) to (0.75,0.25) and then linear to (1,1)).

- It measures current income rather than lifetime income. A society in which everyone earned the same over a lifetime would appear unequal because of people at different stages in their life; a society in which students study rather than save can never have a coefficient of 0. However, Gini coefficient can also be calculated for any kind of single-variable distribution, e.g. for wealth.

- Gini coefficients do include investment income; however, the Gini coefficient based on net income does not accurately reflect differences in wealth—a possible source of misinterpretation. For example, Sweden has a low Gini coefficient for income distribution but a significantly higher Gini coefficient for wealth (for instance 77% of the share value owned by households is held by just 5% of Swedish shareholding households). In other words, the Gini income coefficient should not be interpreted as measuring effective egalitarianism.

- Too often only the Gini coefficient is quoted without describing the proportions of the quantiles used for measurement. As with other inequality coefficients, the Gini coefficient is influenced by the granularity of the measurements. For example, five 20% quantiles (low granularity) will usually yield a lower Gini coefficient than twenty 5% quantiles (high granularity) taken from the same distribution. This is an often encountered problem with measurements.

- Care should be taken in using the Gini coefficient as a measure of egalitarianism, as it is properly a measure of income dispersion. For example, if two equally egalitarian countries pursue different immigration policies, the country accepting higher proportion of low-income or impoverished migrants will be assessed as less equal (gain a higher Gini coefficient).

- The Gini coefficient is a point-estimate of equality at a certain time, hence it ignores life-span changes in income. Typically, increases in the proportion of young or old members of a society will drive apparent changes in equality. Because of this, factors such as age distribution within a population and mobility within income classes can create the appearance of differential equality when none exist taking into account demographic effects. Thus a given economy may have a higher Gini coefficient at any one point in time compared to another, while the Gini coefficient calculated over individuals' lifetime income is actually lower than the apparently more equal (at a given point in time) economy's. Essentially, what matters is not just inequality in any particular year, but the composition of the distribution over time.

General problems of measurement

- Comparing income distributions among countries may be difficult because benefits systems may differ. For example, some countries give benefits in the form of money while others give food stamps, which might not be counted by some economists and researchers as income in the Lorenz curve and therefore not taken into account in the Gini coefficient. Income in the United States is counted before benefits, while in France it is counted after benefits, which may lead the United States to appear somewhat more unequal vis-a-vis France. In another example, the Soviet Union was measured to have relatively high income inequality: by some estimates, in the late 1970s, Gini coefficient of its urban population was as high as 0.38, which is higher than many Western countries today. This number would not reflect those benefits received by Soviet citizens that were not monetized for measurement, which may include child care for children as young as two months, elementary, secondary and higher education, cradle-to-grave medical care, and heavily subsidized or provided housing. In this example, a more accurate comparison between the 1970s Soviet Union and Western countries may require one to assign monetary values to all benefits – a difficult task in the absence of free markets. Similar problems arise whenever a comparison between pure free-market economies and partially socialist economies is attempted. Benefits may take various and unexpected forms: for example, major oil producers such as Venezuela and Iran provide indirect benefits to its citizens by subsidizing the retail price of gasoline.

- Similarly, in some societies people may have significant income in other forms than money, for example through subsistence farming or bartering. Like non-monetary benefits, the value of these incomes is difficult to quantify. Different quantifications of these incomes will yield different Gini coefficients.

- The measure will give different results when applied to individuals instead of households. When different populations are not measured with consistent definitions, comparison is not meaningful.

- As for all statistics, there may be systematic and random errors in the data. The meaning of the Gini coefficient decreases as the data become less accurate. Also, countries may collect data differently, making it difficult to compare statistics between countries.

As one result of this criticism, in addition to or in competition with the Gini coefficient *entropy measures* are frequently used (e.g. the Theil Index and the Atkinson index). These measures attempt to compare the distribution of resources by intelligent agents in the market with a maximum entropy random distribution, which would occur if these agents acted like non-intelligent particles in a closed system following the laws of statistical physics.

Credit risk

The Gini coefficient is also commonly used for the measurement of the discriminatory power of rating systems in credit risk management.

The discriminatory power refers to a credit risk model's ability to differentiate between defaulting and non-defaulting clients. The above formula G_1 may be used for the final model and also at individual model factor level, to quantify the discriminatory power of individual factors. This is as a result of too many non defaulting clients falling into the lower points scale e.g. factor has a 10 point scale and 30% of non defaulting clients are being assigned the lowest points available e.g. 0 or negative points. This indicates that the factor is behaving in a counter-intuitive manner and would require further investigation at the model development stage.

Other uses

Although the Gini coefficient is most popular in economics, it can in theory be applied in any field of science that studies a distribution. For example, in ecology the Gini coefficient has been used as a measure of biodiversity, where the cumulative proportion of species is plotted against cumulative proportion of individuals. In health, it has been used as a measure of the inequality of health related quality of life in a population. In education, it has been used as a measure of the inequality of universities. In chemistry it has been used to express the selectivity of protein kinase inhibitors against a panel of kinases. In engineering, it has been used to evaluate the fairness achieved by Internet routers in scheduling packet transmissions from different flows of traffic. In statistics, building decision trees, it is used to measure the purity of possible child nodes, with the aim of maximising the average purity of two child nodes when splitting.

See also

- Atkinson index
- Human Poverty Index
- Income inequality metrics

- Pareto distribution
- Robin Hood index
- ROC analysis
- Social welfare provision
- Suits index

- *The Spirit Level: Why More Equal Societies Almost Always Do Better*
- Theil index
- Wealth condensation
- Welfare economics
- List of countries by income equality
- List of countries by Human Development Index

Further reading

- Amiel, Y.; Cowell, F.A. (1999). *Thinking about Inequality*. Cambridge. ISBN 0521466962.
- Anand, Sudhir (1983). *Inequality and Poverty in Malaysia*. New York: Oxford University Press. ISBN 0195201531.
- Brown, Malcolm (1994). "Using Gini-Style Indices to Evaluate the Spatial Patterns of Health Practitioners: Theoretical Considerations and an Application Based on Alberta Data". *Social Science Medicine* **38** (9): 1243–1256. doi:10.1016/0277-9536(94)90189-9 [1]. PMID 8016689 [2].
- Chakravarty, S. R. (1990). *Ethical Social Index Numbers*. New York: Springer-Verlag. ISBN 0387522743.
- Deaton, Angus (1997). *Analysis of Household Surveys*. Baltimore MD: Johns Hopkins University Press. ISBN 0585237875.
- Dixon, PM, Weiner J., Mitchell-Olds T, Woodley R. (1987). "Bootstrapping the Gini coefficient of inequality" [3]. *Ecology* (Ecological Society of America) **68** (5): 1548–1551. doi:10.2307/1939238 [4].
- Dorfman, Robert (1979). "A Formula for the Gini Coefficient" [5]. *The Review of Economics and Statistics* (The MIT Press) **61** (1): 146–149. doi:10.2307/1924845 [6].
- Firebaugh, Glenn (2003). *The New Geography of Global Income Inequality*. Cambridge MA: Harvard University Press. ISBN 0674010671.
- Gastwirth, Joseph L. (1972). "The Estimation of the Lorenz Curve and Gini Index" [7]. *The Review of Economics and Statistics* (The MIT Press) **54** (3): 306–316. doi:10.2307/1937992 [8].
- Giles, David (2004). "Calculating a Standard Error for the Gini Coefficient: Some Further Results". *Oxford Bulletin of Economics and Statistics* **66**: 425–433. doi:10.1111/j.1468-0084.2004.00086.x [9].
- Gini, Corrado (1912). "Variabilità e mutabilità" Reprinted in Memorie di metodologica statistica (Ed. Pizetti E, Salvemini, T). Rome: Libreria Eredi Virgilio Veschi (1955).
- Gini, Corrado (1921). "Measurement of Inequality of Incomes" [10]. *The Economic Journal* (Blackwell Publishing) **31** (121): 124–126. doi:10.2307/2223319 [11].
- Karagiannis, E. and Kovacevic, M. (2000). "A Method to Calculate the Jackknife Variance Estimator for the Gini Coefficient". *Oxford Bulletin of Economics and Statistics* **62**: 119–122. doi:10.1111/1468-0084.00163 [12].
- Mills, Jeffrey A.; Zandvakili, Sourushe (1997). "Statistical Inference via Bootstrapping for Measures of Inequality". *Journal of Applied Econometrics* **12**: 133–150. doi:10.1002/(SICI)1099-1255(199703)12:2<133::AID-JAE433>3.0.CO;2-H [13].
- Modarres, Reza and Gastwirth, Joseph L. (2006). "A Cautionary Note on Estimating the Standard Error of the Gini Index of Inequality". *Oxford Bulletin of Economics and Statistics* **68**: 385–390. doi:10.1111/j.1468-0084.2006.00167.x [14].
- Morgan, James (1962). "The Anatomy of Income Distribution" [15]. *The Review of Economics and Statistics* (The MIT Press) **44** (3): 270–283. doi:10.2307/1926398 [16].

- Ogwang, Tomson (2000). "A Convenient Method of Computing the Gini Index and its Standard Error". *Oxford Bulletin of Economics and Statistics* **62**: 123–129. doi:10.1111/1468-0084.00164 [17].

- Ogwang, Tomson (2004). "Calculating a Standard Error for the Gini Coefficient: Some Further Results: Reply". *Oxford Bulletin of Economics and Statistics* **66**: 435–437. doi:10.1111/j.1468-0084.2004.00087.x [18].

- Xu, Kuan (January 2004). *How Has the Literature on Gini's Index Evolved in the Past 80 Years?* [19]. Department of Economics, Dalhousie University. Retrieved 2006-06-01. The Chinese version of this paper appears in Xu, Kuan (2003). "How Has the Literature on Gini's Index Evolved in the Past 80 Years?". *China Economic Quarterly* **2**: 757–778.

- Yitzhaki, S. (1991). "Calculating Jackknife Variance Estimators for Parameters of the Gini Method" [20]. *Journal of Business and Economic Statistics* (American Statistical Association) **9** (2): 235–239. doi:10.2307/1391792 [21].

External links

- Deutsche Bundesbank: Do banks diversify loan portfolios? [22], 2005 (on using e.g. the Gini coefficient for risk evaluation of loan portfolios)
- Forbes Article, In praise of inequality [23]
- Measuring Software Project Risk With The Gini Coefficient [24], an application of the Gini coefficient to software
- The World Bank: Measuring Inequality [25]
- Travis Hale, University of Texas Inequality Project:The Theoretical Basics of Popular Inequality Measures [3], online computation of examples: 1A [4], 1B [5]
- United States Census Bureau List of Gini Coefficients by State for Families and Households [26]
- Article from The Guardian analysing inequality in the UK 1974 - 2006 [27]
- World Income Inequality Database [28]
- Income Distribution and Poverty in OECD Countries [29]
- Software:
    - A Matlab Inequality Package [21], including code for computing Gini, Atkinson, Theil indexes and for plotting the Lorenz Curve. Many examples are available.
    - Free Online Calculator [15] computes the Gini Coefficient, plots the Lorenz curve, and computes many other measures of concentration for any dataset
    - Free Calculator: Online [30] and downloadable scripts [18] (Python and Lua) for Atkinson, Gini, and Hoover inequalities
    - Users of the R [20] data analysis software can install the "ineq [31]" package which allows for computation of a variety of inequality indices including Gini, Atkinson, Theil.

- LORENZ 2.0 [32] is a Mathematica notebook which draw sample Lorenz curves and calculates Gini coefficients and Lorenz asymmetry coefficients from data in an Excel sheet.

Private Product Remaining

Private Product Remaining or **PPR** is a means of national income accounting similar to, the more commonly encountered GNP. Since government is financed through taxation and any resulting output is not (usually) sold on the market, what value is ascribed to it is disputed (see calculation problem), and it is counted in GNP. Murray Rothbard developed the **GPP** (Gross Private Product) and **PPR** measures. GPP is GNP minus income originating in government and government enterprises. PPR is GPP minus the higher of government expenditures and tax revenues plus interest received.

For example, in an economy in which the private expenditures total $1,000 and government expenditures total $200, the GNP would be $1,200, GPP would be $1,000, and PPR would be $800.

See also

- Gross Domestic Product

External links

- *GNP, PPR, and the Standard of Living* [1] by Robert Batemarco, from the journal *Review of Austrian Economics*

Happy Planet Index

The **Happy Planet Index (HPI)** is an index of human well-being and environmental impact that was introduced by the New Economics Foundation (NEF) in July 2006. The index is designed to challenge well-established indices of countries' development, such as Gross Domestic Product (GDP) and the Human Development Index

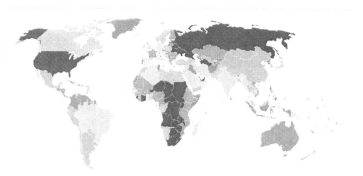

Map showing countries shaded by their position in the Happy Planet Index (2006). The highest-ranked countries are bright green; the lowest are brown

(HDI), which are seen as not taking sustainability into account. In particular, GDP is seen as inappropriate, as the usual ultimate aim of most people is not to be rich, but to be happy and healthy. Furthermore, it is believed that the notion of sustainable development requires a measure of the environmental costs of pursuing those goals.

Outline

The HPI is based on general utilitarian principles — that most people want to live long and fulfilling lives, and the country which is doing the best is the one that allows its citizens to do so, whilst avoiding infringing on the opportunity of future people and people in other countries to do the same. In effect it operationalises the IUCN's (World Conservation Union) call for a metric capable of measuring 'the production of human well-being (not necessarily material goods) per unit of extraction of or imposition upon nature'. Human well-being is operationalised as Happy Life Years. Extraction of or imposition upon nature is proxied for using the ecological footprint per capita, which attempts to estimate the amount of natural resources required to sustain a given country's lifestyle. A country with a large per capita ecological footprint uses more than its fair share of resources, both by drawing resources from other countries, and also by causing permanent damage to the planet which will impact future generations.

As such, the HPI is *not* a measure of which are the happiest countries in the world. Countries with relatively high levels of life satisfaction, as measured in surveys, are found from the very top (Colombia in 6th place) to the very bottom (the USA in 114th place) of the rank order. The HPI is best conceived as a measure of the *environmental efficiency of supporting well-being* in a given country. Such efficiency could emerge in a country with a medium environmental impact (e.g. Costa Rica) and very high well-being, but it could also emerge in a country with only mediocre well-being, but very low environmental impact (e.g. Vietnam).

Each country's HPI value is a function of its average subjective life satisfaction, life expectancy at birth, and ecological footprint per capita. The exact function is a little more complex, but conceptually it approximates multiplying life satisfaction and life expectancy, and dividing that by the ecological footprint. Most of the life satisfaction data is taken from the World Values Survey and World Database of Happiness, but some is drawn from other surveys, and some is estimated using statistical regression techniques.

178 countries were surveyed in 2006, compared to 143 in 2009. The best scoring country in 2009 was Costa Rica, followed by the Dominican Republic, Jamaica and Guatemala, with Tanzania, Botswana and Zimbabwe featuring at the bottom of the list.

International rankings

2006 Happy Planet Index

Rank	Country	HPI
1	Vanuatu	68.21
2	Colombia	67.24
3	Costa Rica	66.00
4	Dominica	64.55
5	Panama	63.54
6	Cuba	61.86
7	Honduras	61.75
8	Guatemala	61.69
9	El Salvador	61.66
10	Saint Vincent and the Grenadines	61.37
11	Saint Lucia	61.31
12	Vietnam	61.23
13	Bhutan	61.08
14	Samoa	60.98
15	Sri Lanka	60.31
16	Antigua and Barbuda	59.23
17	Philippines	59.17
18	Nicaragua	59.09
19	Kyrgyzstan	59.05

20	Solomon Islands	58.93
21	Tunisia	58.92
22	São Tomé and Príncipe	57.92
23	Indonesia	57.90
24	Tonga	57.90
25	Tajikistan	57.66
26	Venezuela	57.55
27	Dominican Republic	57.14
28	Guyana	56.65
29	Saint Kitts and Nevis	56.14
30	Seychelles	56.07
31	China	55.99
32	Thailand	55.39
33	Peru	55.14
34	Suriname	55.03
35	Yemen	55.00
36	Fiji	54.47
37	Morocco	54.43
38	Mexico	54.39
39	Maldives	53.52
40	Malta	53.26
41	Bangladesh	53.20
42	Comoros	52.92
43	Barbados	52.73
44	Malaysia	52.69
45	Palestinian Authority	52.64
46	Cape Verde	52.41
47	Chile	52.20
48	Timor-Leste	52.04
49	Argentina	51.96
50	Trinidad and Tobago	51.87
51	Belize	51.32

52	Paraguay	51.13
53	Jamaica	51.01
54	Nepal	49.95
55	Mauritius	49.65
56	Mongolia	49.59
57	Uruguay	49.31
58	Ecuador	49.29
59	Uzbekistan	49.22
60	Grenada	48.96
61	Austria	48.77
62	The Gambia	48.67
63	Brazil	48.59
64	Iceland	48.35
65	Switzerland	48.30
66	Italy	48.26
67	Iran	47.23
68	Ghana	46.98
69	Bolivia	46.17
70	Netherlands	46.00
71	Madagascar	45.99
72	Cyprus	45.99
73	Algeria	45.89
74	Luxembourg	45.62
75	Bahamas	44.90
76	Papua New Guinea	44.75
77	Myanmar	44.55
78	Belgium	44.04
79	Slovenia	44.03
80	Oman	43.94
81	Germany	43.83
82	Croatia	43.71
83	Lebanon	43.64

84	Taiwan	43.41
85	Haiti	43.34
86	Syria	43.23
87	Spain	43.04
88	Hong Kong	42.88
89	Saudi Arabia	42.65
90	India	42.46
91	Cambodia	42.15
92	Albania	42.13
93	Jordan	42.05
94	New Zealand	41.92
95	Japan	41.70
96	Republic of the Congo	41.59
97	Egypt	41.58
98	Turkey	41.40
99	Denmark	41.40
100	Brunei	41.16
101	Georgia	41.15
102	South Korea	41.11
103	Bosnia and Herzegovina	40.96
104	Senegal	40.81
105	Azerbaijan	40.69
106	Gabon	40.52
107	Libya	40.33
108	United Kingdom	40.29
109	Laos	40.26
110	Benin	40.10
111	Canada	39.76
112	Pakistan	39.40
113	Ireland	39.38
114	Poland	39.29
115	Norway	39.18

116	Macedonia	39.14
117	Israel	39.07
118	Namibia	38.41
119	Sweden	38.17
120	Romania	37.72
121	Hungary	37.64
122	Guinea	37.42
123	Finland	37.36
124	Mauritania	37.30
125	Kazakhstan	36.92
126	Togo	36.86
127	Kenya	36.70
128	Czech Republic	36.5
129	France	36.42
130	Armenia	36.15
131	Singapore	36.14
132	Slovakia	35.81
133	Greece	35.71
134	Tanzania	35.08
135	Guinea-Bissau	35.08
136	Portugal	34.83
137	Eritrea	34.49
138	Bahrain	34.35
139	Australia	34.06
140	Mali	33.68
141	Mozambique	33.01
142	Cameroon	32.76
143	Djibouti	32.72
144	Ethiopia	32.53
145	Bulgaria	31.59
146	Nigeria	31.14
147	Moldova	31.12

148	Burkina Faso	30.08
149	Lithuania	29.29
150	United States	28.83
151	Côte d'Ivoire	28.80
152	Rwanda	28.35
153	Sierra Leone	28.24
154	United Arab Emirates	28.20
155	Angola	27.88
156	South Africa	27.80
157	Sudan	27.74
158	Uganda	27.68
159	Kuwait	27.67
160	Latvia	27.27
161	Niger	26.80
162	Malawi	26.66
163	Zambia	25.91
164	Central African Republic	25.90
165	Belarus	25.78
166	Qatar	25.50
167	Botswana	25.42
168	Chad	25.37
169	Turkmenistan	23.96
170	Equatorial Guinea	23.77
171	Lesotho	23.05
172	Russia	22.76
173	Estonia	22.68
174	Ukraine	22.21
175	Democratic Republic of the Congo	20.69
176	Burundi	19.02
177	Swaziland	18.38
178	Zimbabwe	16.64

2009 Happy Planet Index

Rank	Country	HPI
1	Costa Rica	76.1
2	Dominican Republic	71.8
3	Jamaica	70.1
4	Guatemala	68.4
5	Vietnam	66.5
6	Colombia	66.1
7	Cuba	65.7
8	El Salvador	61.5
9	Brazil	61.0
10	Honduras	61.0
11	Nicaragua	60.5
12	Egypt	60.3
13	Saudi Arabia	59.7
14	Philippines	59.0
15	Argentina	59.0
16	Indonesia	58.9
17	Bhutan	58.5
18	Panama	57.4
19	Laos	57.3
20	China	57.1
21	Morocco	56.8
22	Sri Lanka	56.5
23	Mexico	55.6
24	Pakistan	55.6
25	Ecuador	55.5
26	Jordan	54.6
27	Belize	54.5
28	Peru	54.4
29	Tunisia	54.3

30	Trinidad and Tobago	54.2
31	Bangladesh	54.1
32	Moldova	54.1
33	Malaysia	54.0
34	Tajikistan	53.5
35	India	53.0
36	Venezuela	52.5
37	Nepal	51.9
38	Syria	51.3
39	Burma	51.2
40	Algeria	51.2
41	Thailand	50.9
42	Haiti	50.8
43	Netherlands	50.6
44	Malta	50.4
45	Uzbekistan	50.1
46	Chile	49.7
47	Bolivia	49.3
48	Armenia	48.3
49	Singapore	48.2
50	Yemen	48.1
51	Germany	48.1
52	Switzerland	48.1
53	Sweden	48.0
54	Albania	47.9
55	Paraguay	47.8
56	Palestinian Authority	47.7
57	Austria	47.7
58	Serbia	47.6
59	Finland	47.2
60	Croatia	47.2
61	Kyrgyzstan	47.1

62	Cyprus	46.2
63	Guyana	45.6
64	Belgium	45.4
65	Bosnia and Herzegovina	45.0
66	Slovenia	44.5
67	Israel	44.5
68	South Korea	44.4
69	Italy	44.0
70	Romania	43.9
71	France	43.9
72	Georgia	43.6
73	Slovakia	43.5
74	United Kingdom	43.3
75	Japan	43.3
76	Spain	43.2
77	Poland	42.8
78	Ireland	42.6
79	Iraq	42.6
80	Cambodia	42.3
81	Iran	42.1
82	Bulgaria	42.0
83	Turkey	41.7
84	Hong Kong	41.6
85	Azerbaijan	41.2
86	Lithuania	40.9
87	Djibouti	40.4
88	Norway	40.4
89	Canada	39.4
90	Hungary	38.9
91	Kazakhstan	38.5
92	Czech Republic	38.3
93	Mauritania	38.2

94	Iceland	38.1
95	Ukraine	38.1
96	Senegal	38.0
97	Greece	37.6
98	Portugal	37.5
99	Uruguay	37.2
100	Ghana	37.1
101	Latvia	36.7
102	Australia	36.6
103	New Zealand	36.2
104	Belarus	35.7
105	Denmark	35.5
106	Mongolia	35.0
107	Malawi	34.5
108	Russia	34.5
109	Chad	34.3
110	Lebanon	33.6
111	Macedonia	32.7
112	Republic of the Congo	32.4
113	Madagascar	31.5
114	United States	30.7
115	Nigeria	30.3
116	Guinea	30.3
117	Uganda	30.2
118	South Africa	29.7
119	Rwanda	29.6
120	Democratic Republic of the Congo	29.0
121	Sudan	28.5
122	Luxembourg	28.5
123	United Arab Emirates	28.2
124	Ethiopia	28.1

125	Kenya	27.8
126	Cameroon	27.2
127	Zambia	27.2
128	Kuwait	27.0
129	Niger	26.9
130	Angola	26.8
131	Estonia	26.4
132	Mali	25.8
133	Mozambique	24.6
134	Benin	24.6
135	Togo	23.3
136	Sierra Leone	23.1
137	Central African Republic	22.9
138	Burkina Faso	22.4
139	Burundi	21.8
140	Namibia	21.1
141	Botswana	20.9
142	Tanzania	17.8
143	Zimbabwe	16.6

Views

Much criticism of the index has been due to commentators falsely understanding it to be a measure of happiness, when it is in fact a measure of the ecological *efficiency* of supporting well-being (see, for example, the following blogs in Heavy Lifting and Spiked).

Aside from that, criticism has focused on the following:

- That the HPI completely ignores issues like political freedom, human rights and labor rights.
- That the World Values Survey covers only a minority of the world's nations and is only done every five years. As a result, much of the data for the index must come from other sources, or is estimated using regressions.
- General suspicion of subjective measures of well-being.
- That the Ecological Footprint is a controversial concept with many criticisms.

Nevertheless, the HPI and its subcomponents have been considered in political circles. The Ecological Footprint, championed by the WWF, is widely used by both local and national governments, as well as supranational organisations such as the European Commission. The HPI itself was recently cited in the British Conservative Party as a possible substitute for GDP,. A recent review of progress indicators produced by the European Parliament, lists the following pros and cons to using the HPI as a measure of national progress:

Pros:

- Considers the actual 'ends' of economic activity in the form of life satisfaction and longevity
- Combines wellbeing and environmental aspects
- Simple and easily understandable scheme for calculating the index
- Comparability of results ('EF' and 'life expectancy' can be applied to different countries)
- Data online available, although some data gaps remain
- Mixture of 'soft' and 'hard' criteria; takes into account people's well-being and resource use of countries

Cons:

- 'Happiness' or 'life satisfaction' are very subjective and personal: cultural influences and complex impact of policies on happiness
- Confusion of name: index is not a measure of happiness but rather measure of environmental efficiency of supporting well-being in a given country

See also

- Global Peace Index
- Gross national happiness
- Satisfaction with Life Index
- Genuine Progress Indicator
- Legatum Prosperity Index

External links

- The Happy Planet Index [1]
- Official website of the New Economics Foundation [2]

Subjective life satisfaction

Subjective life satisfaction is a measure of an individual's perceived level of well-being (quality of life) and happiness. It is frequently assessed in surveys, by asking individuals how satisfied they are with their own lives. It is sometimes used as a synonym for subjective happiness and subjective well-being, however questions tapping life satisfaction and happiness are slightly different, and well-being can be seen as a broader term.

The most commonly used question probing life satisfaction, as found in the World Values Survey is as follows:

"All things considered, how satisfied are you with your life as a whole these days?"

Respondents are typically asked to respond on a scale of 1-10.

Life satisfaction index was used as one of the three main components in the new economics foundation's (**nef**) Happy Planet Index, published in July 2006.

See also

- Personality psychology
- Negative affectivity

External links

- Global Projection of Subjective Well-Being [1]

Developing Country

Developing country

Developing country is a term generally used to describe a nation with a low level of material well-being (not to be confused with third world countries). Since no single definition of the term *developed country* is recognized internationally, the levels of development may vary widely within so-called developing countries, with some developing countries having high average standards of living.

Countries with more advanced economies than other developing nations, but which have not yet fully demonstrated the signs of a developed country, are categorized under the term *newly industrialized countries.*

Advanced economies   Emerging and developing economies (not least developed)   Emerging and developing economies (least developed)Classifications by the IMF and the UN

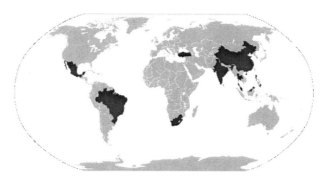

Newly industrialized countries as of 2009

Definition

Kofi Annan, former Secretary General of the United Nations, defined a developed country as follows. "A   developed   country   is one that allows all its citizens to enjoy a free and healthy life in a safe environment." But according to the United Nations Statistics Division,

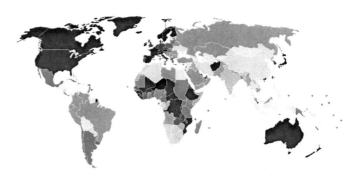

> There is no established convention for the designation of "developed" and "developing" countries or areas in the United Nations system.

World map indicating the Human Development Index (based on 2007 data, published on October 5, 2009) See the color-blind compliant map for red-green color vision problems.

And it notes that

> The designations "developed" and "developing" are intended for statistical convenience and do not necessarily express a judgment about the stage reached by a particular country or area in the development process.

The UN also notes

> In common practice, Japan in Asia, Canada and the United States in northern America, Australia and New Zealand in Oceania, and Europe are considered "developed" regions or areas. In international trade statistics, the Southern African Customs Union is also treated as a developed region and Israel as a developed country; countries emerging from the former Yugoslavia, except for Slovenia, are treated as developing countries; and countries of eastern Europe and the Commonwealth of Independent States (code 172) in Europe are not included under either developed or developing regions.

According to the classification from IMF before April 2004, all the countries of Eastern Europe (including Central European countries which still belongs to "Eastern Europe Group" in the UN institutions) as well as the former Soviet Union (U.S.S.R.) countries in Central Asia (Kazakhstan, Uzbekistan, Kyrgyzstan, Tajikistan and Turkmenistan) and Mongolia, were not included under either developed or developing regions, but rather were referred to as "countries in transition"; however they are now widely regarded (in the international reports) as "developing countries". In the 21st century, the original Four Asian Tigers regions (Hong Kong, Singapore, South Korea, and Taiwan), along with Cyprus,, Malta, and Slovenia, are considered "developed countries".

The IMF uses a flexible classification system that considers "(1) per capita income level, (2) export diversification—so oil exporters that have high per capita GDP would not make the advanced classification because around 70% of its exports are oil, and (3) degree of integration into the global financial system."

The World Bank classifies countries into four income groups. These are set each year on July 1. Economies were divided according to 2008 GNI per capita using the following ranges of income:

- Low income countries had GNI per capita of US$975 or less.
- Lower middle income countries had GNI per capita of US$976–$3,855.
- Upper middle income countries had GNI per capita between US$3,856–$11,905.
- High income countries had GNI above $11,906.

The World Bank classifies all low- and middle-income countries as developing but notes, "The use of the term is convenient; it is not intended to imply that all economies in the group are experiencing similar development or that other economies have reached a preferred or final stage of development. Classification by income does not necessarily reflect development status."

Measure and concept of development

The development of a country is measured with statistical indexes such as income per capita (per person) (GDP), life expectancy, the rate of literacy, et cetera. The UN has developed the HDI, a compound indicator of the above statistics, to gauge the level of human development for countries where data is available.

Developing countries are in general countries which have not achieved a significant degree of industrialization relative to their populations, and which have, in most cases a medium to low standard of living. There is a strong correlation between low income and high population growth.

The terms utilized when discussing developing countries refer to the intent and to the constructs of those who utilize these terms. Other terms sometimes used are less developed countries (LDCs), least economically developed countries (LEDCs), "underdeveloped nations" or Third World nations, and "non-industrialized nations". Conversely, the opposite end of the spectrum is termed developed countries, most economically developed countries (MEDCs), First World nations and "industrialized nations".

To moderate the euphemistic aspect of the word *developing*, international organizations have started to use the term Less economically developed country (LEDCs) for the poorest nations which can in no sense be regarded as developing. That is, LEDCs are the poorest subset of LDCs. This may moderate against a belief that the standard of living across the entire developing world is the same.

The concept of the developing nation is found, under one term or another, in numerous theoretical systems having diverse orientations — for example, theories of decolonization, liberation theology, Marxism, anti-imperialism, and political economy.

Criticism of the term 'developing country'

There is criticism of the use of the term 'developing country'. The term **implies** inferiority of a 'developing country' compared to a 'developed country', which many countries dislike. It assumes a desire to 'develop' along the traditional 'Western' model of economic development which a few countries, such as Cuba, have chosen not to follow. Thus Cuba remains classed as 'developing' due to its low gross national income but has a lower infant mortality rate than the USA.

The term 'developing' implies mobility and does not acknowledge that development may be in decline or static in some countries, particularly those southern African states worst affected by HIV/AIDS. In such cases, the term *developing country* may be considered a euphemism. The term implies homogeneity between such countries, which vary widely. The term also implies homogeneity within such countries when wealth (and health) of the most and least affluent groups varies widely.[citation needed]

In general, development entails a modern infrastructure (both physical and institutional), and a move away from low value added sectors such as agriculture and natural resource extraction. Developed countries, in comparison, usually have economic systems based on continuous, self-sustaining economic growth in the tertiary sector of the economy and quaternary sector of the economy and high material standards of living. However, there are notable exceptions, as some countries considered developed have a significant component of primary industries in their national economies, e.g. Norway, Canada, Australia. The USA and Western Europe have a very important agricultural sector, both are major players in international agricultural markets. Also, natural resource extraction can be a very profitable industry (high value added) e.g. oil extraction.

List of emerging and developing economies

The following are considered **emerging and developing economies** according to the International Monetary Fund's World Economic Outlook Report, April 2010.

- Afghanistan
- Albania
- Algeria
- Angola
- Antigua and Barbuda
- Argentina
- Armenia
- Azerbaijan
- The Bahamas
- Bahrain
- Bangladesh

- Barbados
- Belarus
- Belize
- Benin
- Bhutan
- Bolivia
- Botswana
- Bosnia and Herzegovina
- Brazil
- Bulgaria
- Burkina Faso
- Burma
- Burundi
- Cameroon
- Cape Verde
- Central African Republic
- Chad
- Chile
- China
- Colombia
- Comoros
- Democratic Republic of the Congo
- Republic of the Congo
- Costa Rica
- Côte d'Ivoire
- Croatia
- Djibouti
- Dominica
- Dominican Republic
- Ecuador
- Egypt
- El Salvador
- Equatorial Guinea
- Eritrea
- Estonia
- Ethiopia
- Fiji
- Gabon

- The Gambia
- Georgia
- Ghana
- Grenada
- Guatemala
- Guinea
- Guinea-Bissau
- Guyana
- Haiti
- Honduras
- Hungary
- Indonesia
- India
- Iran
- Iraq
- Jamaica
- Jordan
- Kazakhstan
- Kenya
- Kiribati
- Kuwait
- Kyrgyzstan
- Laos
- Latvia
- Lebanon
- Lesotho
- Liberia
- Libya
- Lithuania
- Macedonia
- Madagascar
- Malawi
- Malaysia
- Maldives
- Mali
- Marshall Islands
- Mauritania
- Mauritius

- Mexico
- Federated States of Micronesia
- Moldova
- Mongolia
- Montenegro
- Morocco
- Mozambique
- Namibia
- Nauru
- Nepal
- Nicaragua
- Niger
- Nigeria
- Oman
- Pakistan
- Palau
- Panama
- Papua New Guinea
- Paraguay
- Peru
- Philippines
- Poland
- Qatar
- Romania
- Russia
- Rwanda
- Saudi Arabia
- Samoa
- São Tomé and Príncipe
- Senegal
- Serbia
- Seychelles
- Sierra Leone
- Solomon Islands
- South Africa
- Somalia
- Sri Lanka
- Saint Kitts and Nevis

- Saint Lucia
- Saint Vincent and the Grenadines
- Sudan
- Suriname
- Swaziland
- Syria
- Tajikistan
- Tanzania
- Thailand
- Timor-Leste
- Togo
- Tonga
- Trinidad and Tobago
- Tunisia
- Turkey
- Turkmenistan
- Tuvalu
- Uganda
- Ukraine
- United Arab Emirates
- Uruguay
- Uzbekistan
- Vanuatu
- Venezuela
- Vietnam
- Yemen
- Zambia
- Zimbabwe

Developing countries not listed by IMF

- Cuba
- North Korea

List of graduated developing economies (Four Asian Tigers and New Euro countries), now considered advanced economies

- Hong Kong (after 1997)
- Singapore (after 1997)
- South Korea (after 1997)
- Taiwan (after 1997)
- Cyprus (after 2001)
- Slovenia (after 2007)
- Malta (after 2008)
- Czech Republic (after 2009)
- Slovakia (after 2009)

Typology and names of countries

Countries are often loosely placed into four categories of development. Each category includes the countries listed in their respective article. The term "developing nation" is not a label to assign a specific, similar type of problem.

1. Newly industrialized countries (NICs) are nations with economies more advanced and developed than those in the developing world, but not yet with the full signs of a developed country. NIC is a category between developed and developing countries. It includes Brazil, China, India, Malaysia, Mexico, Philippines, South Africa, Thailand and Turkey.
2. The Advanced Emerging Markets are: Brazil, Hungary, Mexico, Poland, South Africa and Taiwan.
3. Countries with long-term civil war or large-scale breakdown of rule of law ("failed states") (e.g. Democratic Republic of Congo, Afghanistan, Pakistan, Somalia) or non-development-oriented dictatorship (North Korea, Myanmar, Zimbabwe).
4. Some developing countries have been classified as "Developed countries" such as Antigua and Barbuda, The Bahamas, Bahrain, Barbados, Brunei, Equatorial Guinea, Kuwait, Oman, Qatar, Saudi Arabia and Trinidad and Tobago by the World Bank.

New Industrialized Country

Newly industrialized country

The category of **newly industrialized country** (**NIC**) is a socioeconomic classification applied to several countries around the world by political scientists and economists.

NICs are countries whose economies have not yet reached First World status but have, in a macroeconomic sense, outpaced their developing counterparts.

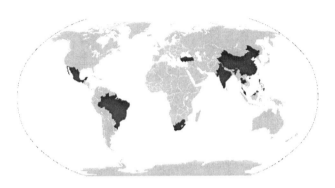

Newly industrialized countries as of 2009.

Another characterization of NICs is that of nations undergoing rapid economic growth (usually export-oriented). Incipient or ongoing industrialization is an important indicator of a NIC. In many NICs, social upheaval can occur as primarily rural, or agricultural, populations migrate to the cities, where the growth of manufacturing concerns and factories can draw many thousands of laborers.

NICs usually share some other common features, including:

- Increased social freedoms and civil rights.
- Strong political leaders.
- A switch from agricultural to industrial economies, especially in the manufacturing sector.
- An increasingly open-market economy, allowing free trade with other nations in the world.
- Large national corporations operating in several continents.
- Strong capital investment from foreign countries.
- Political leadership in their area of influence.
- Lowered poverty rates.

NICs often receive support from international organizations such as the WTO and other internal support bodies. However, as environmental, labor and social standards tend to be significantly weaker in NICs, many fair trade supporters have advocated standards for importing their products and criticized the outsourcing of jobs to NICs.

Historical context

The term began to be used *circa* 1970 when the Four Asian Tigers of Hong Kong, Singapore, South Korea and Taiwan rose to global prominence as NICs in the 1970s and 80s, with exceptionally fast industrial growth since the 1960s; all four regions have since graduated into advanced economies and high-income economies. There is a clear distinction between these countries and the nations now considered to be NICs. In particular, the combination of an open political process, high GNI per capita and a thriving, export-oriented economic policy has shown that these countries have now not only reached but surpassed the ranks of many developed countries.

All four economies are classified as High-income economies by the World Bank and Advanced economies by the IMF and CIA. All of them also possess Human Development Index over 0.9, equal to Western European countries. South Korea in particular, is the only OECD member and a "full democracy" in Asia along with Japan. Japan is a parliamentary constitutional monarchy.

Current NICs

The following table presents the list of countries consistently considered NICs by different authors and experts. Turkey, and South Africa are classified as developed countries by the CIA. Turkey is a founding member of the OECD since 1961 and Mexico joined in 1994. The G8+5 group is composed by G8 members plus China, India, Mexico, South Africa and Brazil.

Note: Green-colored cells indicate higher value or best performance in index, while yellow-colored cells indicate the opposite.

Continent	Country	GDP (PPP) (Billions of USD, 2009 IMF)	GDP per capita (PPP) (USD, 2009 IMF)	Income equality (GINI) 2006	Human Development Index (HDI, 2007)	GDP (real) growth rate	GDP (real) growth rate per capita
Africa	South Africa	505.214	10,243	**57.8**	0.683 (medium)	4.50	4.92
North America	Mexico	1,465.726	13,628	46.3	**0.854** (high)	**3.00**	**3.30**
South America	Brazil	2,013.186	10,513	54	0.813 (high)	5.70	4.50

Asia	China	8,765.240	6,567	44.7	0.772 (medium)	11.10	9.95
	India	3,526.124	2,940	32.5	0.612 (medium)	9.70	7.02
	Malaysia	382.257	13,769	49.2	0.829 (high)	5.40	3.65
	Philippines	324.692	3,520	44.5	0.751 (medium)	7.50	7.40
	Thailand	539.871	8,059	42	0.783 (medium)	4.40	3.93
Europe	Turkey	880.061	12,476	38	0.806 (high)	5.20	4.10

According to Goldman Sachs review of emerging economies, by 2050 the largest economies in the world will be as follows: China, USA, India, Brazil, and Mexico.

For China and India, the immense population of these two nations (each with over 1.1 billion people as of January 2009) means that per capita income will remain low even if either economy surpasses that of the United States in overall GDP. When GDP per capita is calculated according to Purchasing Power Parity (PPP), this takes into account the lower costs of living in each newly industrialized country.

Brazil, China, India, Mexico and South Africa meet annually with the G8 countries to discuss financial topics and climate change, due to their economic importance in today's global market and environmental impact, in a group known as G8+5. This group is expected to be expanded to G14 by adding Egypt alongside the five forementioned countries.

Other NICs

Each author set a list of countries accordingly to the methods or type of economic analysis. This sometimes results in a country being mentioned as NIC in a particular work, but that is rarely considered as such by the other authors. This is the case of nations such as Argentina, Chile, Egypt, Indonesia and Russia.

Brief economic analysis

NICs usually benefit from comparatively low labor costs, which translates into lower input prices for suppliers. As a result, it is often easier for producers in NICs to outperform and outproduce factories in developed countries, where the cost of living is higher, and labor unions and other organizations have more political sway.

This comparative advantage is often criticized by advocates of the fair trade movement.

Issues

Economic freedom is not always associated with political freedom in nations such as the People's Republic of China, where Internet censorship and human rights violations are common. The case is diametrically opposite for India. While being a liberal democracy throughout its post-colonial history, India has been widely criticized for its inefficient government and widespread corruption. Thus, while in China where political freedoms remain tight, the average Chinese citizen enjoys a higher standard of living than his counterpart in India.

South Africa faces an influx of immigrants from countries such as Zimbabwe.[citation needed]

See also

- Emerging markets
- Science in newly industrialized countries
- Flying Geese Paradigm

Groupings:

- G8+5
- G20 industrial nations
- G20 developing nations
- BRIMC
- BRIC
- Next Eleven

References

15. The Planning Commission, Government of India

Measure and Concept of Development for Developing Countries

Per capita

Per capita is a term adapted from the Latin phrase *pro capite* meaning "per (each) head" with *pro* meaning "per" or "for each", and *capite* (*caput* ablative) meaning "head." Both words together equate to the phrase "for each head", i.e. per individual or per person. The term is used in a wide variety of social sciences and statistical research contexts, including government statistics, economic indicators, and built environment studies.

It is commonly and usually used in the field of statistics in place of saying "for each person" or "per person".[1][2]

It is also used in wills to indicate that each of the named beneficiaries should receive, by devise or bequest, equal shares of the estate. This is in contrast to a per stirpes division, in which each branch of the inheriting family inherits an equal share of the estate.

See also

- Per capita income

Life expectancy

Life expectancy is the expected (in the statistical sense) number of years of life remaining at a given age. It is denoted by e_x, which means the average number of subsequent years of life for someone now aged x, according to a particular mortality experience. (In technical literature, this symbol means the average number of *complete* years of life remaining, excluding fractions of a year. The corresponding statistic including fractions of a year, the normal meaning of life expectancy, has a symbol with a small circle over the e.) The life expectancy of a group of individuals is heavily dependent on the criteria used to select the group. Life expectancy is usually calculated separately for males and females. Females live longer than males in countries with modern obstetric care.

The term that is known as life expectancy is most often used in the context of human populations, but is also used in plant or animal ecology; it is calculated by the analysis of life tables (also known as actuarial tables). The term life expectancy may also be used in the context of manufactured objects although the related term shelf life is used for consumer products and the terms "mean time to breakdown" (MTTB) and "mean time before failures" (MTBF) are used in engineering literature.

A common misunderstanding is that life expectancy means average life span. This is untrue since, for example, life expectancy takes into account infant mortality and hence while in some age life expectancy may had been low, several people may had had long lives.

Interpretation of life expectancy

In countries with high infant mortality rates, the life expectancy at birth is highly sensitive to the rate of death in the first few years of life. Because of this sensitivity to infant mortality, simple life expectancy at age zero can be subject to gross misinterpretation, leading one to believe that a population with a low overall life expectancy will necessarily have a small proportion of older people. For example, in a hypothetical stationary population in which half the population dies before the age of five, but everybody else dies exactly at 70 years old, the life expectancy at age zero will be about 35 years, while about 25% of the population will be between the ages of 50 and 70. Another measure such as life expectancy at age 5 (e_5) can be used to exclude the effect of infant mortality to provide a simple measure of overall mortality rates other than in early childhood—in the hypothetical population above, life expectancy at age 5 would be 70 years. Aggregate population measures such as the proportion of the population in various age classes should also be used alongside individual-based measures like formal life expectancy when analyzing population structure and dynamics.

One example of this common misinterpretation can be seen in the *In Search of...* episode "The Man Who Would Not Die" (About Count of St. Germain) where it is stated "Evidence recently discovered in the British Museum indicates that St. Germain may have well been the long lost third son of Rákóczi born in Transylvania in 1694. If he died in Germany in 1784, he lived 90 years. The average life expectancy in the 18th century was 35 years. Fifty was a ripe old age. *Ninety*... was forever." This ignores the fact that life expectancy *changes* depending on age and the one often presented is the "at birth" number. For example, a Roman Life Expectancy table at the University of Texas [1] shows that *at birth* the life expectancy was 25 but if one lived to the age of 5 one's life expectancy jumped to 48. Similar papers such as Plymouth Plantation; "Dead at Forty" [2] and Life Expectancy by Age, 1850–2004 [3] show dramatic increases in life expectancy after childhood.

Human life expectancy patterns

Humans live on average 39.5 years in Swaziland and 81 years in Japan (2008 est.), although Japan's recorded life expectancy may have been very slightly increased by counting many infant deaths as stillborn. The oldest confirmed recorded age for any human is 122 years (see Jeanne Calment). This is referred to as the "maximum life span", which is the upper boundary of life, the maximum number of years any human is known to have lived.

Life expectancy variation over time

The following information is derived from *Encyclopaedia Britannica*, 1961 and other sources, and unless otherwise stated represents estimates of the life expectancies of the population as a whole. In many instances life expectancy varied considerably according to class and gender.

Sometimes, mainly in the past, life expectancy increased during the years of childhood, as the individual survived the high mortality rates then associated with childhood. The life expectancies at birth listed below take account of infant mortality but not pre-natal mortality (miscarriage or abortion).

Humans by Era	Average Lifespan at Birth (years)	Comment
Upper Paleolithic	33	At age 15: 39 (to age 54)
Neolithic	20	
Bronze Age and Iron Age	35+	
Classical Greece	28	
Classical Rome	28	
Pre-Columbian North America	25-30	
Medieval Islamic Caliphate	35+	
Medieval Britain	30	
Early Modern Britain	40+	

Early 20th Century	30-45	
Current world average	67.2	2010 est.

While different sample attributes and sizes, methodologies, and theoretical assumptions produce sometimes notable variations, in general, interpretations of the available data indicate that the occurrence of older age became more common late in human evolution. This increased longevity is attributed by some writers to cultural adaptations rather than phylogenetic change, although some research indicates that during the Neolithic Revolution there was a selection effect of extrinsic mortality risk upon genotypic expressions favouring increased longevity in subsequent populations. Nevertheless, all researchers acknowledge the effect of cultural adaptations upon life expectancy.

The average life expectancy in Colonial America was under 25 years in the Virginia colony, and in New England about 40% of children failed to reach adulthood. During the Industrial Revolution, the life expectancy of children increased dramatically. The percentage of children born in London who died before the age of five decreased from 74.5% in 1730-1749 to 31.8% in 1810-1829.

Public health measures are credited with much of the recent increase in life expectancy. During the 20th century, the average lifespan in the United States increased by more than 30 years, of which 25 years can be attributed to advances in public health.

In order to assess the quality of these additional years of life, 'healthy life expectancies' have been calculated for the last 30 years. Since 2001, the World Health Organization publishes statistics called Healthy life expectancy (HALE), defined as the average number of years that a person can expect to live in "full health", excluding the years lived in less than full health due to disease and/or injury. Since 2004, Eurostat publishes annual statistics called Healthy Life Years (HLY) based on reported activity limitations. The United States of America uses similar indicators in the framework of their nationwide health promotion and disease prevention plan "Healthy People 2010". An increasing number of countries are using health expectancy indicators to monitor the health of their population.

Regional variations

There are great variations in life expectancy between different parts of the world, mostly caused by differences in public health, medical care and diet. Much of the excess mortality (higher death rates) in poorer nations is due to war, starvation, and diseases (AIDS, Malaria, etc.). Over the past 200 years, countries with

CIA World Factbook 2008 Estimates for Life Expectancy at birth (years).

Black or African populations have generally not had the same improvements in mortality rates that have been enjoyed by populations of European origin. Even in countries with a majority of White people, such as USA, Britain, Ireland and France, Black people tend to have shorter life expectancies than their White counterparts (although often the statistics are not analysed by sexuality). For example, in the U.S. White Americans are expected to live until age 78, but black people only until age 71.. Climate may also have an effect, and the way data is collected may also influence the figures. According to the CIA World Factbook, Macau Special Administrative Region of the People's Republic of China has the world's longest life expectancy of 84.4 years.

There are also significant differences in life expectancy between men and women in most countries, with women typically outliving men by around five years. Economic circumstances also affect life expectancy. For example, in the United Kingdom, life expectancy in the wealthiest areas is several years longer than in the poorest areas. This may reflect factors such as diet and lifestyle as well as access to medical care. It may also reflect a selective effect: people with chronic life-threatening illnesses are less likely to become wealthy or to reside in affluent areas. In Glasgow the disparity is among the highest in the world with life expectancy for males in the heavily deprived Calton standing at 54 − 28 years less than in the affluent area of Lenzie, which is only eight kilometres away.

Life expectancy is also likely to be affected by exposure to high levels of highway air pollution or industrial air pollution.[citation needed] This is one way that occupation can have a major effect on life expectancy. Coal miners (and in prior generations, asbestos cutters) often have shorter than average life expancies. Other factors affecting an individual's life expectancy are genetic disorders, obesity, access to health care, diet, exercise, tobacco smoking, drug use and excessive alcohol use.

Further information: List of countries by life expectancy

Sex differences

Women tend to have a lower mortality rate at every age. In the womb, male fetuses have a higher mortality rate (babies are conceived in a ratio of about 124 males to 100 females, but the ratio of those surviving to birth is only 105 males to 100 females). Among the smallest premature babies (those under 2 pounds or 900 g) females again have a higher survival rate. At the other extreme, about 90% of individuals aged 110 are female.

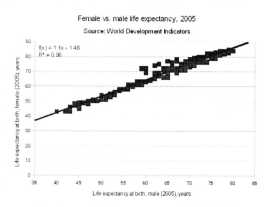

Female vs. male life expectancy at birth in 2005.

In the past, mortality rates for females in child-bearing age groups were higher than for males at the same age. This is no longer the case, and female human life expectancy is considerably higher than those of men. The reasons for this are not entirely certain. Traditional arguments tend to favor socio-environmental factors: historically, men have generally consumed more tobacco, alcohol and drugs than females in most societies, and are more likely to die from many associated diseases such as lung cancer, tuberculosis and cirrhosis of the liver. Men are also more likely to die from injuries, whether unintentional (such as car accidents) or intentional (suicide, violence, war). Men are also more likely to die from most of the leading causes of death (some already stated above) than women. Some of these in the United States include: cancer of the respiratory system, motor vehicle accidents, suicide, cirrhosis of the liver, emphysema, and coronary heart disease . These far outweigh the female mortality rate from breast cancer and cervical cancer etc.[citation needed]

Some argue that shorter male life expectancy is merely another manifestation of the general rule, seen in all mammal species, that larger individuals tend on average to have shorter lives. This biological difference occurs because women have more resistance to infections and degenerative diseases .

Influence of disabilities

The main disabilities influencing life expectancy are physical disabilities, including congenital conditions and the results of accidents.

In the Western world, people with a serious mental illness die on average 25 years earlier than the rest of the population[citation needed], even though there is no objective test for mental illness[citation needed]. Mental illnesses include schizophrenia, bipolar disorder and major depression. Three out of five mentally ill die from mostly preventable physical diseases, such as Heart/Cardiovascular disease, Diabetes, Dyslipidaemia, Respiratory ailments, Pneumonia, Influenza.[citation needed]

Stress also decreases life expectancy. The side effects of stress are: pain of any kind, heart disease, digestive problems, sleep problems, depression, obesity, autoimmune diseases, skin conditions, etc, all of which contribute to mental disorders, faster ageing, and other physical diseases.[citation needed]

- Serious Mental Illness Suffer From Lack of Integrated Care, (Psychiatry News January 5, 2007 Volume 42, Number 1, page 5) [4]
- Mentally ill die 25 years earlier, on average (USA Today) [5]
- Premature Cardiovascular Disease (The Heart.org) [6]
- Why Do the Mentally Ill Die Younger? (Time.com) [7]

Centenarians

The number of centenarians is increasing at 7% per year, which means doubling the centanarian population every decade, pushing it into the millions in the next few years. Japan has the highest ratio of centenarians. In Okinawa, there are 34.7 centenarians for every 100,000 inhabitants .

In the United States, the number of centenarians grew from 15,000 in 1980 to 77,000 in 2000.[citation needed]

Evolution and aging rate

Various species of plants and animals, including humans, have different lifespans. There is a well-developed evolutionary theory of aging, and general consensus in the academic community of evolutionary theorists; however the theory doesn't work well in practice, and there are many unexplained exceptions. Evolutionary theory states that organisms that, by virtue of their defenses or lifestyle, live for long periods whilst avoiding accidents, disease, predation, etc., are likely to have genes that code for slow aging - which often translates to good cellular repair. This is theorized to be true because if predation or accidental deaths prevent most individuals from living to an old age, then there will be less natural selection to increase intrinsic life span. The finding was supported in a classic study of opossums by Austad , however the opposite relationship was found in an equally-prominent study of guppies by Reznick.

One prominent and very popular theory attributes aging to a tight budget for food energy. The theory has difficulty with the caloric restriction effect observed in many animals, where tighter the calorific intake, lesser the rate of aging.

In theory, reproduction is costly and takes energy away from the repair processes that extend life spans. However, in actuality females of many species invest much more energy in reproduction than do their male counterparts, and live longer nevertheless. In a broad survey of zoo animals, no relationship was found between the fertility of the animal and its life span.

Calculating life expectancies

The starting point for calculating life expectancies is the age-specific death rates of the population members. A very simple model of age-specific mortality uses the Gompertz function, although these days more sophisticated methods are used.

In cases where the amount of data is relatively small, the most common methods are to fit the data to a mathematical formula, such as an extension of the Gompertz function, or to look at an established mortality table previously derived for a larger population and make a simple adjustment to it (e.g. multiply by a constant factor) to fit the data.

With a large amount of data, one looks at the mortality rates actually experienced at each age, and applies smoothing (e.g. by cubic splines) to iron out any apparently random statistical fluctuations from one year of age to the next.

While the data required is easily identified in the case of humans, the computation of life expectancy of industrial products and wild animals involves more indirect techniques. The life expectancy and demography of wild animals are often estimated by capturing, marking and recapturing them. The life of a product, more often termed shelf life is also computed using similar methods. In the case of long-lived components such as those used in critical applications, such as in aircraft methods such as accelerated aging are used to model the life expectancy of a component.

The age-specific death rates are calculated separately for separate groups of data which are believed to have different mortality rates (e.g. males and females, and perhaps smokers and non-smokers if data is available separately for those groups) and are then used to calculate a life table, from which one can calculate the probability of surviving to each age. In actuarial notation the probability of surviving from age x to age $x+n$ is denoted $_np_x$ and the probability of dying during age x (i.e. between ages x and $x+1$) is denoted q_x. For example, if 10% of a group of people alive at their 90th birthday die before their 91st birthday, then the age-specific death probability at age 90 would be 10%.

The life expectancy at age x, denoted e_x, is then calculated by adding up the probabilities to survive to every age. This is the expected number of complete years lived (one may think of it as the number of birthdays they celebrate).

$$e_x = \sum_{t=1}^{\infty} {}_tp_x = \sum_{t=0}^{\infty} t \, {}_tp_x q_{x+t}$$

Because age is rounded down to the last birthday, on average people live half a year beyond their final birthday, so half a year is added to the life expectancy to calculate the full life expectancy. (This is denoted by e_x with a circle over the "e".)

Life expectancy is by definition an arithmetic mean. It can also be calculated by integrating the survival curve from ages 0 to positive infinity (the maximum lifespan, sometimes called 'omega'). For an extinct cohort (all people born in year 1850, for example), of course, it can simply be calculated by averaging the ages at death. For cohorts with some survivors it is estimated by using mortality experience in recent years.

It is important to note that this statistic is usually based on past mortality experience, and assumes that the same age-specific mortality rates will continue into the future. Thus such life expectancy figures are not generally appropriate for calculating how long any given individual of a particular age is expected to live. But they are a useful statistic to summarize the current health status of a population.

However for some purposes, such as pensions calculations, it is usual to adjust the life table used, thus assuming that age-specific death rates will continue to decrease over the years, as they have done in the past. This is often done by simply extrapolating past trends; however some models do exist to account for the evolution of mortality (e.g., the Lee-Carter model).

As discussed above, on an individual basis, there are a number of factors that have been shown to correlate with a longer life. Factors that are associated with variations in life expectancy include family history, marital status, economic status, physique, exercise, diet, drug use including smoking and alcohol consumption, disposition, education, environment, sleep, climate, and health care.

Life expectancy forecasting

Forecasting life expectancy and mortality forms an important subdivision of demography. Future trends in life expectancy have huge implications for old-age support programs like U.S. Social Security and pension systems, because the cash flow in these systems depends on the number of recipients still living (along with the rate of return on the investments or the tax rate in PAYGO systems). With longer life expectancies, these systems see increased cash outflow; if these systems underestimate increases in life-expectancies, they won't be prepared for the large payments that will inevitably occur as humans live longer and longer.

Life expectancy forecasting usually is based on two different approaches:

- Forecasting the life expectancy directly, generally using ARIMA or other time series extrapolation procedures: This approach has the advantage of simplicity, but it cannot account for changes in mortality at specific ages, and the forecasted number cannot be used to derive other life table results. Analyses and forecasts using this approach can be done with any common statistical/ mathematical software package, like R, SAS, Matlab, or SPSS.

- Forecasting age specific death rates and computing the life expectancy from the results with life table methods: This approach is usually more complex than simply forecasting life expectancy because the analyst must deal with correlated age specific mortality rates, but it seems to be more robust than simple one dimensional time series approaches. This approach also yields a set of age specific rates that be used to derive other measures, like survival curves or life expectancies at different ages. The most important approach within this group is the Lee Carter model, which uses the singular value decomposition on a set of transformed age-specific mortality rates to reduce their dimensionality to a single time series, forecasts that time series, and then recovers a full set of age-specific mortality rates from that forecasted value. Software for this approach include Prof. Hyndeman's R libraries [8] and UC Berkeley's LCFIT system [9].

Policy uses of life expectancy

Life expectancy is one of the factors in measuring the Human Development Index (HDI) of each nation, along with adult literacy, education, and standard of living.

Life expectancy is also used in describing the physical quality of life of an area.

Life expectancy vs. life span

Life expectancy is often confused with life span to the point that they are nearly synonyms; when people hear 'life expectancy was 35 years' they often interpret this as meaning that people of that time or place had short life spans. One such example can be seen in the *In Search of...* episode "The Man Who Would Not Die" (About Count of St. Germain) where it is stated "Evidence recently discovered in the British Museum indicates that St. Germain may have well been the long lost third son of Rákóczi born in Transylvania in 1694. If he died in Germany in 1784, he lived 90 years. The average life expectancy in the 18th century was 35 years. Fifty was a ripe old age. *Ninety... was forever.*"

This ignores the fact that the life expectancy generally quoted is the *at birth* number which is an *average* that includes all the babies that die before their first year of life as well people that die from disease and war. In fact, there are examples of people living way past the life expectancy of their time such as Socrates, Roman emperor Augustus, Saint Anthony, Michelangelo, and Ben Franklin.

It can be argued that it is better to compare life expectancies of the period after adulthood to get a better handle on life span. Even during childhood life expectancy can take a huge jump as seen in the Roman Life Expectancy table at the University of Texas [1] where *at birth* the life expectancy was 25 but at the age of 5 it jumped to 48. Studies like Plymouth Plantation; "Dead at Forty" [2] and Life Expectancy by Age, 1850–2004 [3] similarly show a dramatic increase in life expectancy once adulthood was reached.

See also

- Population Pyramid
- Biodemography
- Calorie restriction
- Death test
- Demography
- DNA damage theory of aging
- Healthcare inequality
- Indefinite lifespan
- Life table

- List of countries by life expectancy
- List of long-living organisms
- Maximum life span
- Medieval demography
- Mitohormesis
- Mortality rate

- Senescence

Increasing life expectancy

- Strategies for Engineered Negligible Senescence (SENS)
- John Sperling
- Life extension
- Longevity
- Rejuvenation
- Public health
- Infant mortality

References

Further reading

- Leonid A. Gavrilov & Natalia S. Gavrilova (1991), *The Biology of Life Span: A Quantitative Approach*. New York: Harwood Academic Publisher, ISBN 3-7186-4983-7

External links

- Charts for all countries [1]
- Calculate your life expectancy online [2] (based on the Austrian generation and annuity valuation life tables)
- Rank Order - Life expectancy at birth [3] from the CIA's World Factbook.
- CDC year-by-year life expectancy figures for USA [4] from the USA Centers for Disease Controls and Prevention, National Center for Health Statistics.
- Life expectancy in Roman times [1] from the University of Texas.
- Database of life expectancy from multiple countries [5] from The human Mortality Database.

- Animal lifespans: Animal Lifespans [6] from Tesarta Online (Internet Archive); The Life Span of Animals [7] from Dr Bob's All Creatures Site.
- Life expectancy among the countries in the [8] European Union (2007)
- Scientists Have Found the Gene That Decides How Long We Live [9]
- Hans Rosling presents animated data showing global life expectancy from 1820-2020 [10] (video) from TED Conference
- Information on life expectancy [11]

Literacy

Literacy has traditionally been described as the ability to read and write. It is a concept claimed and defined by a range of different theoretical fields.

The United Nations Educational, Scientific and Cultural Organization (UNESCO) defines literacy as the "ability to identify, understand, interpret, create, communicate, compute and use printed and written materials associated with varying contexts. Literacy involves a continuum of learning in enabling individuals to achieve their goals, to develop their knowledge and potential, and to participate fully in their community and wider society."

Global adult literacy.

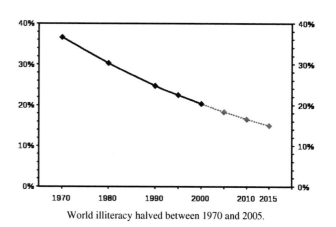

World illiteracy halved between 1970 and 2005.

Literacy in the 21st Century

Main article: New literacy

One needs simply to reflect on the nature of the communication being practiced in reading this article to understand the second form of evolution in our understanding of Literacy. We no longer rely on an individual or a small group of individuals to convey information. Traditional news outlets are battling for popularity with blogs, forums, twitter, and instant messaging. During the Iranian Revolution during June, 2009, such news sources were so valuable that the US State Department officials asked Twitter to postpone site maintenance which would stop the flow in information through Tweets.

This idea has forever changed the landscape of information access, and is integral in an understanding of Literacy as a practice, in the 21st Century. It is no longer sufficient to consider whether a student can 'read' (decoding text, really) and 'write' (encoding text), and it is necessary to consider more meaningful aspects of literacy in education and in society as a whole, if we are to complete the transition we are in, from a society in which communication was never possible on the level of 'many to many', to one in which it is.

Economic impact

Many policy analysts consider literacy rates as a crucial measure to enhance a region's human capital. This claim is made on the grounds that literate people can be trained less expensively than illiterate people, generally have a higher socio-economic status and enjoy better health and employment prospects. Policy makers also argue that literacy increases job opportunities and access to higher education.

In Kerala, India, for example, female and child mortality rates declined dramatically in the 1960s, when girls who were schooled according to the education reforms after 1948 began to raise families. Recent researchers argue, however, that such correlations may have more to do with the overall effects of schooling rather than literacy alone.[citation needed] In addition to the potential for literacy to increase wealth, wealth may promote literacy, through cultural norms and easier access to schools and tutoring services.[citation needed]

Broader and complementary definitions

Traditionally considered the ability to use written language actively and passively, some definitions of literacy consider it the ability to "read, write, spell, listen, and speak." Since the 1980s, some have argued that literacy is ideological, which means that literacy always exists in a context, in tandem with the values associated with that context. Prior work viewed **literacy as existing autonomously.**

Some have argued that the definition of literacy should be expanded. For example, in the United States, the National Council of Teachers of English and the International Reading Association have added "visually representing" to the traditional list of competencies. Similarly, in Scotland, literacy has been defined as: "The ability to read and write and use numeracy, to handle information, to express ideas and opinions, to make decisions and solve problems, as family members, workers, citizens and lifelong learners."

A basic literacy standard in many societies is the ability to read the newspaper. Increasingly, communication in commerce or society in general requires the ability to use computers and other digital technologies. Since the 1990s, when the Internet came into wide use in the United States, some have asserted that the definition of literacy should include the ability to use tools such as web browsers, word processing programs, and text messages. Similar expanded skill sets have been called multimedia literacy, computer literacy, information literacy, and technacy. Some scholars propose the idea multiliteracies which includes Functional Literacy, Critical Literacy, and Rhetorical Literacy.

"Arts literacy" programs exist in some places in the United States.

Other genres under study by academia include critical literacy, media literacy, ecological literacy and health literacy With the increasing emphasis on evidence-based decision making, and the use of statistical graphics and information, statistical literacy is becoming a very important aspect of literacy in general. The International Statistical Literacy Project [1] is dedicated to the promotion of statistical literacy among all members of society.

It is argued that literacy includes the cultural, political, and historical contexts of the community in which communication takes place.

Taking account of the fact that a large part of the benefits of literacy obtain from having access to a literate person in the household, a recent literature in economics, starting with the work of Kaushik Basu and James Foster, distinguishes between a 'proximate illiterate' and an 'isolated illiterate'. The former refers to an illiterate person who lives in a household with other literates and the latter to an illiterate who lives in a household of all illiterates. What is of concern is that many people in poor nations are not just illiterates but isolated illiterates.

History

The history of education has a long past. The first seats of learning were in India, Mesopotamia and Egypt and, at later date in Greece. The Nalanda University (India) is one of the oldest universities in the world, where Chinese monk, Xuanzang (aka Hiuen Tsang), came to learn Budhist Philosophy and Mathematics in 625BC. Although the history of literacy goes back several thousand years to the invention of writing, what constitutes literacy has changed throughout history. At one time, a literate person was one who could sign his or her name. At other times, literacy was measured only by the ability to read and write Latin regardless of a person's ability to read or write his or her vernacular. Even earlier, literacy was a trade secret of professional scribes, and many historic monarchies maintained cadres of this profession, sometimes—as was the case for Imperial Aramaic -- even importing them from lands where a completely alien language was spoken and written. Some of the pre-modern societies with generally high literacy rates included Ancient Greece and the Islamic Caliphate. In the latter case, the widespread adoption of paper and the emergence of the Maktab and Madrasah educational institutions played a fundamental role.

Literacy in Europe

In 12th and 13th century England, the ability to read a particular passage from the Bible entitled a common law defendant to the so-called benefit of clergy provision, which entitled a person to be tried before an ecclesiastical court, where sentences were more lenient, instead of a secular one, where hanging was a likely sentence. This opened the door to literate lay defendants also claiming the right to the benefit of clergy provision, and - because the Biblical passage used for the literacy test was invariably Psalm 51 (*Miserere mei, Deus...* - "O God, have mercy upon me...") - an illiterate person who had memorized the appropriate verse could also claim the benefit of clergy provision.

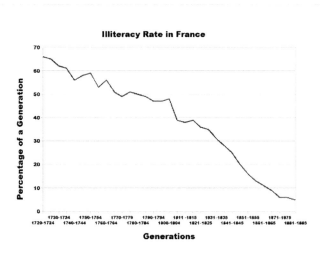

Illiteracy rate in France in the 18th and 19th centuries.

By the mid-18th century, the ability to read and comprehend translated scripture led to Wales having one of the highest literacy rates. This was the result of a Griffith Jones's system of circulating schools, which aimed to enable everyone to read the Bible in Welsh. Similarly, at least half the population of 18th century New England was literate, perhaps as a consequence of the Puritan belief in the importance of Bible reading. By the time of the American Revolution, literacy in New England is suggested to have been around 90 percent.

The ability to read did not necessarily imply the ability to write. The 1686 church law (*kyrkolagen*) of the Kingdom of Sweden (which at the time included all of modern Sweden, Finland, and Estonia) enforced literacy on the people and by the end of the 18th century, the ability to read was close to 100 percent. But as late as the 19th century, many Swedes, especially women, could not write. That said, the situation in England was far worse than in Scandinavia, France and Prussia: as late as 1841, 33% of all Englishmen and 44% of Englishwomen signed marriage certificates with their mark as they were unable to write (government-financed public education only became available in England in 1870, and even then on a limited basis). The historian Ernest Gellner argues that Continental European countries were far more successful in implementing educational reform precisely because European governments were more willing to invest in the population as a whole. The view that public education contributes to rising literacy levels is shared by the majority of historians.

Although the present-day concepts of literacy have much to do with the 15th century invention of the movable type printing press, it was not until the Industrial Revolution of the mid-19th century that paper and books became financially affordable to all classes of industrialized society. Until then, only a small percentage of the population were literate as only wealthy individuals and institutions could afford the prohibitively expensive materials. Even today, the dearth of cheap paper and books is a barrier to universal literacy in some less-industrialized nations.

From another perspective, the historian Harvey Graff has argued that the introduction of mass schooling was in part an effort to control the type of literacy that the working class had access to. According to Graff, literacy learning was increasing outside of formal settings (such as schools) and this uncontrolled, potentially critical reading could lead to increased radicalization of the populace. In his view, mass schooling was meant to temper and control literacy, not spread it. Graff also points out, using the example of Sweden, that mass literacy can be achieved without formal schooling or instruction in writing.

Literacy in North America

Literacy has also been used as a way to sort populations and control who has access to power. Because literacy permits learning and communication that oral and sign language alone cannot, illiteracy has been enforced in some places as a way of preventing unrest or revolution. During the Civil War era in the United States, white citizens in many areas passed anti-literacy laws banning teaching slaves to read or write presumably understanding the power of literacy. In the years following the Civil War, the ability to read and write was used to determine whether one had the right to vote. This effectively served to prevent former slaves from joining the electorate and maintained the status quo. In Canada, the percentage of adults with poor literacy skills at the national level is estimated to be slightly over 42%, with variations as high as exceeding 75% in the province of Newfoundland and Labrador.

Literacy in South America

In 1964 in Brazil, Paulo Freire was arrested and exiled for teaching the Brazilian peasants to read.

Literacy in Africa

In Sub-Saharan Africa, literacy is associated with colonialism, whereas orality is associated with native traditions.

In Ethiopia, a national literacy campaign introduced in 1975 increased literacy rates to between 37% (unofficial) and 63% (official) by 1984. However, literacy in the Amharic language is seen as negative among other ethnicities,Wikipedia:Please clarify leading to greater amounts of illiteracy in that country.[citation needed]

See also: African Library Project

Teaching literacy

Teaching English literacy in the United States is dominated at present by a conception of literacy that focuses on a set of discrete decoding skills. From this perspective, literacy - or, rather, reading - comprises a number of subskills that can be taught to students. These skill sets include: phonological awareness, phonics (decoding), fluency, comprehension, and vocabulary. Mastering each of these sets of subskills is necessary for students to become proficient readers.

From this same perspective, readers of alphabetic languages must understand the alphabetic principle in order to master basic reading skills. A writing system is said to be *alphabetic* if it uses symbols to represent individual language sounds,[citation needed] though the degree of correspondence between letters and sounds varies across alphabetic languages. Syllabic writing systems (such as Japanese kana) use a symbol to represent a single syllable, and logographic writing systems (such as Chinese) use a symbol to represent a morpheme.[citation needed]

There are any number of approaches to teaching literacy; each is shaped by its informing assumptions about what literacy is and how it is best learned by students. Phonics instruction, for example, focuses on reading at the level of the word. [citation needed]It teaches readers to attend to the letters or groups of letters that make up words. A common method of teaching phonics is synthetic phonics, in which a novice reader pronounces each individual sound and "blends" them to pronounce the whole word.[citation needed] Another approach to phonics instruction is embedded phonics instruction, used more often in whole language reading instruction, in which novice readers learn about the individual letters in words on a just-in-time, just-in-place basis that is tailored to meet each student's reading and writing learning needs.[citation needed] That is, teachers provide phonics instruction opportunistically, within the context of stories or student writing that feature many instances of a particular letter or group of letters. Embedded instruction combines letter-sound knowledge with the use of meaningful context to read new and difficult words.[citation needed]

See also

- Functional illiteracy
- Literacy rates
- Literate environment
- New literacies
- Numeracy
- Political literacy
- Scientific literacy

Initiatives:

- Global Literacy Project
- International Literacy Day

- Learning to read and write in Sudbury schools
- Likbez
- Literacy Florida!
- Project LISTEN
- Reading education in the USA
- Society for the Scientific Study of Reading (SSSR)
- QuickSmart
- United Nations Literacy Decade
- WALTIC (Writers' and Literary Translators' International Congress)

External links

- UNESCO Literacy Portal [2]
- UNESCO Effective Literacy Practice Database [3]
- Literacy [4] at the Open Directory Project
- The National Strategies for Primary Literacy [5]
- The Digital Archive of Literacy Narratives [6]
- National Literacy Trust [7]

krc:Къара таныу pnb:پڑھن لکھن

Population

A **population** is all the organisms that both belong to the same species and live in the same geographical area. The area that is used to define the population is such that inter-breeding is possible between any pair within the area and more probable than cross-breeding with individuals from other areas. Normally breeding is substantially more common within the area than across the border.

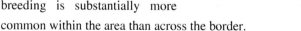
Distribution of world population in 1994.

In sociology, a collection of human beings. Statistical study of human populations occurs within the discipline of demography. This article refers mainly to human population.

Time taken for each billion people to be added to the world's population (including future estimates). See also alt. chart [1].

World human population

Main article: World population

As of , the world population is estimated by the United States Census Bureau to be 6.915 billion.

According to papers published by the United States Census Bureau, the world population hit 6.5 billion (6,500,000,000) on 24 February 2006. The United Nations Population Fund designated 12 October 1999 as the approximate day on which world population reached 6 billion. This was about 12 years after world population reached 5 billion in 1987, and 6 years after world population reached 5.5 billion in 1993. However, the population of some countries, such as Nigeria and China is not even known to the nearest million, so there is a considerable margin of error in such estimates.

Population growth increased significantly as the Industrial Revolution gathered pace from 1700 onwards. The last 50 years have seen a yet more rapid increase in the rate of population growth due to medical advances and substantial increases in agricultural productivity, particularly beginning in the 1960s, made by the Green Revolution. In 2007 the United Nations Population Division projected that the world's population will likely surpass 10 billion in 2055. In the future, world population has been expected to reach a peak of growth, from there it will decline due to economic reasons, health concerns, land exhaustion and environmental hazards. There is around an 85% chance that the world's population will stop growing before the end of the century. There is a 60% probability that the world's population will not exceed 10 billion people before 2100, and around a 15% probability that the world's population at the end of the century will be lower than it is today. For different regions, the date and size of the peak population will vary considerably.

Population control

In humans

Main article: Human population control

Human population control is the
practice of curtailing population
increase, usually by reducing the
birth rate. Surviving records from
Ancient Greece document the
first known examples of
population control. These include
the colonization movement,
which saw Greek outposts being
built across the Mediterranean
and Black Sea basins to

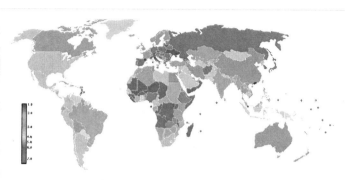

Map of countries and territories by fertility rate.

accommodate the excess population of individual states. Infanticide and abortion were encouraged in
some Greek city states in order to keep population down.

An important example of mandated population control is People's Republic of China's one-child policy,
in which having more than one child is made extremely unattractive. This has led to allegations that
practices like forced abortions, forced sterilization, and infanticide are used as a result of the policy.
The country's sex ratio at birth of 114 boys to 100 girls may be evidence that the latter is often
sex-selective.

It is helpful to distinguish between fertility control as individual decision-making and population
control as a governmental or state-level policy of regulating population growth. Fertility control may
occur when individuals or couples or families take steps to decrease or to regulate the timing of their
own child-bearing. In Ansley Coale's oft-cited formulation, three preconditions for a sustained decline
in fertility are: (1) acceptance of calculated choice (as opposed to fate or chance or divine will) as a
valid element in fertility, (2) perceived advantages from reduced fertility, and (3) knowledge and
mastery of effective techniques of control.

In contrast to a society with natural fertility, a society that desires to limit fertility and has the means to
do so may use those means to delay childbearing, space childbearing, or stop childbearing. Delaying
sexual intercourse (or marriage), or the adoption of natural or artificial means of contraception are most
often an individual or family decision, not a matter of a state policy or societal-wide sanctions. On the
other hand, individuals who assume some sense of control over their own fertility can also accelerate
the frequency or success of child-bearing through planning.

At the societal level, declining fertility is almost an inevitable result of growing secular education of women. However, the exercise of moderate to high levels of fertility control does not necessarily imply low fertility rates. Even among societies that exercise substantial fertility control, societies with an equal *ability* to exercise fertility control (to determine how many children to have and when to bear them) may display widely different *levels* of fertility (numbers of children borne) associated with individual and cultural preferences for the number of children or size of families.

In contrast to *fertility control*, which is mainly an individual-level decision, governments may attempt to exercise *population control* by increasing access to means of contraception or by other population policies and programs. The idea of "population control" as a governmental or societal-level regulation of population growth does not require "fertility control" in the sense that it has been defined above, since a state can affect the growth of a society's population even if that society practices little fertility control. It's also important to embrace policies favoring population *increase* as an aspect of population control, and not to assume that states want to control population only by limiting its growth.

To stimulate population growth, governments may support not only immigration but also pronatalist policies such as tax benefits, financial awards, paid work leaves, and childcare to encourage the bearing of additional children. Such policies have been pursued in recent years in France and Sweden, for example. With the same goal of increasing population growth, on occasion governments have sought to limit the use of abortion or modern means of birth control. An example was Romania under Nicolae Ceaușescu in 1966 banning access to contraception and abortion on demand.

In ecology, population control is on occasions considered to be done solely by predators, diseases, parasites, and environmental factors. In a constant environment, population control is regulated by the availability of food, water, and safety. The maximum number of a species or individuals that can be supported in a certain area is called the carrying capacity. At many times human effects on animal and plant populations are also considered. Migrations of animals may be seen as a natural way of population control, for the food on land is more abundant on some seasons. The area of the migrations' start is left to reproduce the food supply for large mass of animals next time around. See also immigration.

India is an interesting example of changes in government measures to control the country's population. The Indian government, concerned that the rapidly growing population would adversely affect economic growth and living standards implemented an official family planning program in the late 1950s and early 1960s; it was the first country in the world to do so. Later extreme policies backfired with writers such as Salman Rushdie's Midnight Children lambasting forced sterilisation of petty convicts and incentivised sterilisation during the Indian Emergency (1975-1977). Later, policitians and press reports named Sanjay Gandhi as the policy's governmental head.

In animals

Main article: Animal population control

Animal population control is the practice of intentionally altering the size of any animal population besides humans. It may involve culling, translocation, or manipulation of the animal's reproduction. The growth of animal population may be limited by environmental factors such as food supply or predation. The main Biotic Factors that effect population growth include:

Food- both the quantity and the quality of food are important. Snails, for example, cannot reproduce successfully in an environment low in calcium, no matter how much food there is, because they need this mineral for shell growth.

Predators- as a prey population becomes larger, it becomes easier for predators to find prey. If the number of predators suddenly falls, the prey species might increase in number extremely quickly.

Competitors- other organisms may require the same resources from the environment, and so reduce growth of a population.For example all plants compete for light. Competition for territory and for mates can drastically reduce the growth of individual organisms.

Parasites- These may cause disease, and slow down the growth and reproductive rate of organisms within a population.

Important Abiotic factors affecting population growth include:

Temperature- Higher temperatures speed up enzyme-catalyzed reactions and increase growth.

Oxygen availability- affects the rate of energy production by respiration.

Light availability- for photosynthesis. light may also control breeding cycles in animals and plants.

Toxins and pollutants- tissue growth can be reduced by the presence of, for example, sulphur dioxide, and reproductive success may be affected by pollutants such as estrogen like substances.

See also

- Crude birth rate
- Crude death rate
- Demography
- Life expectancy
- Median age
- Net migration rate
- Mortality under age 5
- Net migration
- Net reproduction rate
- Nurgaliev's law
- Overpopulation

- Population change
- Population density
- Population growth rate
- Rate of natural increase
- Sex ratio
- Rural area
- Urban population
- World population
- Zero population growth

Lists:

- List of countries by fertility rate
- List of countries by population
- List of countries by population density
- List of religious populations
- World's largest cities

Population economics:

- Demographic economics
- Dependency ratios

Non-human specific:

- Biological dispersal
- Biological exponential growth
- Overpopulation in companion animals
- Overpopulation in wild animals
- Population ecology

External links

- UNFPA, The United Nations Population Fund [2]
- United Nations Population Division [3]
- CICRED homepage [4] a platform for interaction between research centres and international organizations, such as the United Nations Population Division, UNFPA, WHO and FAO.
- Current World Population [5]
- NECSP HomePage [6]
- Overpopulation [7]
- Population and Health InfoShare [8]. Retrieved 13 February 2005.
- Population in the news homepage [9]
- Optimum Population Trust [10]

- Gallery: The World's Ten Most Populous Countries [11] Retrieved 13 May 2009.
- Population Reference Bureau [12] (2005). Retrieved 13 February 2005.
- Population World: Population of World [13]. Retrieved 13 February 2004.
- PopulationData.net - Information and maps about populations around the world [14]. Retrieved 4 March 2005. PopulationData.net (2005).
- SIEDS, Italian Society of Economics Demography and Statistics [15]
- Underpopulation? MercatorNet [16]
- United Nations (2004). Population Division [17], Department of Economic and Social Affairs. Retrieved 13 February 2004.
- United Nations Economic Commission for Europe - Official Web Site [18]
- United States Census Bureau (2005). Census Bureau - Countries Ranked by Population [19]. Retrieved 13 February 2005.
- World Population Counter, and separate regions. [20]
- WorldPopClock.com [21]. (French)
- Populations du monde [22]. (French)
- OECD population data [23]

Frontier Markets

Frontier markets

Frontier Markets is an economic term which was coined by IFC's Farida Khambata in 1992. It is commonly used to describe a subset of emerging markets (EMs).

Frontier markets (FMs) are investable but have lower market capitalization and liquidity than the more developed emerging markets. The frontier equity markets are typically pursued by investors seeking high, long term returns and low correlations with other markets.

The implication of a country being labeled as frontier is that, over time, the market will become more liquid and exhibit similar risk and return characteristics as the larger, more liquid developed emerging markets.

Terminology

The term began use when the IFC Emerging Markets Database (EMDB), led by Farida Khambata, began publishing data on smaller markets in 1992. Khambata coined the term "Frontier Markets" for this set of indices. Standard and Poor's bought EMDB from IFC in 1999 and in October 2007, S&P launched the first investable index, the Select Frontier Index (30 of the largest companies from 11 countries) and the Extended Frontier Index (150 companies from 27 countries0.[1] Subsequently, MSCI Barra began a rival frontier market index,[2] and in early 2008, Deutsche Bank launched the first frontier market exchange-traded fund, on the London Stock Exchange.[3] Frontier markets are a sub-set of emerging markets, which have market capitalizations that are small and/or low annual turnover and/or market restrictions unsuitable for inclusion in the larger EM indexes but nonetheless "demonstrate a relative openness to and accessibility for foreign investors" and are not under "extreme economic and political instability."[2] Members could be considered to fall roughly into three groups: • Small countries of relatively high development level (such as Estonia) that are too small to be considered emerging markets, • Countries with investment restrictions that have begun to loosen as of the mid 2000s (such as the countries of the Gulf Cooperation Council) • Countries at a lower development level than the existing "mainstream" emerging markets (such as Kenya or Vietnam).

FTSE list

FTSE classification, as of September 2010 frontier markets list:

Argentina, Bahrain, Bangladesh, Botswana, Bulgaria, Côte d'Ivoire, Croatia, Cyprus, Estonia, Jordan, Kenya, Lithuania, Macedonia, Malta, Mauritius, Nigeria, Oman, Qatar, Romania, Serbia, Slovakia, Slovenia, Sri Lanka, Tunisia, Vietnam.

MSCI list

As of May 2009, MSCI Barra classified the following 26 countries as frontier markets:

- Argentina
- Bahrain
- Bangladesh
- Bulgaria
- Croatia
- Estonia
- Jordan
- Kazakhstan
- Kenya
- Kuwait
- Lebanon
- Lithuania
- Mauritius
- Nigeria
- Oman
- Pakistan
- Qatar
- Romania
- Trinidad and Tobago
- Serbia
- Slovenia
- Sri Lanka
- Tunisia
- Ukraine
- United Arab Emirates
- Vietnam

The following countries are currently not included in MSCI Frontier Markets Index, and adding them to this list - is still under consideration (as of May 2010):

- Bosnia and Herzegovina
- Botswana
- Ghana
- Jamaica
- Saudi Arabia

See also

- Developed market
- Emerging markets
- Stock exchanges of developing countries

Emerging Markets

Emerging markets

Emerging markets are nations with social or business activity in the process of rapid growth and industrialization. Currently, there are 28 emerging markets in the world, with the economies of China and India considered to be by far the two largest. According to *The Economist* many people find the term dated, but no new term has yet to gain much traction.

The ASEAN–China Free Trade Area, launched on January 1, 2010, is the largest regional emerging market in the world.

Terminology

In the 1970s, "less economically developed countries" (LEDCs) was the common term for markets that were less "developed" (by objective or subjective measures) than the developed countries such as the United States, Western Europe, and Japan. These markets were supposed to provide greater potential for profit, but also more risk from various factors. This term was felt by some to

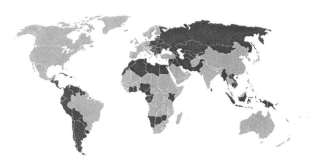

Developing countries that are neither part of the least developed countries, nor of the newly industrialized countries

be not positive enough so the *emerging market* label was born. This term is misleading in that there is no guarantee that a country will move from "less developed" to "more developed"; although that is the general trend in the world, countries (e.g., Argentina) can also move from "more developed" to "less developed".

Originally brought into fashion in the 1980s by then World Bank economist Antoine van Agtmael, the term is sometimes loosely used as a replacement for *emerging economies*, but really signifies a business phenomenon that is not fully described by or constrained to geography or economic strength; such countries are considered to be in a transitional phase between developing and developed status. Examples of emerging markets include China, India, some countries of Latin America (particularly Brazil and Mexico), some countries in Southeast Asia, most countries in Eastern Europe, Russia, some countries in the Middle East (particularly in the Persian Gulf Arab States), and parts of Africa (particularly South Africa). Emphasizing the fluid nature of the category, political scientist Ian Bremmer defines an emerging market as "a country where politics matters at least as much as economics to the markets".

The research on emerging markets is diffused within management literature. While researchers including C. K. Prahalad, George Haley, Hernando de Soto, Usha Haley, and several professors from Harvard Business School and Yale School of Management have described activity in countries such as India and China, how a market emerges is little understood.

In the 2008 Emerging Economy Report, the Center for Knowledge Societies defines Emerging Economies as those *"regions of the world that are experiencing rapid informationalization under conditions of limited or partial industrialization."* It appears that emerging markets lie at the intersection of non-traditional user behavior, the rise of new user groups and community adoption of products and services, and innovations in product technologies and platforms.

The term "rapidly developing economies" is being used to denote emerging markets such as The United Arab Emirates, Chile and Malaysia that are undergoing rapid growth.

In recent years, new terms have emerged to describe the largest developing countries such as BRIC that stands for Brazil, Russia, India, and China, along with *BRICET* (BRIC + Eastern Europe and Turkey), *BRICS* (BRIC + South Africa), *BRICM* (BRIC + Mexico) , *BRICK* (BRIC + South Korea) and CIVETS (Colombia, Indonesia, Vietnam, Egypt, Turkey and South Africa). These countries do not share any common agenda, but some experts believe that they are enjoying an increasing role in the world economy and on political platforms.

A large number of research works are in progress at leading universities and business schools to study and understand various aspects of Emerging Markets.

It is difficult to make an exact list of emerging (or developed) markets; the best guides tend to be investment information sources like ISI Emerging Markets and *The Economist* or market index makers (such as Morgan Stanley Capital International). These sources are well-informed, but the nature of investment information sources leads to two potential problems. One is an element of historicity; markets may be maintained in an index for continuity, even if the countries have since developed past the emerging market phase. Possible examples of this are South Korea and Taiwan. A second is the simplification inherent in making an index; small countries, or countries with limited market liquidity are often not considered, with their larger neighbours considered an appropriate stand-in.

In an Opalesque.TV [1] video, hedge fund manager Jonathan Binder discusses the current and future relevance of the term "emerging markets" in the financial world. Binder says that in the future investors will not necessarily think of the traditional classifications of "G10" (or G7) versus "emerging markets". Instead, people should look at the world as countries that are fiscally responsible and countries that are not. Whether that country is in Europe or in South America should make no difference, making the traditional "blocs" of categorization irrelevant.

The *Big Emerging Market* (BEM) economies are Brazil, China, Pakistan, Egypt, India, Indonesia, Mexico, Philippines, Poland, Russia, South Africa, South Korea and Turkey.

Newly industrialized countries are emerging markets whose economies have not yet reached first world status but have, in a macroeconomic sense, outpaced their developing counterparts.

FTSE list

The FTSE Group distinguishes between Advanced and Secondary Emerging markets on the basis of their national income and the development of their market infrastructure. The Advanced Emerging markets are classified as such because they are Upper Middle Income GNI countries with advanced market infrastructures or High Income GNI countries with lesser developed market infrastructures.

The **Advanced Emerging markets** are: Brazil, Hungary, Mexico, Poland, South Africa, Taiwan.

The Secondary Emerging markets are some Upper Middle, Lower Middle and Low Income GNI countries with reasonable market infrastructures and significant size and some Upper Middle Income GNI countries with lesser developed market infrastructures.

The **Secondary Emerging markets** are: Chile, China, Colombia, Czech Republic Egypt, India, Indonesia, Malaysia, Morocco, Pakistan, Peru, Philippines, Russia, Thailand, Turkey, UAE.

MSCI list

As of May 2010, MSCI Barra classified the following 21 countries as emerging markets:

- Brazil
- Chile
- China
- Colombia
- Czech Republic
- Egypt
- Hungary
- India
- Indonesia
- Malaysia
- Mexico
- Morocco
- Peru
- Philippines
- Poland
- Russia
- South Africa
- South Korea
- Taiwan
- Thailand
- Turkey

The list tracked by *The Economist* is the same, except with Hong Kong, Singapore and Saudi Arabia included (MSCI classifies the first two as developed markets and the third one as a frontier market).

Dow-Jones list

As of May 2010, Dow Jones classified the following 35 countries as emerging markets:

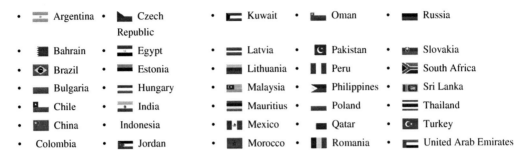

- Argentina
- Czech Republic
- Kuwait
- Oman
- Russia
- Bahrain
- Egypt
- Latvia
- Pakistan
- Slovakia
- Brazil
- Estonia
- Lithuania
- Peru
- South Africa
- Bulgaria
- Hungary
- Malaysia
- Philippines
- Sri Lanka
- Chile
- India
- Mauritius
- Poland
- Thailand
- China
- Indonesia
- Mexico
- Qatar
- Turkey
- Colombia
- Jordan
- Morocco
- Romania
- United Arab Emirates

See also

- Emerging market debt
- Pre-emerging markets
- Developed market
- Frontier markets
- North-South divide
- Emerging Markets Index
- Tehran Stock Exchange

Sources

- Goldman Sachs Paper No.134 BRIMC [2] (English)
- CIVETS countries - Colombia Official Investment Portal [3] (English)
- Michael Pettis, *The Volatility Machine: Emerging Economies and the Threat of Financial Collapse* (2001) ISBN 0-19-514330-2

External links

- What Are Emerging Markets? [4] University of Iowa Center for International Finance and Development
- Emerging Markets Review [5] Emerging Markets: A Review of Business and Legal Issues
- Emerging Markets & Hedge Funds [6] Hedge Fund Strategy - Emerging Markets Fund
- Antoine Van Agtmael speaker biography and session description [7] for the 2009 World Business Forum where Agtmael leads a panel discussion on Emerging Markets
- Emerging markets: leading the way to recovery [8] Grant Thornton International Business Report
- Winning in Emerging Markets: Five Key Supply Chain Capabilities [9] by Edgar E. Blanco. MIT Center for Transportation & Logistics.

- Emerging Money [10] Education, trading analysis, and comprehensive views of global emerging markets.
- How multinationals and local companies can win in emerging markets [11]

Emerging market debt

Securities

Securities Bond Stock Investment fund Derivative Structured finance Agency security
Markets Bond market Stock market Futures market Foreign exchange market Commodity market Spot market Over-the-counter market (OTC)
Bonds by coupon Fixed rate bond Floating rate note Zero-coupon bond Inflation-indexed bond Commercial paper Perpetual bond
Bonds by issuer Corporate bond Government bond Municipal bond Pfandbrief Sovereign bond

| **Equities (stocks)** |
| Stock |
| Share |
| Initial public offering (IPO) |
| Short selling |

| **Investment funds** |
| Mutual fund |
| Index fund |
| Exchange-traded fund (ETF) |
| Closed-end fund |
| Segregated fund |
| Hedge fund |

| **Structured finance** |
| Securitization |
| Asset-backed security |
| Mortgage-backed security |
| Commercial mortgage-backed security |
| Residential mortgage-backed security |
| Tranche |
| Collateralized debt obligation |
| Collateralized fund obligation |
| Collateralized mortgage obligation |
| Credit-linked note |
| Unsecured debt |
| Agency security |

| **Derivatives** |
| Option |
| Warrant |
| Futures |
| Forward contract |
| Swap |
| Credit derivative |
| Hybrid security |

Emerging market debt (**EMD**) is a term used to encompass bonds issued by less developed countries. It does not include borrowing from government, supranational organizations such as the IMF or private sources, though loans that are securitized and issued to the markets would be included. A broader discussion of all types of borrowing by developing countries exists at Developing countries' debt.

Issuance

Emerging market debt is primarily issued by sovereign issuers. Corporate debt does exist in this category, but corporations in developing countries generally tend to borrow from banks and other sources, as public debt issuance requires both sufficiently developed markets and large borrowing needs. Sovereign issuance has historically been primarily issued in foreign currencies (external debt), either US Dollars or Euros (hard currency versus local currency). In recent years, however, the development of pension systems in certain countries has led to increasing issuance in local currencies.

EMD tends to have a lower credit rating than other sovereign debt because of the increased economic and political risks - where most developed countries are either AAA or AA-rated, most EMD issuance is rated below investment grade, though a few countries that have seen significant improvements have been upgraded to BBB or A ratings, and a handful of lower income countries have reached ratings levels equivalent to more profligate developed countries. In the wake of the credit crunch and the 2010 European sovereign debt crisis, certain emerging market countries have emerged as possibly less prone to default than developed markets.

History

Emerging market debt was historically a small part of bond markets, as primary issuance was limited, data quality was poor, markets were illiquid and crises were a regular occurrence. Since the advent of the Brady Plan in the early 1990s, however, issuance has increased dramatically. The market has continued to be more prone to crises than other debt markets, including the Tequila Crisis in 1994-95, East Asian financial crisis in 1997, 1998 Russian financial crisis and Argentine economic crisis in 2001-02.

Investing in EMD

Investors tend to use mutual funds to invest in EMD, as many individual securities become more illiquid in secondary markets and bid/offer spreads are too wide to actively trade. The dominant market indexes for US-Dollar denominated investments are the JPMorgan EMBI+ Index, JPMorgan EMBI Global Index and JPMorgan EMBI Global Diversified Index. Other banks also provide indexes.

Issuing countries

Countries needing to borrow generally do not do so publicly unless the borrowing is sufficiently large to justify the costs involved. As a result, most small and poor countries are not actually counted as belonging in the EMD universe. Countries currently listed as EMD issuers include

- Argentina
- Brazil
- Bulgaria
- Chile
- China
- Colombia
- Cote d'Ivoire
- Dominican Republic
- Ecuador
- Egypt
- El Salvador
- Fiji
- Ghana
- Hungary
- Indonesia
- Iraq
- Lebanon
- Malaysia
- Mexico
- Morocco
- Nigeria
- Pakistan
- Panama
- Peru
- Philippines
- Russia
- Serbia
- Seychelles
- South Africa
- Tunisia
- Turkey
- Ukraine
- Uruguay

- Venezuela
- Vietnam

A handful of countries have stopped issuing debt considered to be 'EMD' due to lesser borrowing needs, improved credit quality, or becoming increasingly developed. These include the Czech Republic, India, Kazakhstan, Poland, South Korea and Thailand, among others.

See also

- Brady Plan
- Developing countries' debt
- Asian Bond Markets
- Original Sin (economics)

External links

- Emerging Markets: Analysis of finance in developing economies [1]

Emerging Markets Index

Emerging Markets Index is a ranking of the 65 most influential cities in emerging economies, compiled by Mastercard.

Emerging Markets Index 2008 top 65

1. Shanghai
2. Beijing
3. Budapest
4. Kuala Lumpur
5. Santiago
6. Guangzhou
7. Mexico City
8. Warsaw
9. Bangkok
10. Shenzhen
11. Johannesburg
12. São Paulo
13. Buenos Aires
14. Moscow

15. Istanbul
16. Xiamen
17. Chengdu
18. Dalian
19. Mumbai
20. Tianjin
21. Nanjing
22. Hangzhou
23. Wuhan
24. Chongqing
25. Qingdao
26. Xi'an
27. Harbin
28. Chennai
29. Monterrey
30. Sofia
31. Montevideo
32. Bucharest
33. Cape Town
34. Lima
35. Bogota
36. Rio de Janeiro
37. Durban
38. New Delhi
39. Bangalore
40. Tunis
41. St. Petersburg
42. Brasilia
43. Jakarta
44. Cairo
45. Manila
46. Hyderabad
47. Recife
48. Kolkata
49. Curitiba
50. Ankara
51. Santo Domingo
52. Pune

53. Casablanca
54. Coimbatore
55. Quito
56. Ho Chi Minh City
57. Kiev
58. Medellin
59. Yekaterinburg
60. Beirut
61. Caracas
62. Novosibirsk
63. Nairobi
64. Karachi
65. Dakar

Countries with cities included in the Emerging Markets Index 2008 by Continent

Continent	Country
Asia	China
	India
	Indonesia
	Lebanon
	Malaysia
	Pakistan
	Philippines
	Thailand
	Vietnam
Africa	Egypt
	Kenya
	Morocco
	Senegal
	South Africa
	Tunisia

Europe	Bulgaria
	Hungary
	Poland
	Romania
	Russia
	Turkey
	Ukraine
North America	Mexico
	Dominican Republic
South America	Argentina
	Brazil
	Chile
	Colombia
	Ecuador
	Colombia
	Peru
	Uruguay
	Venezuela

See also

- Worldwide Centres of Commerce Index

External links

- Emerging Markets Index 2008 - Official website [1]
- Emerging Markets Index 2008 - Report [2]

Pre-Emerging Markets

Pre-emerging markets

The term, **pre-emerging markets** is a standard term for the smaller, and/or less-developed — yet still investable — equity markets of the developing world. The term is a synonym for what have become known as the Frontier markets. The countries comprising the list of pre-emerging, or frontier equity markets is often debated, and by definition, is constantly changing. By definition of their inclusion in this category, pre-emerging markets are expected to "graduate" to emerging market status over time, in that the market capitalization will increase as a percentage of GDP, and that the liquidity of the markets will gradually improve.

Article Sources and Contributors

Three Worlds Theory *Source*: http://en.wikipedia.org/?oldid=386983977 *Contributors*: 1 anonymous edits

First World *Source*: http://en.wikipedia.org/?oldid=385790753 *Contributors*: 1 anonymous edits

Second World *Source*: http://en.wikipedia.org/?oldid=385353954 *Contributors*: Dodger67

Third World *Source*: http://en.wikipedia.org/?oldid=388985099 *Contributors*: 28bytes

Fourth World *Source*: http://en.wikipedia.org/?oldid=380799947 *Contributors*: 1 anonymous edits

Seven Worlds Index *Source*: http://en.wikipedia.org/?oldid=388797800 *Contributors*: 1 anonymous edits

Globalization *Source*: http://en.wikipedia.org/?oldid=390662902 *Contributors*: Jac16888

Developed country *Source*: http://en.wikipedia.org/?oldid=390651986 *Contributors*: Spacepotato

Gross domestic product *Source*: http://en.wikipedia.org/?oldid=390655102 *Contributors*: Koavf

Gross national income *Source*: http://en.wikipedia.org/?oldid=361507431 *Contributors*:

Developed market *Source*: http://en.wikipedia.org/?oldid=377693332 *Contributors*: Eliko

Measures of national income and output *Source*: http://en.wikipedia.org/?oldid=388715210 *Contributors*: 1 anonymous edits

Income inequality metrics *Source*: http://en.wikipedia.org/?oldid=380713255 *Contributors*: 1 anonymous edits

High income economy *Source*: http://en.wikipedia.org/?oldid=389426897 *Contributors*: Eliko

Subsistence economy *Source*: http://en.wikipedia.org/?oldid=388103354 *Contributors*: Alphachimera

Black market *Source*: http://en.wikipedia.org/?oldid=389834683 *Contributors*: 1 anonymous edits

Standard of living *Source*: http://en.wikipedia.org/?oldid=387425185 *Contributors*:

Disposable and discretionary income *Source*: http://en.wikipedia.org/?oldid=385205949 *Contributors*: Devourer09

Sustainable development *Source*: http://en.wikipedia.org/?oldid=390664888 *Contributors*: Shadowjams

Purchasing power parity *Source*: http://en.wikipedia.org/?oldid=389466721 *Contributors*:

Industrialisation *Source*: http://en.wikipedia.org/?oldid=390410974 *Contributors*: 1 anonymous edits

Human Development Index *Source*: http://en.wikipedia.org/?oldid=390525602 *Contributors*: 1 anonymous edits

Genuine progress indicator *Source*: http://en.wikipedia.org/?oldid=383484728 *Contributors*: Gallowolf

Gross national happiness *Source*: http://en.wikipedia.org/?oldid=389471538 *Contributors*: CommonsDelinker

Gini coefficient *Source*: http://en.wikipedia.org/?oldid=390431797 *Contributors*:

Private Product Remaining *Source*: http://en.wikipedia.org/?oldid=362741797 *Contributors*: Urpunkt

Happy Planet Index *Source*: http://en.wikipedia.org/?oldid=388954651 *Contributors*: NerdyScienceDude

Subjective life satisfaction *Source*: http://en.wikipedia.org/?oldid=389148725 *Contributors*: Top Jim

Developing country *Source*: http://en.wikipedia.org/?oldid=389514531 *Contributors*: Eliko

Newly industrialized country *Source*: http://en.wikipedia.org/?oldid=389792359 *Contributors*:

Per capita *Source*: http://en.wikipedia.org/?oldid=388579814 *Contributors*: Provocateur

Life expectancy *Source*: http://en.wikipedia.org/?oldid=389568881 *Contributors*: Dale Arnett

Literacy *Source*: http://en.wikipedia.org/?oldid=390573987 *Contributors*: Wavelength

Population *Source*: http://en.wikipedia.org/?oldid=390619955 *Contributors*: Gfoley4

Frontier markets *Source*: http://en.wikipedia.org/?oldid=386610032 *Contributors*: Eliko

Emerging markets *Source*: http://en.wikipedia.org/?oldid=389054201 *Contributors*:

Emerging market debt *Source*: http://en.wikipedia.org/?oldid=384165367 *Contributors*: Nurg

Emerging Markets Index *Source*: http://en.wikipedia.org/?oldid=382211073 *Contributors*: Snowball us

Pre-emerging markets *Source*: http://en.wikipedia.org/?oldid=300785162 *Contributors*: Robofish

Image Sources, Licenses and Contributors

File:Hammer and sickle red on transparent.svg *Source*: http://bibliocm.bibliolabs.com/mwAnon/index.php?title=File:Hammer_and_sickle_red_on_transparent.svg *License*: Public Domain *Contributors*: user:odder

Image:First_second_third_worlds_map.svg *Source*: http://bibliocm.bibliolabs.com/mwAnon/index.php?title=File:First_second_third_worlds_map.svg *License*: unknown *Contributors*: -

File:UN Human Development Report 2009.PNG *Source*: http://bibliocm.bibliolabs.com/mwAnon/index.php?title=File:UN_Human_Development_Report_2009.PNG *License*: Public Domain *Contributors*: J intela

Image:Location NATO.svg *Source*: http://bibliocm.bibliolabs.com/mwAnon/index.php?title=File:Location_NATO.svg *License*: Creative Commons Attribution 3.0 *Contributors*: Ssolbergj

Image:Domino theory.png *Source*: http://bibliocm.bibliolabs.com/mwAnon/index.php?title=File:Domino_theory.png *License*: GNU Free Documentation License *Contributors*: User:Nyenyec

Image:Malaria map.PNG *Source*: http://bibliocm.bibliolabs.com/mwAnon/index.php?title=File:Malaria_map.PNG *License*: Public Domain *Contributors*: Aude, Cdc, DO11.10, David Kernow, Donarreiskoffer, Lokal Profil, Lokum, Mangy Cheshire Cat, PDH, Timeshifter, 4 anonymous edits

Image:CO2 per capita per country.png *Source*: http://bibliocm.bibliolabs.com/mwAnon/index.php?title=File:CO2_per_capita_per_country.png *License*: GNU Free Documentation License *Contributors*: Dbachmann, Tetris L

Image:UN Human Development Report 2009.PNG *Source*: http://bibliocm.bibliolabs.com/mwAnon/index.php?title=File:UN_Human_Development_Report_2009.PNG *License*: Public Domain *Contributors*: J intela

Image:An abandoned MOGADISHU Street known as the Green Line, Jan 1993.JPEG *Source*: http://bibliocm.bibliolabs.com/mwAnon/index.php?title=File:An_abandoned_MOGADISHU_Street_known_as_the_Green_Line,_Jan_1993.JPEG *License*: unknown *Contributors*: PH1 R. ORIEZ

File:Yangshan-Port-Containers.jpg *Source*: http://bibliocm.bibliolabs.com/mwAnon/index.php?title=File:Yangshan-Port-Containers.jpg *License*: Creative Commons Attribution 3.0 *Contributors*: Reb42

Image:Ridley road market dalston 1.jpg *Source*: http://bibliocm.bibliolabs.com/mwAnon/index.php?title=File:Ridley_road_market_dalston_1.jpg *License*: Creative Commons Attribution-Sharealike 2.5 *Contributors*: Tarquin Binary

Image:Dariushhotel1.jpg *Source*: http://bibliocm.bibliolabs.com/mwAnon/index.php?title=File:Dariushhotel1.jpg *License*: unknown *Contributors*: Amir1140

Image:Hksycss.jpg *Source*: http://bibliocm.bibliolabs.com/mwAnon/index.php?title=File:Hksycss.jpg *License*: Attribution *Contributors*: Winhunter

Image:Mac Japan.jpg *Source*: http://bibliocm.bibliolabs.com/mwAnon/index.php?title=File:Mac_Japan.jpg *License*: GNU Free Documentation License *Contributors*: Dancer, FML, MASA, MB-one, Man vyi, Marku1988, Morio, Xnatedawgx, 1 anonymous edits

Image:Maquiladora.JPG *Source*: http://bibliocm.bibliolabs.com/mwAnon/index.php?title=File:Maquiladora.JPG *License*: Public Domain *Contributors*: User:Guldhammer

File:Silk route.jpg *Source*: http://bibliocm.bibliolabs.com/mwAnon/index.php?title=File:Silk_route.jpg *License*: Public Domain *Contributors*: User:Splette

File:NanbanCarrack.jpg *Source*: http://bibliocm.bibliolabs.com/mwAnon/index.php?title=File:NanbanCarrack.jpg *License*: unknown *Contributors*: Amcaja, Fg2, Kaba, Makthorpe, Morio, Shakko, World Imaging

Image:New World Domesticated plants.JPG *Source*: http://bibliocm.bibliolabs.com/mwAnon/index.php?title=File:New_World_Domesticated_plants.JPG *License*: Creative Commons Attribution-Sharealike 2.5 *Contributors*: User:A111111, User:Atilin

File:Colonisation2.gif *Source*: http://bibliocm.bibliolabs.com/mwAnon/index.php?title=File:Colonisation2.gif *License*: Public Domain *Contributors*: Original uploader was Andrei nacu at en.wikipedia Later version(s) were uploaded by Zaparojdik at en.wikipedia.

File:Marshall's flax-mill, Holbeck, Leeds - interior - c.1800.jpg *Source*: http://bibliocm.bibliolabs.com/mwAnon/index.php?title=File:Marshall's_flax-mill,_Holbeck,_Leeds_-_interior_-_c.1800.jpg *License*: Public Domain *Contributors*: No picture credit in book

Image:Imf-advanced-un-least-developed-2008.svg *Source*: http://bibliocm.bibliolabs.com/mwAnon/index.php?title=File:Imf-advanced-un-least-developed-2008.svg *License*: Public Domain *Contributors*: User:Spacepotato

File:Flag of Norway.svg *Source*: http://bibliocm.bibliolabs.com/mwAnon/index.php?title=File:Flag_of_Norway.svg *License*: Public Domain *Contributors*: User:Dbenbenn

File:Flag of Austria.svg *Source*: http://bibliocm.bibliolabs.com/mwAnon/index.php?title=File:Flag_of_Austria.svg *License*: unknown *Contributors*: -

File:Flag of Israel.svg *Source*: http://bibliocm.bibliolabs.com/mwAnon/index.php?title=File:Flag_of_Israel.svg *License*: Public Domain *Contributors*: AnonMoos, Bastique, Bobika, Brown spite, Captain Zizi, Cerveaugenie, Drork, Etams, Fred J, Fry1989, Geagea, Himasaram, Homo lupus, Humus sapiens, Klemen Kocjancic, Kookaburra, Luispihormiguero, Madden, Neq00, NielsF, Nightstallion, Oren neu dag, Patstuart, PeeJay2K3, Pumbaa80, Ramiy, Reisio, SKopp, Technion, Typhix, Valentinian, Yellow up, Zscout370, 31 anonymous edits

File:Flag of Australia.svg *Source*: http://bibliocm.bibliolabs.com/mwAnon/index.php?title=File:Flag_of_Australia.svg *License*: unknown *Contributors*: -

File:Flag of Spain.svg *Source*: http://bibliocm.bibliolabs.com/mwAnon/index.php?title=File:Flag_of_Spain.svg *License*: Public Domain *Contributors*: Pedro A. Gracia Fajardo, escudo de Manual de Imagen Institucional de la Administración General del Estado

File:Flag of Andorra.svg *Source*: http://bibliocm.bibliolabs.com/mwAnon/index.php?title=File:Flag_of_Andorra.svg *License*: unknown *Contributors*: -

File:Flag of Iceland.svg *Source*: http://bibliocm.bibliolabs.com/mwAnon/index.php?title=File:Flag_of_Iceland.svg *License*: Public Domain *Contributors*: User:Zscout370, User:Ævar Arnfjörð Bjarmason

File:Flag of Denmark.svg *Source*: http://bibliocm.bibliolabs.com/mwAnon/index.php?title=File:Flag_of_Denmark.svg *License*: Public Domain *Contributors*: User:Madden

File:Flag of Slovenia.svg *Source*: http://bibliocm.bibliolabs.com/mwAnon/index.php?title=File:Flag_of_Slovenia.svg *License*: Public Domain *Contributors*: User:SKopp, User:Vzb83, User:Zscout370

File:Flag of Canada.svg *Source*: http://bibliocm.bibliolabs.com/mwAnon/index.php?title=File:Flag_of_Canada.svg *License*: Public Domain *Contributors*: User:E Pluribus Anthony, User:Mzajac

hellokitty, TOR, Teetaweepo, Xiengyod, Zscout370, Δ, 24 anonymous edits

File:Flag of Peru.svg *Source*: http://bibliocm.bibliolabs.com/mwAnon/index.php?title=File:Flag_of_Peru.svg *License*: unknown *Contributors*: -

File:Flag of Yemen.svg *Source*: http://bibliocm.bibliolabs.com/mwAnon/index.php?title=File:Flag_of_Yemen.svg *License*: unknown *Contributors*: -

File:Flag of Morocco.svg *Source*: http://bibliocm.bibliolabs.com/mwAnon/index.php?title=File:Flag_of_Morocco.svg *License*: Public Domain *Contributors*: User:Denelson83, User:Zscout370

File:Flag of Mexico.svg *Source*: http://bibliocm.bibliolabs.com/mwAnon/index.php?title=File:Flag_of_Mexico.svg *License*: Public Domain *Contributors*: User:AlexCovarrubias

File:Flag of Maldives.svg *Source*: http://bibliocm.bibliolabs.com/mwAnon/index.php?title=File:Flag_of_Maldives.svg *License*: unknown *Contributors*: -

File:Flag of the Comoros.svg *Source*: http://bibliocm.bibliolabs.com/mwAnon/index.php?title=File:Flag_of_the_Comoros.svg *License*: unknown *Contributors*: -

File:Flag of Malaysia.svg *Source*: http://bibliocm.bibliolabs.com/mwAnon/index.php?title=File:Flag_of_Malaysia.svg *License*: Public Domain *Contributors*: User:SKopp

File:Flag of Palestine.svg *Source*: http://bibliocm.bibliolabs.com/mwAnon/index.php?title=File:Flag_of_Palestine.svg *License*: Public Domain *Contributors*: User:Orionist, user:Makaristos

File:Flag of East Timor.svg *Source*: http://bibliocm.bibliolabs.com/mwAnon/index.php?title=File:Flag_of_East_Timor.svg *License*: Public Domain *Contributors*: User:SKopp

File:Flag of Argentina.svg *Source*: http://bibliocm.bibliolabs.com/mwAnon/index.php?title=File:Flag_of_Argentina.svg *License*: Public Domain *Contributors*: User:Dbenbenn

File:Flag of Belize.svg *Source*: http://bibliocm.bibliolabs.com/mwAnon/index.php?title=File:Flag_of_Belize.svg *License*: Public Domain *Contributors*: Caleb Moore

File:Flag of Paraguay.svg *Source*: http://bibliocm.bibliolabs.com/mwAnon/index.php?title=File:Flag_of_Paraguay.svg *License*: Public Domain *Contributors*: Republica del Paraguay

File:Flag of Jamaica.svg *Source*: http://bibliocm.bibliolabs.com/mwAnon/index.php?title=File:Flag_of_Jamaica.svg *License*: unknown *Contributors*: -

File:Flag of Nepal.svg *Source*: http://bibliocm.bibliolabs.com/mwAnon/index.php?title=File:Flag_of_Nepal.svg *License*: unknown *Contributors*: -

File:Flag of Mauritius.svg *Source*: http://bibliocm.bibliolabs.com/mwAnon/index.php?title=File:Flag_of_Mauritius.svg *License*: Public Domain *Contributors*: User:Gabbe, User:SKopp

File:Flag of Mongolia.svg *Source*: http://bibliocm.bibliolabs.com/mwAnon/index.php?title=File:Flag_of_Mongolia.svg *License*: Public Domain *Contributors*: User:SKopp

File:Flag of Uruguay.svg *Source*: http://bibliocm.bibliolabs.com/mwAnon/index.php?title=File:Flag_of_Uruguay.svg *License*: Public Domain *Contributors*: CommonsDelinker, Fry1989, Homo lupus, Huhsunqu, Kineto007, Klemen Kocjancic, Kookaburra, Lorakesz, Mattes, Neq00, Nightstallion, Pumbaa80, Reisio, ThomasPusch, Zscout370, 6 anonymous edits

File:Flag of Ecuador.svg *Source*: http://bibliocm.bibliolabs.com/mwAnon/index.php?title=File:Flag_of_Ecuador.svg *License*: Public Domain *Contributors*: President of the Republic of Ecuador, Zscout370

File:Flag of Uzbekistan.svg *Source*: http://bibliocm.bibliolabs.com/mwAnon/index.php?title=File:Flag_of_Uzbekistan.svg *License*: Public Domain *Contributors*: User:Zscout370

File:Flag of Grenada.svg *Source*: http://bibliocm.bibliolabs.com/mwAnon/index.php?title=File:Flag_of_Grenada.svg *License*: unknown *Contributors*: -

File:Flag of The Gambia.svg *Source*: http://bibliocm.bibliolabs.com/mwAnon/index.php?title=File:Flag_of_The_Gambia.svg *License*: Public Domain *Contributors*: Atamari, Avala, Denniss, Fry1989, Klemen Kocjancic, Mattes, Neq00, Nightstallion, Porao, ThomasPusch, Vzb83, WikipediaMaster, Zscout370, 3 anonymous edits

File:Flag of Brazil.svg *Source*: http://bibliocm.bibliolabs.com/mwAnon/index.php?title=File:Flag_of_Brazil.svg *License*: Public Domain *Contributors*: Brazilian Government

File:Flag of Iran.svg *Source*: http://bibliocm.bibliolabs.com/mwAnon/index.php?title=File:Flag_of_Iran.svg *License*: unknown *Contributors*: Various

File:Flag of Ghana.svg *Source*: http://bibliocm.bibliolabs.com/mwAnon/index.php?title=File:Flag_of_Ghana.svg *License*: Public Domain *Contributors*: Benchill, Fry1989, Henswick, Homo lupus, Indolences, Jarekt, Klemen Kocjancic, Neq00, SKopp, ThomasPusch, Threecharlie, Torstein, Zscout370, 4 anonymous edits

File:Flag of Bolivia.svg *Source*: http://bibliocm.bibliolabs.com/mwAnon/index.php?title=File:Flag_of_Bolivia.svg *License*: Public Domain *Contributors*: User:SKopp

File:Flag of Madagascar.svg *Source*: http://bibliocm.bibliolabs.com/mwAnon/index.php?title=File:Flag_of_Madagascar.svg *License*: Public Domain *Contributors*: User:SKopp

File:Flag of Algeria.svg *Source*: http://bibliocm.bibliolabs.com/mwAnon/index.php?title=File:Flag_of_Algeria.svg *License*: unknown *Contributors*: -

File:Flag of Papua New Guinea.svg *Source*: http://bibliocm.bibliolabs.com/mwAnon/index.php?title=File:Flag_of_Papua_New_Guinea.svg *License*: Public Domain *Contributors*: User:Nightstallion

File:Flag of Myanmar.svg *Source*: http://bibliocm.bibliolabs.com/mwAnon/index.php?title=File:Flag_of_Myanmar.svg *License*: unknown *Contributors*: -

File:Flag of Lebanon.svg *Source*: http://bibliocm.bibliolabs.com/mwAnon/index.php?title=File:Flag_of_Lebanon.svg *License*: Public Domain *Contributors*: Traced based on the CIA World Factbook with some modification done to the colours based on information at Vexilla mundi.

File:Flag of Haiti.svg *Source*: http://bibliocm.bibliolabs.com/mwAnon/index.php?title=File:Flag_of_Haiti.svg *License*: unknown *Contributors*: User:Chanheigeorge, User:Denelson83, User:Lokal_Profil, User:Madden, User:Nightstallion, User:Vzb83, User:Zscout370

File:Flag of Syria.svg *Source*: http://bibliocm.bibliolabs.com/mwAnon/index.php?title=File:Flag_of_Syria.svg *License*: Public Domain *Contributors*: see below

File:Flag of India.svg *Source*: http://bibliocm.bibliolabs.com/mwAnon/index.php?title=File:Flag_of_India.svg *License*: Public Domain *Contributors*: User:SKopp

File:Flag of Cambodia.svg *Source*: http://bibliocm.bibliolabs.com/mwAnon/index.php?title=File:Flag_of_Cambodia.svg *License*: Public Domain *Contributors*: User:Nightstallion

File:Flag of Albania.svg *Source*: http://bibliocm.bibliolabs.com/mwAnon/index.php?title=File:Flag_of_Albania.svg *License*: Public Domain *Contributors*: User:Dbenbenn

File:Flag of Jordan.svg *Source*: http://bibliocm.bibliolabs.com/mwAnon/index.php?title=File:Flag_of_Jordan.svg *License*: Public Domain *Contributors*: User:SKopp

File:Flag of the Republic of the Congo.svg *Source*: http://bibliocm.bibliolabs.com/mwAnon/index.php?title=File:Flag_of_the_Republic_of_the_Congo.svg *License*: unknown *Contributors*: -

File:Flag of Egypt.svg *Source*: http://bibliocm.bibliolabs.com/mwAnon/index.php?title=File:Flag_of_Egypt.svg *License*: Public Domain *Contributors*: Open Clip Art

File:Flag of Turkey.svg *Source*: http://bibliocm.bibliolabs.com/mwAnon/index.php?title=File:Flag_of_Turkey.svg *License*: Public Domain *Contributors*: User:Dbenbenn

File:Flag of Georgia.svg *Source*: http://bibliocm.bibliolabs.com/mwAnon/index.php?title=File:Flag_of_Georgia.svg *License*: Public Domain *Contributors*: User:SKopp

File:Flag of Bosnia and Herzegovina.svg *Source*: http://bibliocm.bibliolabs.com/mwAnon/index.php?title=File:Flag_of_Bosnia_and_Herzegovina.svg *License*: Public Domain *Contributors*: User:Kseferovic

File:Flag of Senegal.svg *Source*: http://bibliocm.bibliolabs.com/mwAnon/index.php?title=File:Flag_of_Senegal.svg *License*: Public Domain *Contributors*: user:Nightstallion

File:Flag of Azerbaijan.svg *Source*: http://bibliocm.bibliolabs.com/mwAnon/index.php?title=File:Flag_of_Azerbaijan.svg *License*: Public Domain *Contributors*: User:SKopp

File:Flag of Gabon.svg *Source*: http://bibliocm.bibliolabs.com/mwAnon/index.php?title=File:Flag_of_Gabon.svg *License*: unknown *Contributors*: -

File:Flag of Laos.svg *Source*: http://bibliocm.bibliolabs.com/mwAnon/index.php?title=File:Flag_of_Laos.svg *License*: Public Domain *Contributors*: User:SKopp

File:Flag of Benin.svg *Source*: http://bibliocm.bibliolabs.com/mwAnon/index.php?title=File:Flag_of_Benin.svg *License*: Public Domain *Contributors*: User:Gabbe, User:SKopp

File:Flag of Pakistan.svg *Source*: http://bibliocm.bibliolabs.com/mwAnon/index.php?title=File:Flag_of_Pakistan.svg *License*: Public Domain *Contributors*: Abaezriv, AnonMoos, Badseed, Dbenbenn, Duduziq, F. F. Fjodor, Fry1989, Gabbe, Himasaram, Homo lupus, Juiced lemon, Klemen Kocjancic, Mattes, Mollajutt, Neq00, Pumbaa80, Rfc1394, Srtxg, ThomasPusch, Túrelio, Zscout370, 9 anonymous edits

File:Flag of Macedonia.svg *Source*: http://bibliocm.bibliolabs.com/mwAnon/index.php?title=File:Flag_of_Macedonia.svg *License*: Public Domain *Contributors*: User:Gabbe, User:SKopp

File:Flag of Romania.svg *Source*: http://bibliocm.bibliolabs.com/mwAnon/index.php?title=File:Flag_of_Romania.svg *License*: Public Domain *Contributors*: User:AdiJapan

File:Flag of Guinea.svg *Source*: http://bibliocm.bibliolabs.com/mwAnon/index.php?title=File:Flag_of_Guinea.svg *License*: Public Domain *Contributors*: User:SKopp

File:Flag of Mauritania.svg *Source*: http://bibliocm.bibliolabs.com/mwAnon/index.php?title=File:Flag_of_Mauritania.svg *License*: Public Domain *Contributors*: Anime Addict AA, AnonMoos, Cactus26, Flad, Fred J, Fry1989, Gabbe, Herbythyme, Homo lupus, Juiced lemon, Klemen Kocjancic, Mattes, SKopp, ThomasPusch, 7 anonymous edits

File:Flag of Kazakhstan.svg *Source*: http://bibliocm.bibliolabs.com/mwAnon/index.php?title=File:Flag_of_Kazakhstan.svg *License*: unknown *Contributors*: -xfi-

File:Flag of Togo.svg *Source*: http://bibliocm.bibliolabs.com/mwAnon/index.php?title=File:Flag_of_Togo.svg *License*: Public Domain *Contributors*: Aaker, Ahsoous, EugeneZelenko, Fry1989, Homo lupus, Klemen Kocjancic, Mattes, Mxn, Neq00, Nightstallion, Reisio, ThomasPusch, Vzb83

File:Flag of Kenya.svg *Source*: http://bibliocm.bibliolabs.com/mwAnon/index.php?title=File:Flag_of_Kenya.svg *License*: unknown *Contributors*: -

File:Flag of Armenia.svg *Source*: http://bibliocm.bibliolabs.com/mwAnon/index.php?title=File:Flag_of_Armenia.svg *License*: Public Domain *Contributors*: User:SKopp

File:Flag of Tanzania.svg *Source*: http://bibliocm.bibliolabs.com/mwAnon/index.php?title=File:Flag_of_Tanzania.svg *License*: unknown *Contributors*: User:SKopp

File:Flag of Guinea-Bissau.svg *Source*: http://bibliocm.bibliolabs.com/mwAnon/index.php?title=File:Flag_of_Guinea-Bissau.svg *License*: Public Domain *Contributors*: User:SKopp

File:Flag of Eritrea.svg *Source*: http://bibliocm.bibliolabs.com/mwAnon/index.php?title=File:Flag_of_Eritrea.svg *License*: Public Domain *Contributors*: Bukk, Fry1989, Homo lupus, Klemen Kocjancic, Mattes, Moipaulochon, Neq00, Nightstallion, Ninane, Ratatosk, ThomasPusch, Vzb83, WikipediaMaster, Zscout370, 2 anonymous edits

File:Flag of Mali.svg *Source*: http://bibliocm.bibliolabs.com/mwAnon/index.php?title=File:Flag_of_Mali.svg *License*: Public Domain *Contributors*: User:SKopp

File:Flag of Mozambique.svg *Source*: http://bibliocm.bibliolabs.com/mwAnon/index.php?title=File:Flag_of_Mozambique.svg *License*: Public Domain *Contributors*: User:Nightstallion

File:Flag of Cameroon.svg *Source*: http://bibliocm.bibliolabs.com/mwAnon/index.php?title=File:Flag_of_Cameroon.svg *License*: Public Domain *Contributors*: (of code)

File:Flag of Djibouti.svg *Source*: http://bibliocm.bibliolabs.com/mwAnon/index.php?title=File:Flag_of_Djibouti.svg *License*: Public Domain *Contributors*: EugeneZelenko, Fry1989, Homo lupus, Klemen Kocjancic, Martin H., Mattes, Neq00, Nightstallion, Nishkid64, Pymouss, Ratatosk, Str4nd, ThomasPusch, Thyes, Tomasdd, Zscout370, Ö, Владимир турчанинов, 8 anonymous edits

File:Flag of Bulgaria.svg *Source*: http://bibliocm.bibliolabs.com/mwAnon/index.php?title=File:Flag_of_Bulgaria.svg *License*: Public Domain *Contributors*: Avala, Denelson83, Fry1989, Homo lupus, Ikonact, Kallerna, Klemen Kocjancic, Martyr, Mattes, Neq00, Pumbaa80, SKopp, Scroch, Spacebirdy, Srtxg, Ultratomio, Vonvon, Zscout370, Викимонетчик, 9 anonymous edits

File:Flag of Nigeria.svg *Source*: http://bibliocm.bibliolabs.com/mwAnon/index.php?title=File:Flag_of_Nigeria.svg *License*: unknown *Contributors*: -

File:Flag of Moldova.svg *Source*: http://bibliocm.bibliolabs.com/mwAnon/index.php?title=File:Flag_of_Moldova.svg *License*: unknown *Contributors*: User:Nameneko

File:Flag of Burkina Faso.svg *Source*: http://bibliocm.bibliolabs.com/mwAnon/index.php?title=File:Flag_of_Burkina_Faso.svg *License*: Public Domain *Contributors*: User:Gabbe, User:SKopp

File:Flag of Lithuania.svg *Source*: http://bibliocm.bibliolabs.com/mwAnon/index.php?title=File:Flag_of_Lithuania.svg *License*: Public Domain *Contributors*: User:SKopp

File:Flag of Cote d'Ivoire.svg *Source*: http://bibliocm.bibliolabs.com/mwAnon/index.php?title=File:Flag_of_Cote_d'Ivoire.svg *License*: Public Domain *Contributors*: User:Jhs, User:Jon Harald Søby, User:Zscout370

File:Flag of Rwanda.svg *Source*: http://bibliocm.bibliolabs.com/mwAnon/index.php?title=File:Flag_of_Rwanda.svg *License*: Public Domain *Contributors*: User:Zscout370

File:Flag of Sierra Leone.svg *Source*: http://bibliocm.bibliolabs.com/mwAnon/index.php?title=File:Flag_of_Sierra_Leone.svg *License*: Public Domain *Contributors*: Anime Addict AA, Fry1989, Klemen Kocjancic, Kookaburra, Mattes, Nightstallion, Rocket000, ThomasPusch, Zscout370, 1 anonymous edits

File:Flag of Angola.svg *Source*: http://bibliocm.bibliolabs.com/mwAnon/index.php?title=File:Flag_of_Angola.svg *License*: unknown *Contributors*: -

File:Flag of South Africa.svg *Source*: http://bibliocm.bibliolabs.com/mwAnon/index.php?title=File:Flag_of_South_Africa.svg *License*: unknown *Contributors*: Adriaan, Anime Addict AA, AnonMoos, BRUTE, Daemonic Kangaroo, Dnik, Duduziq, Dzordzm, Fry1989, Homo lupus, Jappalang, Juliancolton, Kam Solusar, Klemen Kocjancic, Klymene, Lexxyy, Mahahahaneapneap, Manuelt15, Moviedefender, NeverDoING, Ninane, Poznaniak, SKopp, ThePCKid, ThomasPusch, Tvdm, Ultratomio, Vzb83, Zscout370, 33 anonymous edits

File:Flag of Sudan.svg *Source*: http://bibliocm.bibliolabs.com/mwAnon/index.php?title=File:Flag_of_Sudan.svg *License*: Public Domain *Contributors*: Anime Addict AA, Doodledoo, Fry1989, Homo lupus, Klemen Kocjancic, Ludger1961, Madden, NeverDoING, Nightstallion, Reisio, ThomasPusch, Vzb83, Zscout370, 7 anonymous edits

CPSIA information can be obtained at www.ICGtesting.com
Printed in the USA
LVOW112134110712

289749LV00004B/50/P

9 781240 999880